JN093798

The Fundamentals of Japanese Real Estate

図解
事典

英語で学ぶ
不動産ビジ
ネス

2nd Edition

［第2版］

脇本 和也 Kazuya (Kazu) Wakimoto

Jon Salyards ジョン サリアード

著

秀和システム

Preface

As I mentioned in the previous preface of this book, when I started my career in the real estate business in 1992, I never thought there would come a time when I would be using English every day as part of my job.

Now that real estate is regarded as one of the global investment asset classes like stocks and bonds, cross border real estate transactions have become quite common. Even during the pandemic, I have had more meetings with overseas investors through Zoom and orher tools than ever before. We also continue to see more overseas investment by Japanese reak estate deveropers, so English will continue to become more important tool within the real estate business.

This book is mainly for Japanese readers who have to, or want to, deal with Japanese real estate in English. Jon and I also wanted to target foreigners who are interested in understanding the basics of the real estate business in Japan. We know there are many local terminologies in the Japanese real estate business that are difficult for foreigners to understand without additional explanation. We tried to use a lot of illustrations to make this book more understandable and practical for all readers. However, please do remember that there might be some additional translations possible from what we have used in this book because the real estate terminologies are based on the local culture and have no literal English translation.

Lastly, I would like to give a special thanks to Jon because it would have been really difficult to complete this book without his abundant real estate experience and excellent communication skills both in English and Japanese. Additionally, I would like to give thanks to the following colleagues who checked the contents of this book as experienced professional.

Mr. Yukitoshi Nakamura, Mr. Takahiro Manabe, Mr. Ryan Tenbarge

I also would like to give thanks to my wife, who has always supported my commitment to the book, and to Shuwa System who gave us the opportunity to write and publish this book.

Kazuya Wakimoto

はじめに

　初版の「はじめに」でも述べさせていただいたとおり、1992年に社会人として不動産ビジネスに携わりはじめたときには、将来、英語を使って仕事をすることになるとは夢にも思いませんでした。

　今や不動産は株式や債券と並ぶグローバルな投資対象としての位置を確立し、クロスボーダー取引が当たり前となっています。コロナ禍でも、海外投資家とZoom等でコミュニケーションすることは以前よりも頻繁にありました。日本のデベロッパーによる海外投資も着実に増えています。不動産ビジネスにおけるコミュニケーションツールとして、英語はより重要になっていくでしょう。

　この本は、日本の不動産を英語で取り扱わなければならない、もしくは取り扱いたい日本の読者をメインとしていますが、日本の不動産ビジネスの概要を理解したい外国人にも読んでもらえるように作成したつもりです。多くの不動産用語は日本独特のものですので、何らかの追加的な説明がないと、外国人には理解が難しいのが実情です。そこで、多くの図も用いて、極力、分かりやすく、かつ、実践的な本にすることに努めました。ただ、前述したとおり、多くの不動産用語が日本独特のものであり、正確な英語の定義があるわけではありませんので、本書で記載していない他の様々な英語表現も可能だということに留意していただければと思います。

　最後に、この場をお借りして、ジョンに改めて感謝の意を表したいと思います。彼の豊富な不動産ビジネス経験と、英日での卓越したコミュニケーションスキルがなければ、この本は完成しなかったでしょう。加えて、経験ある専門家としてこの本の内容をチェックいただいた以下の方々にもお礼をさせていただきます。

中村行利氏、真鍋孝弘氏、Ryan Tenbarge氏

　また、執筆作業中、常にサポートしてくれた妻、本書執筆・出版の機会を与えていただいた秀和システムの方々にも、お礼の言葉を述べさせていただきます。

脇本和也

Preface

It has been 12 years since we first published "The Fundamentals of Japanese Real Estate", and I have had the pleasure of being able to continue my work in the real estate field with Savills Japan over the past decade. We are delighted to update and refresh the materials in this edition to hopefully help foreign and Japanese real estate professionals better understand our market in both English and Japanese.

The Japanese real estate market has continued to evolve and mature over the past decade, providing a more transparent and professional landscape for investors to acquire and manage real estate in Japan. But challenges remain in understanding the details of our market, the investment structures that are used, and the local practices that are unique to our market.

Our hope in this second edition is to provide a clear and simple look into the many aspects of Japanese real estate, and we hope this book can be used as a reference to better understand the terms and details in both Japanese and English.

I would like to give a special thanks to my friend and colleague, Wakimoto-san, without whom this book would not be possible. It has been a pleasure and privilege to work together on this second edition, and I look forward to our continued friendship in the next decade together.

I would also like to thank the many friends and colleagues whom I have had the good fortune to meet and work with in Japan, and I remain confident and optimistic in our market and future together. I hope to continue to be a part of Japanese real estate for many years to come.

Jon Salyards

はじめに

　「英語で学ぶ不動産ビジネス」の初版を出版してから 12 年、この間、私は、サヴィルズジャパンで引き続き不動産業界での仕事を続けてきました。今回、本書の内容をアップデートできることは大変嬉しいことですし、この本が、外国そして日本の不動産専門家にとって、英語及び日本語で日本不動産市場をさらに理解するための助けになれば幸いです。

　過去 10 年で、日本の不動産市場は、発展し、より成熟してきています。投資家が不動産の投資や運用を行うにあたって、市場の透明性が増し専門性も充実してきました。しかし、市場の詳細、用いられている投資ストラクチャー、そして独特な日本の市場慣行など、海外投資家が直面する困難も引き続きあります。

　本改訂版が、日本不動産の様々な面についての理解に繋がることを期待していますし、不動産の専門用語について日本語及び英語で調べる際の参考となれば非常に嬉しく思います。

　この場をお借りして、友人であり仲間でもある脇本さんに、感謝の意を示したいと思います。彼なしではこの本を出すことはできませんでした。本改訂版を一緒に出すことができて非常に嬉しく思いますし、今後も友人としてあり続けていければ幸いです。

　また、日本で会った多くの友人や一緒に働いてきた同僚にも感謝の意を示させていただきます。日本の不動産市場は今後も発展を続けるでしょう。今後の多くの期間にわたり、私自身もその一翼を担うことができればと思っています。

ジョン　サリアード

The Fundamentals of Japanese Real Estate [2nd Edition]

図解事典
英語で学ぶ不動産ビジネス[第2版]

Chapter 5　Real Estate Businesses in Japan

第5章　日本の不動産ビジネス

Chapter 1

Fundamental Knowledge of Japanese Real Estate

日本の不動産に関する
基礎知識

1-1 What is real estate?

Q : How is real estate officially defined in Japan?

A : Article 86 of the **Civil Law** says that "land and any fixtures thereto are immovables." Also, according to the **Japanese Real Estate Appraisal Standards**, "real estate is land and improvements upon the land." A fixture or improvement usually refers to a building located on the land. Therefore, in Japan, **land** and **buildings** are each regarded as independent pieces of **real estate**.

Q : How is real estate used in daily life in Japan?

A : In Japan there are three main types of real estate: residential, office and retail properties. **Residential real estate** is usually used as a place to live and includes **detached houses, condominiums** and **rental apartments**. **Office buildings** are used as places for people to work and **retail properties** are used as places for businesses to sell something or provide a service, like a jewelry shop or restaurant. Real estate can also be used for other things, such as **logistics properties, hotels, nursing homes**, and **public facilities**.

Q : How is real estate used as a business?

A : Real estate can be used as a way to make money. For example, detached houses and condominiums are built by **real estate developers** and then sold to people for a profit. Sometimes **real estate agent companies** help people buy houses and condominiums and they charge a fee and make money.

Real estate can also be leased to individuals and companies for a profit. When a property is leased to a **tenant**, it is called an **income-producing property**, an **investment property**, or a **commercial proparty**.

Since about the late 1990s, income-producing property has been regarded as a **financial product** in Japan. This change has attracted both Japanese and foreign professional investors and created a global real estate market in Japan.

1-1 不動産とは何か？

Q：日本では、正式には、不動産はどのように定義されていますか？

A：民法第86条で、「土地及びその定着物は、不動産とする」と記載されています。また、**不動産鑑定評価基準**では、「不動産は、通常、土地とその定着物をいう」とされています。定着物の代表的なものは、土地の上に建てられた建物ですので、日本では、**土地**と建物がそれぞれ独立した**不動産**とみなされています。

Q：日本では、不動産は、日常生活でどのように利用されているのですか？

A：日本では、不動産は、主に、住居、オフィス、商業の3つの用途で用いられています。**住宅用不動産**は、住む場所として利用され、例えば、**戸建住宅、分譲マンション、賃貸マンション**があります。**オフィスビル**は、働く場所として利用され、**商業施設**は、宝石店やレストランのように、何かを売ったり、サービスを提供する場所として利用されています。不動産は、他の目的にも、例えば、**物流施設、ホテル、老人ホーム、公共施設**としても、利用されています。

Q：不動産は、ビジネスではどのように利用されていますか？

A：不動産は、収入を得る手段としても用いられています。例えば、**不動産開発会社（デベロッパー）**は、戸建住宅や分譲マンションを作って、個人に売って利益を得ています。また、**不動産仲介会社**は、個人が戸建住宅や分譲マンションを探すのを手伝うことで、手数料収入を得ています。

不動産は、また、人や会社に貸すことで、収入を得ることもできます。**テナント（賃借人）**に貸している不動産は、**収益不動産（収益物件）、投資不動産**、あるいは、**商業用不動産**と呼ばれています。

1990年代後半くらいから、日本では、収益不動産は、**金融商品**としてみなされるようになりました。その結果、日本の投資家だけでなく、外国人投資家も、日本での不動産投資に関心を持つようになり、今や、日本の不動産市場は、グローバルな市場となっています。

What is real estate?

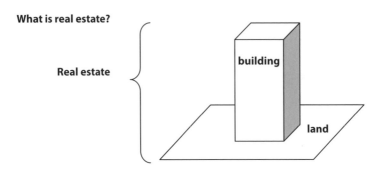

Real estate

building

land

Types of Real Estate

Residential   Office   Retail

Logistics   Hotel   Norsing Home

What is an income-producing property?

*A property owner can earn **rental income** by leasing its space to one or more tenants. The property which can be rented out is called "**income-producing property**".*

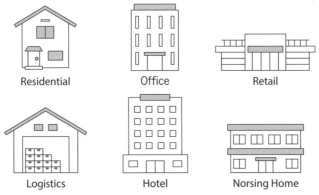

Lease

**Tenants
(Lessee)**

Rent

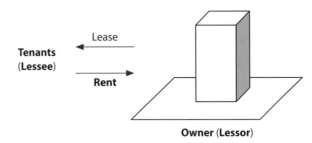

Owner (Lessor)

不動産とは何か？

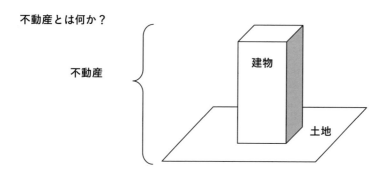

不動産の種類

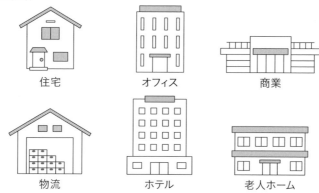

収益物件とは何か？

*不動産所有者は保有不動産の空間をテナントに貸すことで**賃料収入**を得ることができます。テナントに貸すことができる不動産を「**収益不動産（収益物件）**」と呼びます。*

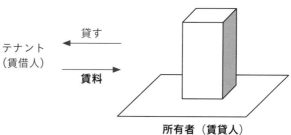

1-2 What kinds of real estate ownership are possible in Japan?

Q : What are the major rights related to the use of real estate in Japan?

A : The most common right of real estate usage is **ownership**. Article 206 of the Civil Law states, "an **owner** has the right to freely use, profit from and dispose of the thing owned, within the limits of laws and regulations". Since land and buildings are regarded as independent real estate in Japan, there are two types of real estate ownership: **land ownership and buildin**.

Q : Can individuals or companies own real estate together?

A : This type ownership includes joint ownership and sectional ownership.

Joint ownership (**co-ownership**) means two or more individuals or companies own land or a building together.

Sectional ownership (**strata-title**) means each individual or company owns sectional parts of a building. A condominium building is a good example of sectional ownership where each person in the building owns their individual unit independently from the other owners. Interestingly, the land underneath the condominium building is collectively owned in percentage form by all the owners according to the share (or size) of their unit.

Q : Are there any other rights related to the use of real estate?

A : Another major right of property usage is called **leasehold** (Chinshaku Ken). This means an individual or a company leases the real estate (land, or building, or both) from the owner. The **lessee** can then use the real estate for their own needs.

A similar right to land leasehold is called **superficies** (Chijyo Ken), which is explained in the Civil Law. Both land leasehold and superficies offer basically the same rights to the owners by the **Land Lease and Building Lease Law**. Unlike land leaseholds, superficies must be legally registered. So, superficies has not generally been used. The law describes a land leasehold or superficies for the purpose of owning and using a building as a "**land lease right** (Shakuchi Ken)".

1-2 不動産の権利には どのようなものがあるか？

Q：不動産の使用に係る日本での代表的な権利を教えてもらえますか？

A：最も一般的な不動産利用に係る権利は、**所有権**です。民法第206条は、「**所有者**は、法令の制限内において、自由にその所有物の使用、収益及び処分をする権利を有する。」と規定しています。日本では、土地と建物はそれぞれ独立した不動産とみなされていますので、不動産には、**土地所有権**と**建物所有権**という2種類の所有権形態があります。

Q：個人や会社が共同で不動産を所有することは可能ですか？

A：所有権には、共有と区分所有も含まれます。

共有は、複数の人や会社が、土地や建物を共同して所有している場合です。

区分所有は、ある人や会社が、建物の区分された部分を所有している場合を意味します。分譲マンションの建物のように、各個人が各戸を、他の人とは独立して所有している形態が、区分所有の代表的な例です。そして、この建物の下の土地は、建物の持分に応じてそれぞれが持分を有する共有の形態となっています。

Q：不動産を利用するための他の権利には何がありますか？

A：その他の不動産を利用する代表的な権利としては、**賃借権**があります。賃借権により、個人や会社は、土地や建物、あるいは土地建物の所有者から、それらを借りて、**賃借人**として、その不動産を自らのニーズに合わせて使用することができます。

土地賃借権に似た権利として、民法に定められている地上権があります。土地賃借権と**地上権**は、実質的に同様の権利が、**借地借家法**により与えられています。しかし、土地賃借権とは異なり、地上権は登記しなければなりません。したがって、地上権はあまり用いられていません。同法では、建物の所有を目的とする地上権又は土地の賃借権を、「**借地権**」と定めています。

Ownership

"XYZ company has ownership of the real estate".

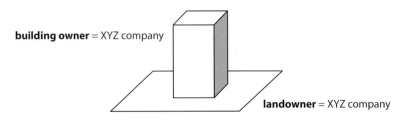

building owner = XYZ company

landowner = XYZ company

Sectional ownership(strata-title)

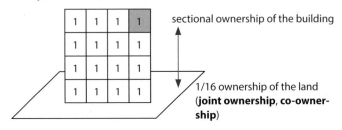

sectional ownership of the building

1/16 ownership of the land
(**joint ownership, co-owner-ship**)

Leasehold

*"XYZ company leases the land from ABC company. So, XYZ company has the **land lease right** of the land and can own the building on this land by themselves". On the other hand, ABC company has **land with leasehold interest** and can receive **ground rent** from XYZ company.*

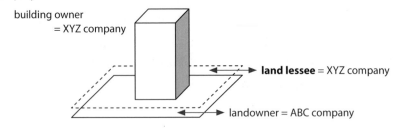

building owner
= XYZ company

land lessee = XYZ company

landowner = ABC company

所有権

XYZ社は、その不動産を所有しています。

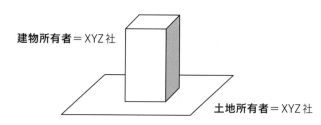

建物所有者＝XYZ社

土地所有者＝XYZ社

区分所有権

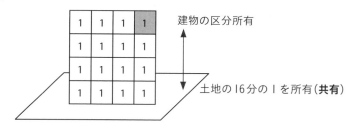

建物の区分所有

土地の16分の1を所有（**共有**）

賃借権

*XYZ社は、ABC社から土地を賃借しており、その土地の上に建物を所有するための**借地権**を持っています。一方、ABC社は**底地**を持っており、XYZ社から**地代**を受け取ることができます。*

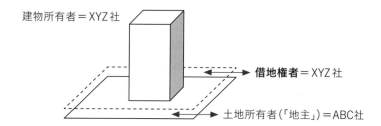

建物所有者＝XYZ社

借地権者＝XYZ社

土地所有者（「地主」）＝ABC社

1-3 How is real estate ownership recorded in Japan?

Q : How does the **real estate registration system** in Japan work ?

A : The real estate registration system is governed by the **Real Estate Registration Law**. Properties are registered in the **real estate registry**, which gives an overview of the property and the property's rights. The contents of the registry can be reviewed at the local **Legal Affairs Bureau,** or more conveniently, they may be accessed through the Internet. The law defines which contents can be listed on the registry, who may register them and how registration procedures are conducted.

Q : What contents are registered?

A : There are two main sections within the real estate registry: the description of the property and the rights of the property. The description of the property mainly describes the address, area and type of land, the **gross floor area** (**GFA**), the structure and the number of stories of the building. The term "right of the property" refers to the contents of ownership, **superficies, mortgages** and any other rights of the real estate. Corporations or individuals who have registered ownership of a piece of land or a building hold the **title deed** of the land or the building.

Q : Where is **real estate registration** conducted?

A : Real property registration is conducted at the Legal Affairs Bureau, which is governed by the **Justice Ministry.** Each Legal Affairs Bureau in Japan has a specific section where property registration takes place.

Q : Who are the key players in the real estate registration system?

A : The **registered land and house investigators** are responsible for preparing documents necessary for the description of the property aspect of real estate registration. **Judicial scriveners** are responsible for preparing documents related to the real property rights registration.

1-3 不動産の所有権は どのように登記されるのか?

Q：日本の**不動産登記制度**の概要を教えてもらえますか?

A：不動産登記制度は、**不動産登記法**により定められています。不動産の概要や権利を登記した帳簿を**不動産登記簿**と呼んでいます。不動産登記簿の内容は、**法務局**において閲覧することができます。また、インターネットでより簡単に見ることもできます。不動産登記法は、どのような内容を登記簿に登記できるか、誰が登記を行うか、どのように登記を行うか、などを定めています。

Q：どんな内容が登記されるのですか?

A：不動産登記簿の内容としては、不動産の表示と不動産の権利の2つが挙げられます。不動産の表示には、土地の所在、面積（地積）、種類（地目）などが、また、建物の所在地、**延床面積**、構造、階数などが記載されます。登記される不動産の権利には、所有権、**地上権**、**抵当権**などがあります。所有権登記をした法人や個人は、**権利証**（登記済権利証／登記識別情報）を保有します。

Q：**不動産登記**はどこで行われるのですか?

A：不動産登記が行われる場所は、法務局と呼ばれ、**法務省**の管轄です。各法務局は、それぞれ管轄の地域を持っており、その対象地域に所在する不動産の登記は、当該法務局で行わなければなりません。

Q：不動産登記制度で重要な役割を果たしているのは誰なのですか?

A：**土地家屋調査士**は、不動産表示登記に必要な書類の作成を行います。**司法書士**は、不動産権利登記に必要な書類の作成を行います。

Overview of real estate registration

The **Real Estate Registry** is usually divided into the **Land Registry** and the **Building Registry**. However, the registration of each unit in a sectionally owned condominium is combined into one registry, including joint ownership of the land and sectional ownership of the building.

Major Contents of a **Land Registry**

Description of the land *Address, lot number, usage, land area*	**registered land and building investigator**
Matters related to ownership of the land *Reason for ownership transfer, date of ownership transfer, date of ownership transfer registration, name, and address of the new owner*	**judicial scrivener**
Matters related to other rights other than ownership of the land *mortgage, superficies, etc.*	

Major Contents of a **Building Registry**

Description of the building *Site address, building number, type, structure, gross floor area, completion date of the building*	**registered land and building investigator**
Matters related to ownership of the building *Reason for ownership transfer, date of ownership transfer, date of ownership transfer registration, name and address of the new owner*	**judicial scrivener**
Matters related to other rights other than ownership of the building *mortgage, etc.*	

不動産登記の概要

*不動産登記簿*は、通常、*土地登記簿*（*全部事項証明書（土地）*）と*建物登記簿*（*全部事項証明書（建物）*）に分けられます。しかし、分譲マンションのような区分所有建物のそれぞれの区画の登記簿は、土地の共有持分と建物の区分所有が1つの登記簿にまとめられています。

土地登記簿（全部事項証明書（土地））の主な内容

表題部（土地の表示） *所在、地番、地目、地積*	土地家屋調査士
権利部（甲区：所有権に関する事項） *所有権移転の原因、所有権移転日及び登記日、所有者の名前及び住所*	司法書士
権利部（乙区：所有権以外の権利に関する事項） *抵当権、地上権など*	

建物登記簿（全部事項証明書（建物））の主な内容

表題部（建物の表示） *所在、家屋番号、種類、構造、床面積、建築年月日*	土地家屋調査士
権利部（甲区：所有権に関する事項） *所有権移転の原因、所有権移転日及び登記日、所有者の名前及び住所*	司法書士
権利部（乙区：所有権以外の権利に関する事項） *抵当権など*	

1-4 What laws govern real estate?

Q : What laws govern the rights of real estate?

A : The **Civil Law** describes the general rules for the purchase, sale and lease of real estate. The Civil Law regulates ownership and superficies and also provides the definition of security rights such as a pledge and a mortgage.

The **Land and Building Lease Law,** which is a special law of the Civil Law, provides the general rules of land leases and building leases.

The **Sectional Ownership Law** provides the general rules on sectional ownership for owners.

Q : What are the major laws that regulate the use of real estate?

A : The **City Planning Law** and the **Building Standards Law** mainly deal with how we can use land and what kinds of buildings we can build according to the zoning regulations. More detailed information on these laws will be explained in the next two sections. Additionally, land transactions over a certain land area size are usually required to be notified after the transaction to the prefectural governor where the subject property is located based on the **National Land Use Planning Law**.

Other major laws, which regulate the use of real estate, include the **Agricultural Land Law**, which regulates agricultural land transactions and the **Land Readjustment Law**, which focuses on the reallocation of land to improve a town.

Q : Are there any other important laws related to real estate?

A : The **Real Estate Brokerage Law**, which governs **real estate transactions**, provides essential guidelines for real estate developers and real estate agent companies that deal with real estate as a commercial product.

Regarding the due diligence process of investment properties, compliance with the **Fire Protection Law** must be checked carefully because this law stipulates what equipment is required for the building to guard against the danger posed by fire.

不動産はどのような法律で規制されているのか?

Q：不動産の権利を規制する法律にはどのようなものがあるのですか？

A：**民法**は、不動産の売買や賃貸借に関するルールを定めています。民法には、所有権や地上権、また、担保権としての質権や抵当権についての記載もあります。

借地借家法は、民法の特別法で、土地賃貸借や建物賃貸借に係る基本ルールを定めている法律です。

建物の区分所有等に関する法律は、区分所有建物に住む区分所有者間のルールを定めた法律です。

Q：不動産の利用を規制する主な法律には何がありますか？

A：**都市計画法**と**建築基準法**は、主に、用途規制に応じて、どのように土地を利用できるか、また、どのような建物を建築することが可能か、を定めている法律です。詳細は、本章第5節及び第6節で説明します。また、一定面積以上の土地の取引では**国土利用計画法**に基づき、通常、事後届出が求められます。

不動産の利用を規制する他の主な法律としては、農地取引を規制する**農地法**や、街並みを整備するために土地を区画整理する**土地区画整理法**があります。

Q：不動産に関連する他の主な法律には何がありますか？

A：**不動産取引**を規制する**宅地建物取引業法**は、不動産を商品として扱う**デベロッパー**や**不動産仲介会社**にとっては必須の法律です。

投資不動産のデューデリジェンス手続きにおいては、**消防法**を遵守しているか否かも重要です。同法は、火災での危険から建物内の人を守るために必要な設備を規定しているからです。

Major Laws Related to Real Estate Investigation

Real estate buyers usually investigate the ownership structure, zoning, and building restrictions based on the following laws before purchasing real estate. In Japan, licensed real estate brokers are required to explain the above points to buyers by providing the **Property Disclosure Statement of Important Issues.**

Ownership structure: **Civil Law, Land Lease and Building Lease Law, Sectional Ownership Law.**

Zoning and building restrictions: **City Planning Law, Building Standards Law, Agricultural Land Law, Land Readjustment Law**, etc.

Laws Related to Real Estate Transactions

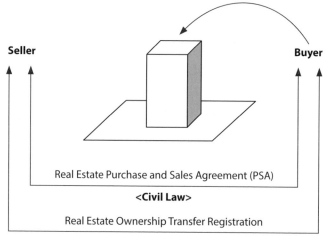

Seller   **Buyer**

Real Estate Purchase and Sales Agreement (PSA)
\<Civil Law\>
Real Estate Ownership Transfer Registration
\<Real Estate Registration Law\>

Real Estate Agent Company
\<Real Estate Brokerage Law\>

不動産調査に関連する主な法律

*不動産の購入者は、通常、対象不動産の所有形態、用途規制や建築規制などを、下記のような法律に基づいて事前に調査します。日本では、これらの調査事項は、不動産仲介会社が**重要事項説明書**により購入者に説明することが求められています。*

所有形態：**民法、借地借家法、建物の区分所有等に関する法律**
用途規制・建築規制：**都市計画法、建築基準法、農地法、土地区画整理法**など

不動産取引に関連する法律

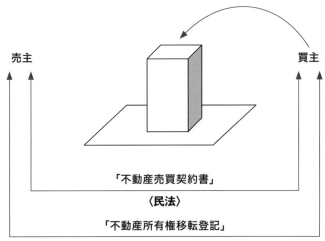

売主　　　　　　　　　　　　　　　買主

「不動産売買契約書」
〈民法〉
「不動産所有権移転登記」
〈不動産登記法〉

「不動産仲介会社」
〈宅地建物取引業法〉

1-5 | What is the City Planning Law?

Q : What is the purpose of the City Planning Law?

A : The **City Planning Law**, which is supervised by the **Ministry of Land, Infrastructure, Transport and Tourism** (**MLIT**), exists to regulate urban development.

The law divides all of Japan into mainly two parts; **City Planning Areas,** which are regulated by the City Planning Law and Non-City Planning Areas, which are not regulated by this law.

A City Planning Area is mainly divided into **Urbanization Promotion Areas,** where development is promoted, and **Urbanization Restricted Areas,** where development is restricted. Urbanization restricted areas consist primarily of agriculture, forestry, and fishery projects and are do not generally allow residential, office, or retail properties to be built.

Q : What kinds of major regulations are there in the urbanization promotion areas?

A : The law defines thirteen **zoning districts** within urbanization promotion areas. Of these zoning districts, three have a primary effect on real estate projects; **residential districts, commercial districts,** and **industrial districts.** Specific regulations for each district, such as allowable use, building coverage ratio, and floor area ratio, are defined by the Building Standards Law, which is explained in the next section.

Q : Are there any other major City Planning Law regulations?

A : Other important zoning regulations include the **fire prevention districts** and **semi-fire prevention districts,** where building structures must take extra fire precautions.

The City Planning Law also requires real estate developers to receive **land development permission** from the relevant local government before they develop a certain size of land within an urbanization promotion area.

1-5 都市計画法とはどのような法律か?

Q:都市計画法の概要を教えてもらえますか?

A:都市計画法は、**国土交通省**により所管されている、計画的なまちづくりのための法律です。

そのために、都市計画法では、日本全体を大まかに、同法の規制の対象となる**都市計画区域**と、規制の対象とならない**都市計画区域外**に分けています。

都市計画区域は、主に、市街化を推進する**市街化区域**と、市街化を抑制する**市街化調整区域**に分けられます。市街化調整区域は、主に農業、林業、漁業の用地として使用され、原則として、住宅、事務所、店舗を建設することができません。

Q:市街化区域では、主にどのような規制がありますか?

A:都市計画法は、市街化区域で、13種類の地域(**用途地域**)を定めています。用途地域は、どのような不動産の用途が可能かで、主に**住居地域**、**商業地域**、**工業地域**という3つに分けることができます。それぞれの用途地域における具体的な建築規制、例えば、建築可能な用途、許容されている建ぺい率や容積率は、次節で説明する建築基準法が定めています。

Q:都市計画法による他の主な規制には何がありますか?

A:上記の用途地域以外の、主要な用途規制としては、その地域内の建物はその構造を燃えにくいものにしなければならないという**防火地域**や**準防火地域**があります。

また、市街化区域内における一定の開発行為においては、不動産開発会社は、都市計画法に基づき、当該地域を所管する地方公共団体から**開発許可**を得る必要があります。

Overview of regulations by the City Planning Law

All land in Japan

City Planning Area: Approx. 27%	Non-City Planning Area: Approx. 73%
Urbanization Restricted Areas *agricultural land, etc.*	*Forests, Mountainous areas.*
Urbanization Promotion Areas: Approx. 4% *residential real estate, office buildings, retail properties, industrial properties, etc.*	

Thirteen Zoning Districts

Eight Residential Districts:
    class one exclusive zone for low-rise residences
    class two exclusive zone for low-rise residences
    class one exclusive zone for medium and high-rise residences
    class two exclusive zone for medium and high-rise residences
    class one residential zone
    class two residential zone
    semi-residential zone
    rural residential zone

Two Commercial Districts:
    neighborhood commercial zone
    commercial zone

Three Industrial Districts:
    semi-industrial zone
    industrial zone
    exclusive industrial zone

都市計画法による規制の概要

日本全国の土地

都市計画区域：約27%　　　　　**都市計画区域外**：約73%

市街化調整区域 *農地など*	*森林や山岳地帯*
市街化区域：約4% *住宅用不動産、オフィスビル、商業施設、産業施設など*	

13の用途地域

8つの住居系地域：
- **第一種低層住居専用地域**
- **第二種低層住居専用地域**
- **第一種中高層住居専用地域**
- **第二種中高層住居専用地域**
- **第一種住居地域**
- **第二種住居地域**
- **準住居地域**
- **田園住居地域**

2つの商業系地域：
- **近隣商業地域**
- **商業地域**

3つの工業系地域：
- **準工業地域**
- **工業地域**
- **工業専用地域**

1-6 What is the Building Standards Law?

Q : What is the purpose and mission of the Building Standards Law?

A : The **Building Standards Law** is supervised by the MLIT to provide basic rules for constructing a building and stipulates minimum engineering safety requirements with regard to fires, earthquakes, and other **natural disasters.** It also stipulates the types of buildings we can build according to each zoning district under the **City Planning Law.** The **height limit** of each building is also stipulated in order to maintain adequate **sunshine** and/or **ventilation** for adjacent roads and buildings.

A building not constructed to meet these requirements is regarded as an **illegal building.** However, a building previously constructed in compliance with standards existing at the time of construction but which no longer meets current construction standards is not considered an illegal building but rather a **legal nonconforming building.**

Q : What is the procedure for constructing a building in Japan?

A : Before any construction begins, a **building permit** must be received from the relevant local government or a **designated confirmation and inspection body.** These procedures ensure the building is constructed in compliance with the Building Standards Law. Upon completion, buildings in compliance with the law receive a **Building Inspection Certificate;** which provides legal documentation that the building meets or exceeds requirements as stipulated in the law.

Q : What are the building coverage ratio and the floor area ratio?

A : The law also governs the building coverage ratio and the floor area ratio of a new building based on the thirteen zoning district requirements.

The **building coverage ratio (BCR)** is the allowable area of land that the building will sit on. The **floor area ratio (FAR)** is the building's total size in relation to the land size. Usually in Japan, this refers to how high (number of floors) you can build based on the size of the land on which the building sits.

1-6 建築基準法とはどのような法律か？

Q：建築基準法の目的や役割を教えてもらえますか？

A：**建築基準法**は、**国土交通省**により所管されている、建物を建築する場合の基本的なルールを定めた法律で、火災や地震などの**自然災害**から建物の安全を確保するために最低限守らなければならないルールは何かを定めています。また、**都市計画法**で定められたそれぞれの用途地域でどのような建物が建築できるかも定められています。また、道路や隣接地の**日当たり**や通風（**風通し**）を確保するための**高さ制限**も定められています。

　建築基準法に違反している建物は、**違法建築物**とみなされます。しかし、竣工したときの建築基準法には適合していたのに、その後の法改正で現在の建築基準法には適合していない建物は、違法ではなく、**既存不適格建築物**と呼ばれます。

Q：建物を建築するのにどんな手続きが必要なのですか？

A：建物を建築する場合には、当該地域を管轄する地方公共団体、もしくは**指定確認検査機関**から**建築確認**を得る必要があります。建築確認手続きは、当該建物が建築基準法を遵守しているかどうかを確認するものです。建築基準法を遵守している建物には、竣工時に、**検査済証**が発行されます。検査済証は、当該建物が建築基準法に記載されている要件を満たしていることを示す法的な書面となります。

Q：建ぺい率と容積率とは何ですか？

A：建築基準法は、13種類の用途地域に応じて、建物の建ぺい率と容積率を規制しています。

　建ぺい率とは、敷地面積に対する建築面積の割合のことです。**容積率**とは、敷地面積に対してどれくらいの床面積の建物が建てられるかを示すものです。通常、日本においては、その建物の敷地においてどのくらいの高さの建物が建てられるかを示す数値といえます。

Case A: *Residential District (Building Coverage Ratio: 50% Floor Area Ratio: 100%)*

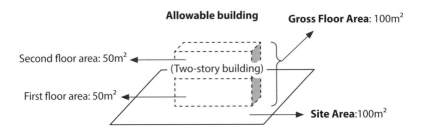

Allowable building

Gross Floor Area: 100m²

Second floor area: 50m² ← (Two-story building)

First floor area: 50m²

Site Area:100m²

Case B: *Commercial District (Building Coverage Ratio: 80% Floor Area Ratio: 800%)*

Allowable building

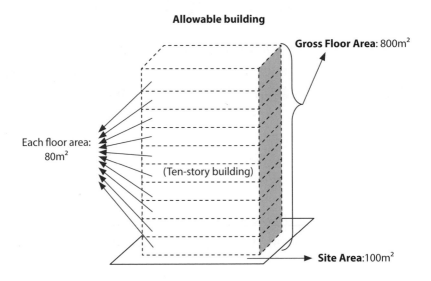

Gross Floor Area: 800m²

Each floor area: 80m²

(Ten-story building)

Site Area:100m²

*The floor area ratio is also restricted according to the **width of the front road** of the subject property.*
*On the other hand, in Japan, there are several ways for developers to build **high-rise buildings** or **high-rise condominiums** (**apartments**) by using a higher floor area ratio than the ratio defined by the law. A typical example is the **comprehensive design system** of the Building Standards Law, which requires developers to secure **public open space**.*

ケースＡ：*住居系地域（建ぺい率：50％、容積率：100％）*

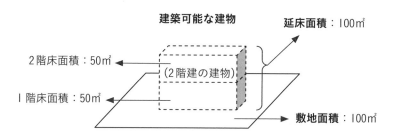

建築可能な建物

延床面積：100㎡

2階床面積：50㎡ ← （2階建の建物）

1階床面積：50㎡ ←

敷地面積：100㎡

ケースＢ：*商業系地域（建ぺい率：80％、容積率：800％）*

建築可能な建物

延床面積：800㎡

各階床面積：
80㎡ ← （10階建の建物）

敷地面積：100㎡

容積率は、対象不動産の***前面道路幅員***によっても制限されます。
一方で、日本には建築基準法に定められている容積率の割増を受けることで、デベロッパーが**高層ビル**や**タワーマンション**を建てられるいくつかの制度があります。代表的な例は、建築基準法に定められた**総合設計制度**です。この制度ではデベロッパーは**公開空地**を確保することが求められます。

1-7 What role do Local Government Ordinances play?

Q : How do local government ordinances differ from central government laws with regard to real estate in Japan?

A : **Ordinances** actually have almost the same effect as laws. **Guidelines**, which are also made by **local governments** and are often confused with ordinances, have a weaker effect than ordinances. Major ordinances in Japan include the number of required parking spaces for a building, the necessary green space on a property site and the necessary facilities for elderly or disabled people.

Q : How does an ordinance regulate parking spaces?

A : The local government ordinance that requires minimum parking spaces in a building primarily applies to condominiums and rental apartments. This ordinance aims to reduce **illegal parking** on public roads. To deal with this requirement, owners of property can provide **parking lots** on the site, or because Japan has limited space, sometimes **machine parking** is used. In the event developers cannot provide sufficient parking on the property, they will then be required to secure parking spaces outside of the subject property.

Q : How does an ordinance regulate green space?

A : Ordinances that require minimum **green space** on a property aim to keep the environment surrounding the property clean and more livable.

Q : How does an ordinance regulate facilities for elderly and/or disabled people?

A : Local ordinances also require facilities for **elderly people** and/or **disabled people**. Retail properties, hotels and especially properties used by the general public require such facilities. Typical examples of this ordinance are the addition of **handrails**, mirrors attached to elevators and a **wheelchair** accessible ramp near the entrance of the building.

地方公共団体の条例はどのような役割を果たしているのか？

Q：地方公共団体が定める条例は、政府が定める法律と、不動産の規制に関してどのように異なるのですか？

A：**条例**は、法律と同様の効力を持ちます。同じように**地方公共団体**が定め、条例と混同する用語に、**要綱**がありますが、これは、条例に比べると効力が弱いものです。主な条例には、駐車場付置義務条例、緑地条例、福祉のまちづくり条例などがあります。

Q：条例は、どのように駐車場を規制しているのですか？

A：駐車場付置義務条例は、分譲マンションや賃貸マンションなどが主な対象になります。この条例は、公道における**違法駐車**を減らすことを目的としています。対象不動産の所有者は、この条例を守るために、平面**駐車場**を確保します。また、日本は敷地が狭いため、**機械式駐車場**を整備する場合もあります。デベロッパーは、対象不動産において十分な駐車場を確保できない場合には、対象不動産の外で駐車場を確保する必要があります。

Q：条例は、どのように緑地を規制しているのですか？

A：緑地条例とは、対象不動産に最低限必要な**緑地面積**を定めたもので、対象不動産の周辺環境をきれいで住みやすくするのが目的です。

Q：条例は、どのように高齢者や障害者のために施設を規制しているのですか？

A：福祉のまちづくり条例は、**高齢者**や**障害者**のための設備を求めています。商業施設やホテル、また、特に不特定多数の人々が利用する不動産においては、そのような設備が求められます。典型的な例としては、エレベーターに障害者用の**手すり**や鏡を設置したり、建物の出入り口に**車椅子**用のスロープを設けたりすることです。

Local governments

*Japan is made up of **47 prefectures** (**47-to-do-fu-ken**). Only Tokyo-to is not called Tokyo prefecture but called **Tokyo Metropolis** in English. Although Hokkai-do, Osaka-fu, and Kyoto-fu are not "ken", they are usually called **Hokkaido prefecture**, **Osaka prefecture**, and **Kyoto prefecture** in English as well.*

Tokyo Metropolis
*Tokyo is made up of 23 **wards(ku)**, 26 **cities(shi)**, 5 **towns** and 8 **villages**.*

Tokyo Metropolitan Government			
Ward Offices	**City Offices**	**Town Offices**	**Village Offices**

*The "**Tokyo 23 Wards**"(Tokyo 23-ku in Japanese) have recently been increasingly referred to as the "Tokyo 23 Cities" in English. For example, the current website of "Chiyoda-ku" now identifies itself in English as "Chiyoda City".*

Other Prefectures
Each prefecture is made up of cities, towns, and villages.

Prefectural Government		
City Offices	Town Offices	Village Offices

__Government-ordinance-designated cities__, which are large, major cities in Japan and known in Japanese as "seirei shitei toshi", are also authorized to have a number of "ku". As an example, the city of Osaka consists of 24 wards (ku), which are totally different from the "ku" that exist in Tokyo. While "ku" within Tokyo are the most similar to an autonomous city, the "ku" within the City of Osaka are governed by the City of Osaka. The "ku" of Tokyo contains a distinct ward Mayor, a distinct ward Assembly, and a distinct ward election process, while the "ku" in the City of Osaka do not have this autonomy or authority.

地方公共団体（地方自治体）

日本は47**都道府県**から構成されています。**東京都**だけは、prefecture ではなく、metropolis が使われています。**北海道**、**大阪府**、**京都府**は県ではありませんが、英語では通常 prefecture が使われています。

東京都

東京都は、23の**区**、26の**市**、5つの**町**、8つの**村**から構成されています。

東京都庁			
区役所	市役所	町役場	村役場

東京23区は、最近では、英語で「Tokyo 23 Cities」と呼ばれています。例えば、千代田区の現在のウェブサイトは「Chiyoda-city」として自らの区を紹介しています。

他の道府県

各道府県は、市、町、村から構成されています。

道庁・府庁・県庁		
市役所	町役場	村役場

日本の主要大都市である**「政令指定都市」**でもいくつかの「区」を持つことが許されています。例えば、大阪市には、24の区があります。しかし、これらの「区」と東京の「区」は、全く異なります。東京の「区」が「市」とほぼ同様のものであるのに対して、大阪市の「区」は大阪市によって統治されています。つまり、東京の「区」は、区長がいて、区議会があって、区議会選挙もありますが、大阪市の「区」には、そのような自治の権限はありません。

1-8 What kinds of taxes are imposed on real estate?

Q : What taxes are there in Japan when acquiring real estate?

A : **Real estate acquisition tax** is paid by individuals and companies that acquire real estate in Japan.

Registration tax is imposed on individuals and companies when they register their ownership of the property or change any contents of the real estate registry.

Real estate acquisition tax and registration tax is calculated by multiplying the **tax assessed value** by a designated tax rate.

Stamp tax is imposed on both parties who sign the real estate purchase and sales agreement.

Q : What taxes are there in Japan when owning real estate?

A : **Property taxes** include **fixed asset tax** and **city planning tax**, which are payable by individuals and companies that own real estate as of January 1st of each year. While fixed asset tax is levied on owners of land, buildings, and **depreciable assets**, city planning tax is levied only on owners of land and buildings in urbanization promotion areas. The fixed asset tax rate is usually 1.4% of the **tax assessed value** of the property. The city planning tax rate is usually 0.3% of the tax assessed value.

Q : What other taxes relating to real estate are there in Japan?

A : **Income tax (personal income tax)** related to real estate is the tax on individuals who gain rental income or capital gain through the sale of real estate.

Corporate tax (corporate income tax) is the tax on companies that have **taxable income**. Therefore, their real estate rental income and any profit from a real estate sale have an impact on their total taxable income level.

Consumption tax within Japan is levied on goods and services. Regarding real estate businesses, consumption tax is levied on the purchase price allocation of the building (not land) and the rent for non-residential building spaces. This **tax rate** is currently 10%.

1-8 不動産にはどのような税金が課せられるのか？

Q：日本では、不動産を取得するときにどのような税金がありますか？

A：**不動産取得税**は、不動産を取得した個人や会社に課せられる税金です。

登録免許税は、不動産を取得した個人や会社が、自らの所有権を登記する際や、登記簿の内容を変更した際に、課せられる税金です。

不動産取得税や登録免許税は、**課税標準額**に税率を乗じて算定されます。

印紙税は、不動産売買契約書に署名する両当事者に課せられます。

Q：日本では、不動産を保有しているときにどのような税金がありますか？

A：**固定資産税**及び**都市計画税**といった**不動産保有税**は、毎年1月1日に不動産を保有する個人や会社に課せられる税金です。固定資産税は、土地、建物、**償却資産**の所有者に課せられますが、都市計画税は、市街化区域における土地、建物の所有者のみに課せられます。通常、固定資産税の税率は**課税標準額**の1.4％で、都市計画税の税率は0.3％です。

Q：日本では、上記以外に不動産に関連したどのような税金がありますか？

A：不動産に関連する**所得税**は、賃貸収入を得たり、不動産の売却により売却益を得た個人に対する税金です。

法人税は、**課税所得**のある法人に課せられる税金です。ですから、賃貸収入や不動産売却益などは、それらの法人の課税所得に影響を及ぼします。

消費税は、物品やサービスに課せられます。不動産ビジネスにおいては、消費税は、建物の取得価格や、非住宅建物を借りる場合の賃料などに課せられます。その**税率**は現在10％です。

Corporate tax

There are several taxes imposed on corporate income. In this book, those taxes are collectively referred to as "corporate tax," or "corporate taxes."

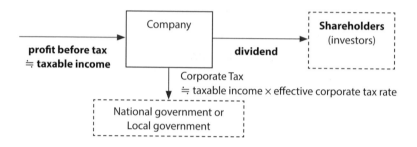

Fixed asset tax & City planning tax

Fixed asset tax and city planning tax are paid to city governments, town governments and village governments.

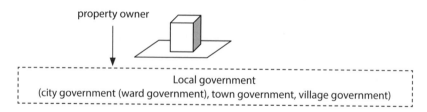

Real estate acquisition tax & Registration tax

Real estate acquisition tax is paid to the prefectural government and registration tax is paid to the national government.

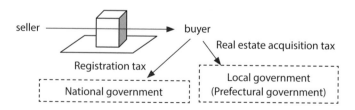

法人税

法人の所得に課税される税金はいくつかあります。本書では、これらの複数の税金をまとめて法人税としています。

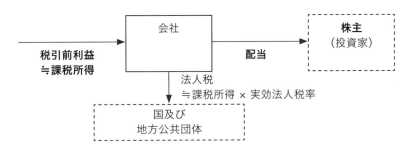

固定資産税 & 都市計画税

固定資産税と都市計画税は、各市町村に支払われます。

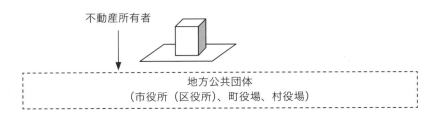

不動産取得税 & 登録免許税

不動産取得税は各県に、登録免許税は国に支払われます。

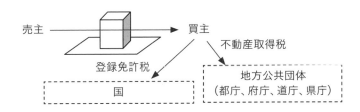

What are Japanese property leases?

Q : What is the leasing system in Japan?

A : The Civil Law provides general rules for leases, but the **Land and Building Lease Law** is more specific than the Civil Law in relation to real estate leases.

In general, there are two types of leases in Japan: **ordinary leases**, where tenants can renew the term and **fixed-term leases** where they can't.

Q : How does the Land and Building Lease Law govern the lease system?

A : Since both land and buildings are considered independent forms of real estate in Japan, the law governs land leases and building leases separately.

With regard to land leases, there are two main types of leases :

Ordinary land lease rights in Japan allow the land lessee to continue using the land with no clear expiration date as long as the lessee keeps paying the agreed upon rent.

Fixed-term land lease rights in Japan allow the landowner (**landlord**) to stipulate a timeline for the lease contract. Land is leased in this fashion, with 10-50 year leases being standard for retail sites and usually 50+ years for land used for residential properties. At the end of the lease term, the lessee must return the land to the landowner unless a new lease contract is agreed upon.

Q : How about building leases?

A : There are also two types of rights: **ordinary building lease rights** and **fixed-term building lease rights**.

If a tenant has a 2-year fixed-term lease, then at the end of the 2 years, the owner(**landlord**) can force the lessee to leave because the contract has expired, or both parties can agree to renegotiate a whole new lease.

On the contrary, in an ordinary term lease, if the owner would like to cancel the contract and force the lessee to leave, they must provide a **justifiable reason** to do so, but this is legally very difficult to accomplish in Japan.

1-9 日本の不動産賃貸借はどのようになっているのか?

Q：日本の賃貸借制度の概要を教えてもらえますか?

A：民法が、賃貸借一般のルールについて規定していますが、不動産の賃貸借に関しては、**借地借家法**がより詳細を定めています。

大きくは、日本には2つの賃貸借があります。1つはテナントが契約期間を更新できる**普通借**で、もう1つはそうではない**定借**です。

Q：借地借家法は、どのように賃貸借制度を定めているのですか?

A：日本では、土地と建物はそれぞれ独立した不動産なので、借地借家法では、借地と借家を別々に規定しています。

借地に関しては、借地借家法は2つの種類の借地権を規定しています。

普通借地権では、賃貸借契約上の期間の定めの有無に関わらず、借地人は、同意した賃料の支払いを継続してさえいれば、土地を利用し続けることができます。

定期借地権は、土地所有者（**地主**）が、賃貸借契約書で借地期間を定めることができます。商業施設用の土地では一般的に10年から50年の間、住宅用の土地では通常50年以上の期間で、賃借されます。賃貸借期間が終わると、借地人は、新たな賃貸借契約が合意されない限り、土地を、所有者に返還する必要があります。

Q：建物の賃貸借はどうなっていますか?

A：建物の賃貸借に関しても、**普通借家権**と**定期借家権**という2つの借家権があります。

2年の定期借家の場合には、所有者（**家主**）は2年後に、借家人を退去させることもできますし、また、新たな契約締結を交渉することも選択できます。

逆に、普通借家の場合には、借家人を退去させようとすると、所有者にはそうするための「**正当事由**」が求められます。所有者にとって、この正当事由の証明は、簡単ではありません。

Two Types of Land Leases(Land Lease Contracts)

Ordinary land lease right: Renewable
A building owner can renew their land-lease term with the landowner and keep owning the building.

Fixed-term land lease right: Non-renewable
The building owner cannot renew their land-lease term. When the term expires, they must demolish the building and give the land back to the landowner. The only way for them to keep holding the building is to persuade the landowner to enter into a new land lease contract with them.

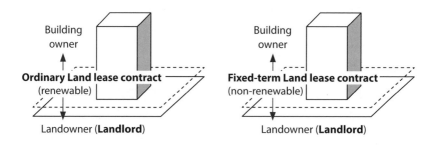

Two Types of Building Leases(Building Lease Contract)

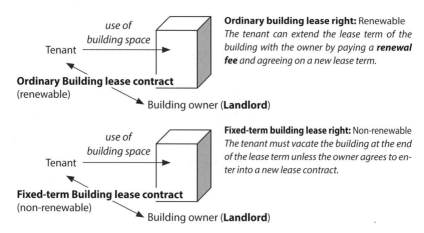

Ordinary building lease right: Renewable
*The tenant can extend the lease term of the building with the owner by paying a **renewal fee** and agreeing on a new lease term.*

Fixed-term building lease right: Non-renewable
The tenant must vacate the building at the end of the lease term unless the owner agrees to enter into a new lease contract.

2種類の借地権（借地契約）

普通借地権：更新可能
建物所有者は、土地所有者との借地期間を更新することができ、建物を保有し続けることができます。

定期借地権：更新不可
建物所有者は、借地期間を更新することができません。期間が満了すると、建物所有者は建物を取り壊し、土地所有者に土地を返還しなければなりません。建物を保有し続ける唯一の方法は、土地所有者に、新たな借地契約を締結してもらうようにすることです。

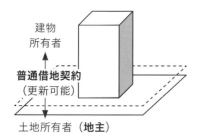 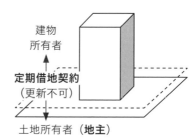

2種類の借家権（借家契約）

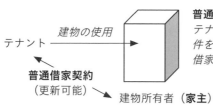

普通借家権：更新可能
*テナントは、**更新料**を払い、賃貸借条件を合意することで、建物所有者との借家契約を延長することができます。*

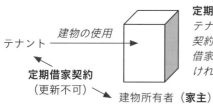

定期借家権：更新不可
テナントは、建物所有者が新たな借家契約の締結に合意してくれない限り、借家期間の終了時には建物を明渡さなければなりません。

1-10 What is the process of purchasing real estate in Japan?

Q : How do individuals or general companies buy real estate in Japan?

A : The first step in the process is locating **real estate for sale** in the market. Usually, when individuals or companies consider purchasing real estate, they consult with several **real estate agent companies**. Real estate agent companies have access to vast amounts of market information and can provide **property tours** for clients. When the seller is a company (as opposed to an individual), the buyer will usually be required to sign a **confidentiality agreement** (**CA**) in order to receive detailed information about a property.

Q : What should buyers do if they want to buy a specific property?

A : The second step in purchasing a property is submitting a **letter of intent** (**LOI**) or a **letter of commitment to purchase** (**LOC**) to the owner. Usually, this is done using a broker to deliver the letter and begin negotiations. If the seller is satisfied with the **terms and conditions** and the price in the LOI/LOC, they can agree at this point and reply to the offer with a **letter of acceptance** (**LOA**) to the buyer.

The third step is the buyer's **due diligence** process, where both parties negotiate in detail and the buyer also talks with lenders about obtaining financing.

The final step in the process is the signing of the **real estate purchase and sales agreement**, which stipulates the details of the negotiations and understandings between the buyer and seller. Once the purchase and sales agreement is concluded, then comes the **settlement**, **property delivery** and **registration** of the new owner.

Q : What role does the real estate agent company have in the transaction?

A : Before concluding the agreement, the real estate agent company has to provide the **Property Disclosure Statement of Important Issues**, which provides all the detailed matters relevant to the subject property. The real estate agent company also signs the purchase and sales agreement as the broker. These obligations of the broker are based on the **Real Estate Brokerage Law**.

1-10 日本における不動産購入手続きはどのように行われるのか?

Q：日本では、個人や一般的な会社はどのようにして不動産を買うのですか?

A：まず、最初のステップは、**売却物件**を探すことです。通常は、不動産を買いたい個人や会社は、**不動産仲介会社**に相談します。不動産仲介会社は、多くの不動産情報を持っており、また、顧客に対して、**物件内覧**も実施してくれます。(個人ではなく)会社が不動産の売主となる場合には、通常、買主は物件の詳細な資料を受領するために、**秘密保持契約**の締結を求められます。

Q：特定の不動産を買いたい場合にはどうするのですか?

A：次のステップとしては、買主は、交渉を始めるために、仲介会社を通じて、売主に対して**購入意向表明書**もしくは**買付証明書**を提示します。もし、売主が、それらに記載された**取引条件**や価格に満足する場合には、売主から買主に対して**売渡承諾書**を提示します。

そして、買主は**詳細な調査**を実施し、両者はより詳細な交渉を行います。買主は、通常、レンダーとの交渉も行います。

最終的に条件がまとまれば、買主と売主との合意条件を記載した**不動産売買契約書**を締結します。売買契約が締結されたら、売買代金の**決済**、新所有者への**不動産の引渡し**と**登記**が実施されます。

Q：取引における不動産仲介会社の役割は何ですか?

A：売買契約締結の前に、不動産仲介会社は、買主に対して対象不動産の詳細を記載した**重要事項説明書**を説明しなければなりません。また、不動産売買契約書にも、不動産仲介会社が仲介者として調印するのが通常です。これらの仲介会社の義務は、**宅地建物取引業法**に基づくものです。

General Real Estate Purchasing Procedure in Japan

These processes apply to the transactions of both commercial and residential properties as well as residential properties between individuals, between companies, and between individuals and companies. The simplified chart below shows these processes.

Unlike these transactions, the transaction of investment properties conducted by professional investors is very complicated and will be detailed in Chapter 4.

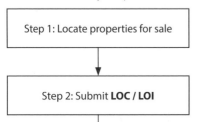

Step 1: Locate properties for sale

Step 2: Submit **LOC / LOI**

In Japan, "Kaitsuke Shomei Sho" literally translated as **LOC (letter of commitment to purchase)** used to be the only letter used in real estate transactions. Its meaning is different from that of the **LOI (letter of intent)**, literally translated as "Konyu Iko Hyomei Sho," which is widely used in current-day real estate investment transactions. This is why misunderstandings between Japanese sellers and foreign investors sometimes occur.

Step 3: Conduct **Due Diligence**

Property defects will be identified in the "**Property Disclosure Statement of Important Issues**" submitted and explained by **a Licensed Real Estate Broker**. An Engineering Report and a Market Report are not usually needed in general real estate transactions.

Step 4: Sign PSA and close the deal

The **contract date** and the **closing date** are usually different. A 10-20% **deposit** is customarily required when the PSA is executed, with the **remaining payment** made at closing. **Ownership transfer registration** is conducted at the closing date.

Lump sum payment on the contract date or the closing date is also available based on the agreement between a buyer and a seller.

Several documents, such as **identity verification documents** (**driver's license**, etc.), **seal registration certificate**, a **residence certificate**, a **power of attorney** to the judicial scrivener, etc., are required for PSA and registration procedures. A **seal** is also used. Regarding foreign individuals and foreign companies, **signature certificate**, **affidavit certificate**, etc. are required.

日本における一般的な不動産購入手続き

　この手続きは、個人間、会社間、あるいは、個人と会社間における**商業不動産**
や住宅用不動産の取引に該当します。下記は、当該手続きを簡素化して示したも
のです。

　この手続きとは異なり、**プロ投資家**による**投資不動産**の取引手続きは非常に複
雑です。この手続きは第4章で取り上げます。

```
┌─────────────────────────────┐
│  ステップ1：売却物件の探索          │
└─────────────────────────────┘
              │
              ▼
┌─────────────────────────────┐
│  ステップ2：買付証明書／           │
│        購入意向表明書の提示          │
└─────────────────────────────┘
              │
```

　　　　日本では、不動産取引においては、もともと「**買付証明
　　　　書**」だけが用いられていました。これは、現在の投資用不
　　　　動産取引で用いられている「**LOI（購入意向表明書）**」とは
　　　　意味が異なります。このことが、日本の売主と海外投資家
　　　　との間でしばしば誤解が発生する原因となっています。

```
              │
              ▼
┌─────────────────────────────┐
│  ステップ3：詳細調査の実施          │
└─────────────────────────────┘
              │
```

　　　　買主は、対象不動産に関する**瑕疵**の有無については、一
　　　　般的に、**宅地建物取引士**によって提示され説明される**重要
　　　　事項説明書**に頼ります。一般的な不動産取引においては、
　　　　エンジニアリングレポートやマーケットレポートは必要と
　　　　されません。

```
              │
              ▼
┌─────────────────────────────┐
│  ステップ4：売買契約書締結          │
│        及び取引完了              │
└─────────────────────────────┘
```

　通常、**契約日**と**決済日**は別に実施されます。この場合、契約日に1割から2割
の**手付金**が求められ、決済日に**残金支払**がなされます。**所有権移転登記**は決済日
に行われます。

　契約日や決済日の**一括払い**も、買主売主の合意により可能です。

　契約や登記手続きでは、**本人確認書類（運転免許証**など）、**印鑑証明書**、住民
票、司法書士への**委任状**などの書類が必要となります。**印鑑**も必要です。外国人
や外国企業の場合には、**サイン証明書**や**宣誓供述書**などが必要となります。

Column   What are some differences when investing in Japan?

When foreign investors make their first real estate investments in Japan, they are often surprised by some key differences in the due diligence and closing processes as compared to their home markets.

In Japan, the **letter of intent (LOI)** that is submitted from the buyer to the seller is treated with a great deal of respect and commitment. In other foreign markets, sometimes the LOI is a starting point in negotiations, whereby the final price, **terms and conditions**, and schedule may have been negotiated and changed many times before closing.

With a Japanese seller, it is very important to understand that the price, terms and schedule put forward in an LOI will be treated as a kind of promise by the buyer and should not be changed unless there are substantial reasons for making amendments.

The **escrow system** is also a big surprise for foreign investors when they first enter Japan because escrow is not used in Japanese transactions. In other markets, the deposit and purchase proceeds would first be paid to the **escrow agent**, sometimes several days in advance of closing. Then, the escrow agent would hold these monies on behalf of the parties until all documents had been confirmed, and the escrow agent would release the money to the seller.

But in Japan, the deposit and purchase proceeds are paid directly from the purchaser to the seller, with no escrow agent being involved.

海外投資家が日本で投資するときに驚くこととは？

海外投資家が日本で不動産に初めて投資する際に、自国と比べて驚くことは、デューデリジェンスと決済手続きにおけるいくつかの違いです。

日本では、買主から売主に提出される**購入意向表明書**は重要なもので購入を約束したものとして扱われます。海外では、しばしば購入意向表明書は、交渉の開始を示すものであり、最終的な価格、**取引条件**、スケジュールは、決済前の交渉により何度も変更されるものです。

日本の売主にとっては、購入意向表明書に記載されている価格、条件、スケジュールを確認することは非常に重要なことです。なぜなら、それらの記載は、買主による一種の約束であり、修正を要するよほどの重大な理由がない限りは変更すべきでないものとして扱われるものだからです。

日本で初めて不動産投資を行う海外投資家にとっては、**エスクロー制度**（不動産の**決済引渡制度**）もまた驚くべき点です。なぜなら、日本の不動産取引においては、エスクローは用いられないからです。他の国では、手付金や決済代金は、取引の数日前に**エスクロー・エージェント**（不動産取引代理会社）に預けられます。そして、すべての書面が確認されるまでは当該エージェントが売主買主のためにその代金を預かり、確認ができて初めて売主に当該エージェントから提供されます。

しかし日本においては、エスクロー・エージェントを介することなく、手付金や決済代金は買主から売主に直接支払われることになります。

Chapter 2

Summary
of
the Real Estate Market
in Japan

日本の
不動産市場の概要

2-1 | Residential Properties

Q : What kinds of **residential properties** are there in Japan?

A : The most common types of residential properties include **detached houses, condominiums** and **rental apartments**. While there are many condominiums and rental apartments in big cities, detached houses are most popular in many local cities. **Company housing, company dormitories for singles** and **student housing** are also included in residential properties.

Q : Which residential area is the best investment area in Japan?

A : The most popular area is the **Tokyo Metropolis**, especially the area called **Tokyo 23 Wards**. The main reason is that this is the economic center of Japan and a growing number of residents **(households)** make their homes here each year. Other residential investment destinations are major cities in the **Greater Tokyo Area** and major local cities including **Osaka City, Nagoya City, Sapporo City, Fukuoka City**, etc., all of which offer fully developed infrastructure.

Q : What are typical rent structures and **lease terms** for rental apartments?

A : The most typical rent structure is **fixed rent**. The lease term is usually two years in duration, regardless of whether it is an **ordinary lease** or **fixed-term lease**. Even though the lease term is short, the stable cash flow of a high demand apartment is the most attractive part of the investment.

Q : What is the most important point to consider when investing in a rental apartment in Japan?

A : Although more people **work from home** than before due to **COVID-19**, most people in Tokyo still commute to work using the train and subway systems. So, the location of the rental apartment in proximity to the **nearest station** is a key point. Usually, a 10-minute walk or less to the station is considered a good location for investment. In addition, **newly built properties** are popular with investors.

2-1 住宅用不動産

Q：日本の**住宅用不動産**にはどのような種類がありますか？

A：**戸建住宅**、**分譲マンション**、**賃貸マンション**が代表的な住宅用不動産です。**大都市**では、分譲マンションや賃貸マンションが多くありますが、多くの**地方都市**では、戸建住宅が最も一般的です。**社宅**、**独身寮**、**学生マンション**なども住宅用不動産に含まれます。

Q：不動産投資の対象として人気がある住宅地域はどこですか？

A：一番人気があるのは**東京都**で、特に**東京23区**と呼ばれる地域です。これらの地域が人気のある最も大きな理由は、東京が日本の経済の中心であり、毎年、より多くの人（**世帯**）が住居を構えているからです。他の住宅投資地域としては、**首都圏（東京圏）**の主要な市や、**大阪市**、**名古屋市**、**札幌市**、**福岡市**といったインフラが整った地方都市が挙げられます。

Q：賃貸マンションの賃料体系や**賃貸借期間**にはどのような種類がありますか？

A：通常の賃料体系は、**固定賃料**です。賃貸借期間は、**普通借**か**定借**かにかかわらず一般的には2年です。賃貸借期間は短いですが、強い需要による安定的なキャッシュフローが得られるのが賃貸マンション投資の最大の魅力です。

Q：賃貸マンションに投資する場合に最も重要な点は何ですか？

A：コロナの影響で以前と比べて多くの人が**在宅勤務をする**ようになりましたが、東京都に住んでいる人の多くは、電車や地下鉄を使って通勤しています。したがって、賃貸マンションの場所、つまり、**最寄駅**からの距離が近いことが最も重要になります。通常、最寄駅から徒歩10分圏内が好立地とされます。また、**築浅物件**が投資家に人気があります。

Detached house

A detached house is usually owned by a single owner and used by his or her family.

Condominium

A condominium has multiple units, each of which is owned by a single owner and used by his or her family.

Individual units

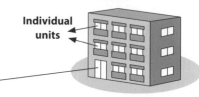

Common Area

*Common areas include **entrance areas**, **elevators**, **hallways**, **stairs**, **rooftops**, etc., and are jointly owned by all unit owners and maintained by the **condominium owners' association**, which tenants are required to join.*

Rental apartment

A rental apartment has multiple units, each of which is leased to tenants. An owner of a rental apartment owns not only their individual unit but also their share of the common areas.

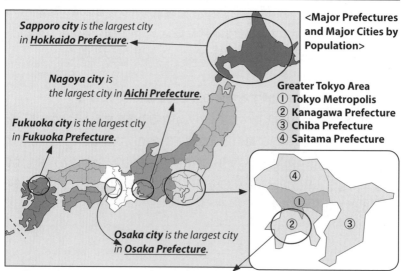

<Major Prefectures and Major Cities by Population>

Sapporo city *is the largest city in* **Hokkaido Prefecture**.

Nagoya city *is the largest city in* **Aichi Prefecture**.

Fukuoka city *is the largest city in* **Fukuoka Prefecture**.

Greater Tokyo Area
① **Tokyo Metropolis**
② **Kanagawa Prefecture**
③ **Chiba Prefecture**
④ **Saitama Prefecture**

Osaka city *is the largest city in* **Osaka Prefecture**.

Yokohama city *is the largest city in* **Kanagawa Prefecture**.

戸建住宅
戸建住宅は、通常、一人の所有者により所有され、
その所有者の家族が住んでいます。

分譲マンション
分譲マンションは、複数のユニット
から成り、各ユニットは一人の所有
者により所有され、その所有者の家
族が住んでいます。

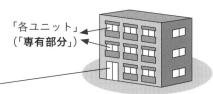

「各ユニット」
（「専有部分」）

共用部分
共用部分は、**エントランス、エレベーター、廊下、階段、屋上**
など、全ての専有部分の所有者により共有され、全所有者が加
入しなければならない**管理組合**により管理されています。

賃貸マンション
賃貸マンションは、複数のユニットから成り、各ユ
ニットはテナントに賃貸されます。所有者は、各ユ
ニットだけでなく、共用部分も所有しています。

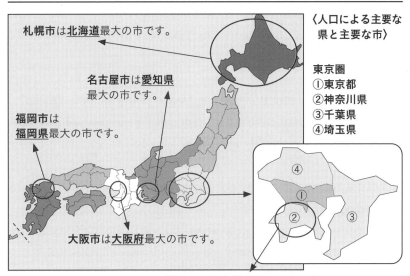

〈人口による主要な
県と主要な市〉

東京圏
①東京都
②神奈川県
③千葉県
④埼玉県

札幌市は北海道最大の市です。

名古屋市は愛知県
最大の市です。

福岡市は
福岡県最大の市です。

大阪市は大阪府最大の市です。

横浜市は神奈川県最大の市です。

2-2 Office Buildings

Q : What kinds of **office buildings** are there in Japan?

A : There are mainly two types of uses for an office building in Japan. The first is an **owner-occupied building**, where the owner of the building will also use the building. The other type is a **rental office building** that is leased to one or more tenants.

Another way to distinguish office buildings is by their size and their building grade. New and very **large sized buildings** usually have a grade referred to as either S-class or A-class. There are also **medium to small sized buildings**, which usually have a grade of B-class or C-class.

Q : Which office areas are the most popular to invest in?

A : The most popular office areas are the **Tokyo Central 3 Wards; Chiyoda Ward, Chuo Ward,** and **Minato Ward.** The second most popular areas are **Shinjuku Ward** and **Shibuya Ward.** These wards are collectively referred to as the **Tokyo Central 5 Wards.** Alternative office investment areas include other Tokyo 23 Wards such as **Shinagawa Ward, Meguro Ward,** and **Toshima Ward**. Other large cities, such as **Yokohama City, Osaka City, Nagoya City, Fukuoka City,** and **Sapporo City** are also major investment destinations.

Q : What are typical rent structures and **lease terms** for rental offices?

A : The typical rent structure is fixed rent under a two-year **ordinary lease** or **fixed term lease.** The rental level can fluctuate according to economic conditions.

Q : What is the most important point to consider when investing in a rental office building?

A : The most important points are **location, size,** and **facility.** Office tenants consider the grade, building specifications and business locations for their activities.

Rent increases based on **value enhancement work** such as **renovation work,** are one of the typical office investment strategies.

Q：日本の**オフィスビル**にはどのような種類がありますか？

A：大きく分けると、2つのタイプのオフィスビルがあります。1つは、所有者が自ら使用している**自社ビル**です。2つ目は、所有者が、単独もしくは複数のテナントに賃貸している**賃貸ビル**です。

　また、その他の区分け方法としては、建物サイズや建物の品質が挙げられます。新しい**大規模ビル**は、通常、SクラスやAクラスなどと呼ばれ、また、**中小ビル**は、通常、BクラスやCクラスなどと呼ばれています。

Q：不動産投資の対象として人気があるオフィス地域はどこですか？

A：最も人気のあるオフィスエリアは、**千代田区**、**中央区**、**港区**の**都心3区**と呼ばれるエリアです。次に人気のあるエリアとしては、**新宿区**や**渋谷区**が挙げられます。上記の3区と合わせて**都心5区**と呼ばれます。他のオフィス立地としては、**品川区**、**目黒区**、**豊島区**といった23区内の他の区や、**横浜市**、**大阪市**、**名古屋市**、**福岡市**、**札幌市**などの大都市が挙げられます。

Q：オフィスの賃料体系や**賃貸借期間**にはどのような種類がありますか？

A：通常の賃料体系は、**普通借**や**定借**に基づく2年間の**固定賃料**です。賃料は経済環境により変動することが多いです。

Q：賃貸オフィスビルに投資する場合に最も重要な点は何ですか？

A：最も重視すべきポイントは、**立地**、**規模**、**設備**です。オフィスビルのテナントは、品質や設備、そして、事業拠点としてふさわしい立地がどうかを考慮します。

　改修工事などのバリューアップ**工事**による設備の向上で賃上げを図るのが、オフィス投資の代表的な投資スタイルの1つです。

Illustrated Real Estate Terminologies

Owner-occupied building

An owner-occupied building is a building that is owned and used by the owner for business activities.

Rental office building

A rental office building is owned by an owner but leased to one or more tenants who use the office space for their business activities.

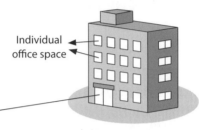

Individual office space

Common Areas

*Common areas include **entrance areas**, **elevators, elevator halls, escalators**, **hallways**, **stairs**, **restrooms**, **rooftops**, etc. Both individual office space and common areas are owned by the building owner but used by one or more tenants.*

Location of the Tokyo Central 5 Wards in the Tokyo 23 Wards

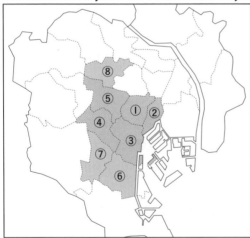

Tokyo Central 5 Wards & Major Business Districts

① **Chiyoda Ward**
(Marunouchi, Otemachi, Yurakucho)
② **Chuo Ward**
(Nihonbashi, Yaesu, Ginza)
③ **Minato Ward**
(Aoyama, Akasaka, Roppongi, Shiodome, Toranomon)
④ **Shibuya Ward**
(Shibuya, Ebisu)
⑤ **Shinjuku Ward**
(Shinjuku)

Other Major Cities for Office Buildings
⑥ **Shinagawa Ward**   ⑦ **Meguro Ward**
⑧ **Toshima Ward**

自社ビル

自社ビルは、所有者により所有され、かつ、その所有者の事業のために使用されているビルです。

賃貸ビル

賃貸ビルは、所有者により所有されますが、オフィススペースはそのスペースで事業活動を行う単独もしくは複数のテナントに賃貸されます。

個々の
オフィス
スペース

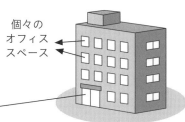

共用部分

*共用部分には、**エントランス、エレベーター、エレベーターホール、エスカレーター、廊下、階段、トイレ、屋上**等が含まれます。個々のオフィススペース（専有部分）と共用部分の両方が、所有者により所有されますが、使用は単独もしくは複数のテナントによりなされます。*

東京23区の中での都心5区の位置

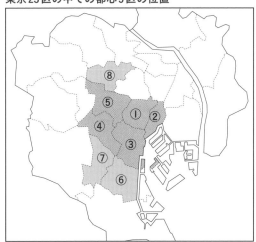

オフィスビルの多い他の主要な区
⑥品川区　⑦目黒区
⑧豊島区

「都心5区」と主なオフィス街

①千代田区
（丸の内、大手町、有楽町）
②中央区
（日本橋、八重洲、銀座）
③港区
（青山、赤坂、六本木、汐留、虎ノ門）
④渋谷区
（渋谷、恵比寿）
⑤新宿区
（新宿）

2-3 Retail Properties

Q : What kinds of **retail properties** are there in Japan?

A : There are three main types of retail properties and location is the defining feature. The first one is **urban retail property,** which is located in the busy streets or **entertainment districts** of urban cities. The second one is **suburban retail property,** which is located in the outlying suburban areas of major cities. The third one is **retail property for daily needs**, which is located near residential areas.

Q : What are some specific examples of these three retail types?

A : Urban retail properties include **department stores, station buildings** directly connected to major train stations, and **high street retail properties** in upscale areas such as **Ginza** and **Omotesando.** The most popular suburban retail property is a large **shopping center**, or **mall**. A typical mall usually has one or two **anchor stores** such as a **general merchandise store (GMS)** and a variety of **specialty shops** within the mall. Entertainment facilities such as movie theaters may also be located there. Typical retail properties for daily needs are **grocery stores** and **drugstores.**

Q : What kinds of rent structures and **lease terms** are there?

A : Typical rent structures are **fixed rent, percentage rent / variable rent**, and **fixed rent with percentage rent**. The lease term is usually 5 to 10 years.

Q : What is the most important point to consider when investing in a retail property in Japan?

A : Because the source of rent is from the subject tenant, the sales of the retailer are very important to consider. In that sense, **location, visibility,** and access from the **nearest station** are important for urban retail. The **catchment area**, or the number of shoppers in the vicinity of the property, and the attractiveness of the **anchor tenant** are important for suburban retail. The operating capability and credit of the **retail operator** who runs the property are also very important for all retail properties.

2-3 商業施設

Q：日本の**商業施設**にはどのような種類がありますか？

A：商業施設は、どこに立地しているかで大きく3つに分けられます。1つ目のタイプは、都市部の人通りの多い通りや繁華街に立地している**都市型商業施設**です。2つ目のタイプは、主要都市の郊外に立地している**郊外型商業施設**です。3つ目のタイプは、住宅地域の近くに立地する**生活密着型商業施設**です。

Q：それら3つのタイプの具体的な例を教えてください。

A：代表的な都市型商業施設には、**百貨店**、主要な鉄道の駅に直結している**駅ビル**、**銀座や表参道**などの**大通り沿いの商業店舗ビル**があります。最も代表的な郊外型商業施設は、**モール**と呼ばれる大規模な**ショッピングセンター**です。代表的なモールは、**総合スーパー**など1つか2つの主要店舗があり、加えて、様々な種類の**専門店**を併設しています。大規模なショッピングモールでは、映画館などの娯楽施設も併設されています。代表的な生活密着型商業施設には、**食料雑貨品店**やドラッグストアなどがあります。

Q：賃料体系や**賃貸借期間**にはどのような種類がありますか？

A：賃料体系の例としては、**固定賃料、売上歩合賃料／変動賃料、売上歩合付固定賃料**があります。賃貸借期間は通常5年から10年です。

Q：商業施設に投資する場合に最も重要な点は何ですか？

A：賃料の原資は、対象商業施設での売上なので、小売業者がそこで稼げるかどうかが最も重要です。その意味では、**立地、視認性**や**最寄駅**からのアクセスは都市型商業施設で重要です。郊外型商業施設では、**商圏**、つまり、その店舗やモールの周辺でどれくらいの人数の購買者が住んでいるかや、**核テナント**がどれくらい人々を引きつける力を持っているかが重要です。そしてまた、対象商業施設を運営する**商業施設運営者**の運営能力や信用力も全ての商業施設において非常に重要です。

Urban retail property

Major Key Success Factors
- Location
- Competitiveness of **anchor tenant**
- Number of the nearest station users
- Accessibility to train or subway
- Concentration level of retail properties

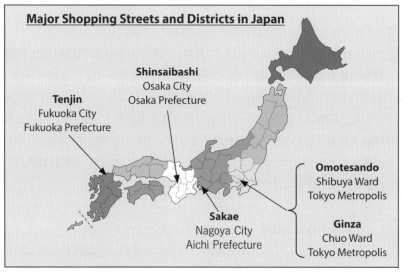

Major Shopping Streets and Districts in Japan

Tenjin
Fukuoka City
Fukuoka Prefecture

Shinsaibashi
Osaka City
Osaka Prefecture

Omotesando
Shibuya Ward
Tokyo Metropolis

Sakae
Nagoya City
Aichi Prefecture

Ginza
Chuo Ward
Tokyo Metropolis

Suburban retail property

Major Key Success Factors
- Competitiveness of anchor tenant
- **Market area population**
- Accessibility mainly by car
- Demographic trends
- Operating capability of the **retail operator**

Another point to consider when analyzing retail properties:
*The rent a retail tenant pays to the owner is sometimes also partially based on the tenant's gross sales amount. In some retail lease contracts, there is the **fixed rent**, which is a set amount, and also the **percentage rent / variable rent,** which can vary depending on the sales performance of the tenant. Understanding both components of the retail lease is important to judge the overall potential income for the owner.*

都市型商業施設

主要な成功要因
- 立地
- **核テナント**の競争力
- 最寄駅の乗降者数
- 鉄道・地下鉄でのアクセス
- 商業集積度

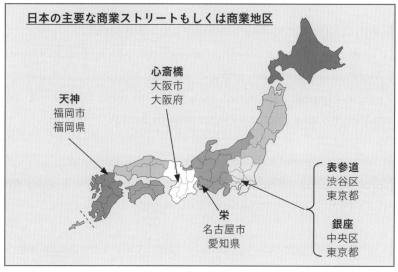

日本の主要な商業ストリートもしくは商業地区

心斎橋
大阪市
大阪府

天神
福岡市
福岡県

表参道
渋谷区
東京都

銀座
中央区
東京都

栄
名古屋市
愛知県

郊外型商業施設

主要な成功要因
- 核テナントの競争力
- **商圏人口**
- 車によるアクセスの容易性
- 人口動態
- **商業施設運営者**の運営能力

商業施設に投資する際の他の留意事項

各テナントが商業施設の所有者に支払う賃料の原資となるのは、各テナントの当該施設での売上高です。したがって、各テナント及び商業施設全体での売上水準に留意しなければなりません。**固定賃料**ではなく、各テナントの売上高に比例して賃料が変動する**売上歩合賃料／変動賃料**を採用する場合には、より留意する必要があります。

2-4 Logistics Properties

Q : What kinds of **logistics properties** are there in Japan?

A : There are two main types of logistics properties in Japan and the number of tenants is the defining point. The first type is the **Build-to-Suit (BTS)** building and facilities which are constructed for one tenant. The second type is the **Multi-Tenant** building and facilities which are constructed for a variety of tenants.

Q : Why is logistics property investment becoming popular?

A : There are mainly two reasons: The first one is due to the increase in demand of **3PL**. More and more companies tend to entrust their logistics functions to specialized logistics companies. The second one is due to the strong demand of **E-commerce**. More and more people tend to buy products through the internet.

Q : What kinds of rent structures and **lease terms** are there?

A : The major rent structure is **fixed rent**. The lease term is usually a long-term lease for BTS and a relatively short-term lease for multi-tenant facilities.

Q : What is the most important point to consider when investing in a logistics property in Japan?

A : The most important point is the **location**. It should be close to areas where many people live like **Greater Tokyo** and **Greater Osaka**. Easy access to production areas through **expressway interchanges**, airports, and seaports is also important.

Building facilities are important as well because the property has to handle a lot of products efficiently. For example, the property must have large loading zones with enough **floor weight capacity**, **ceiling height**, and **column space**. Logistics properties containing the latest facilities are called **modern logistics facilities**.

Additionally, the property must secure a dependable workforce. Services for employees include cafeterias and convenience stores and recently there have been some facilities that provide **nursery schools**.

2-4 物流施設

Q：日本の**物流施設**にはどのような種類がありますか？

A：物流施設は、テナントの数で大きく2つに分けられます。1つ目のタイプは、**ビルド・トゥ・スーツ（BTS）型**で、その建物や設備は1つのテナントに向けて作られます。2つ目のタイプは、**マルチテナント型**で、その建物や設備は様々なテナントに向けて作られます。

Q：なぜ物流施設投資が人気となっているのですか？

A：主には2つの理由があります。1つは、**サードパーティロジスティクス**に対する需要が高まっていることです。多くの企業が物流専門会社に物流機能を委託しています。2つ目の理由は、**電子商取引**に対する強い需要です。多くの人々がインターネットを通じて商品を購入しています。

Q：賃料体系や**賃貸借期間**にはどのような種類がありますか？

A：主要な賃料体系は**固定賃料**です。賃貸借期間は、BTSは長期、マルチテナント型は比較的短期間です。

Q：物流施設に投資する場合に最も重要な点は何ですか？

A：最も重要なのは、**立地**です。**首都圏（東京圏）**や**近畿圏（大阪圏）**など多くの人が住んでいる場所に近いことが必要です。また、**高速道路のインターチェンジ**、空港、港など、生産拠点からのアクセスがよいことも重要です。

　物流施設は大量の商品を効率的に扱うために、建物の設備も重要です。例えば、**十分な床荷重、天井高、柱間隔**を備えた広い荷物を降ろせるスペースが必要です。最新の設備を備えた物流施設を**先進的物流施設**と呼んでいます。

　加えて、働く人を確保しやすいことも重要です。社員食堂やコンビニエンスストアなどのほか、最近では**保育園**を備えた物流施設もあります。

Logistics properties

*Logistics properties in Japan are usually located in outlying areas that are close to large population areas such as the **Greater Tokyo Area**, the **Greater Osaka Area**, and the **Greater Nagoya Area** and are also accessible by car, airplane, and ship.*

*According to the definition of the Statistics Bureau of Japan, the **Three Major Metropolitan Areas** include the Greater Tokyo Area (Tokyo, Kanagawa, Saitama, and Chiba), the Greater Osaka Area (Osaka, Kyoto, Nara, and Hyogo), and the Greater Nagoya (Aichi, Gifu, and Mie). Actually, investment destinations for logistics properties are within about 30 – 60 km from the central point in each area.*

Investment Destinations in **Greater Tokyo Area** (within 60km radius)

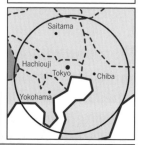

Investment Destinations in **Greater Osaka Area** (within 40km radius)

Investment Destinations in **Greater Nagoya Area** (within 30km radius)

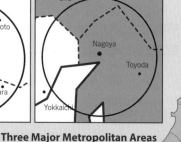

Three Major Metropolitan Areas

*Demand for **modern logistics facilities** is expanding to major cities with populations of 1 million or more, such as Sapporo City, Sendai City, Hiroshima City, Fukuoka City, etc.*

物流施設

物流施設は、**首都圏（東京圏）**、**近畿圏（大阪圏）**、**中部圏（名古屋圏）** といった人口の多い地域に近接し、さらに、それらの地域に車、飛行機、船などでアクセスしやすいところにあります。

総務省統計局の定義によれば、**3大都市圏** は、東京圏（東京都・神奈川県・埼玉県・千葉県）、大阪圏（大阪府・京都府・兵庫県・奈良県）、名古屋圏（愛知県・岐阜県・三重県）です。実際の物流施設の投資対象エリアは、それぞれの中心地からおおよそ30kmから60kmの範囲となっています。

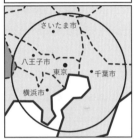

東京圏の物流施設投資エリア
（半径60km圏内）

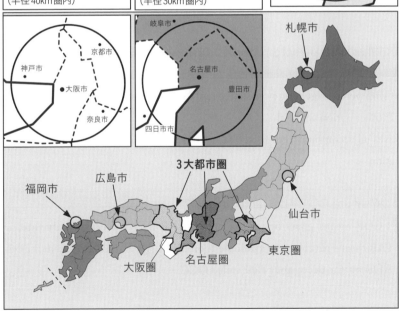

大阪圏の物流施設投資エリア
（半径40km圏内）

名古屋圏の物流施設投資エリア
（半径30km圏内）

札幌市、仙台市、広島市、福岡市など、人口百万人を超える大都市の周辺にも、**先進的物流施設** ニーズは拡大しています。

2-5 | Hotel Properties

Q : What kinds of accommodation properties are there in Japan?

A : Major examples are **full-service hotels,** called city hotels in Japan, **limited-service hotels,** including **business hotels** in Japan, and **resort hotels,** including ryokan (traditional Japanese inns). Other than the above types, there are also **apartment type hotels,** known as **service apartments** in foreign countries, which usually contain a kitchen for long term users.

Q : What is the difference between full-service and limited-service hotels?

A : Full-service hotels not only provide **accommodation facilities,** but also **convention rooms, banquet rooms,** restaurants, etc. On the other hand, limited- service hotels focus on specifically providing accommodation facilities.

Q : What kinds of rent structures and **lease terms** for hotels are there?

A : Rent structures depend on each hotel operator. Examples are **fixed rent, fixed rent with percentage rent, percentage rent / variable rent. Management contracts** are another option where the owner just pays a management fee to the operator and receives all accommodation fees. Lease terms are usually long, such as 10 years in duration.

Q : What are GOP, ADR, and RevPAR?

A : **GOP** means **gross operating profit, ADR** means **average daily rate,** and **RevPAR** means **revenue per available room**. RevPAR is calculated by multiplying the ADR by the **occupancy rate,** called **OCC.**

Q : What should be considered, especially for hotel investment?

A : Whether the owner or operator is responsible for the **FF&E CAPEX** costs is a critical factor. FF&E is the abbreviation for **furniture, fixtures,** and **equipment,** many of which are used in hotel rooms.

2-5 ホテル

Q：日本には、どのような種類の宿泊施設がありますか？

A：代表的な例としては、シティホテルと呼ばれる**フルサービス型ホテル**、ビジネスホテルを含む**リミテッドサービス型ホテル**、日本の伝統的な**旅館**を含む**リゾートホテル**があります。以上のようなタイプのほか、海外で**サービスアパートメント**として知られるキッチンなどを備え付けた長期滞在型の**アパートメント型ホテル**もあります。

Q：フルサービス型ホテルとリミテッドサービス型ホテルの違いは何ですか？

A：フルサービス型ホテルは、**宿泊施設**だけでなく、**会議場**、**宴会場**、レストランなどを併設しています。一方、リミテッドサービス型ホテルは宿泊施設に特化しています。

Q：ホテルの賃料体系や**賃貸借期間**にはどのような種類がありますか？

A：賃料体系は、ホテル運営者によります。例としては、**固定賃料**、**売上歩合付固定賃料**、**売上歩合賃料／変動賃料**があります。また、一定の運営料を運営者に支払い、宿泊料は全て所有者が受け取る**運営委託型**もあります。賃貸借期間は10年の期間など、長期であることが通常です。

Q：GOP、ADR、RevPARとは何ですか？

A：GOPとは**営業総利益**、ADRとは**平均宿泊料（平均客室単価）**、RevPARとは**販売可能客室1室当たり売上**です。RevPARは、ADRにOCCと呼ばれる**客室稼働率**を乗じることで計算できます。

Q：ホテル投資に特有の留意点は何ですか？

A：**FF&E**にかかるCAPEXを所有者が負担するのか、運営者が負担するのかは留意が必要です。FF&Eとは、**家具**、**什器**、**備品**のことで、その多くはホテルの各部屋で使用されているものです。

Economy hotel (Limited-service hotel)
Economy hotels are located in almost all major cities in each prefecture in Japan. Economy hotels greatly outnumber city hotels.

City hotel (Full-service hotel)
***International luxury brand hotels**, operated by international brands like Hyatt or Marriot, are primarily located in the larger cities of Tokyo, Yokohama, Osaka, Kyoto, and Nagoya. They are expanding in other major cities.*
City hotels are also operated by Japanese domestic firms and are located in almost all major cities in each prefecture in Japan.

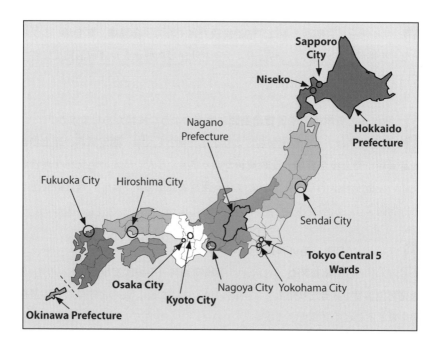

Resort Hotels
*Resort hotels in Japan are located in well-established **tourist destinations** all over Japan. There are many resort hotels especially in Hokkaido Prefecture, Okinawa Prefecture, and Nagano Prefecture. Several popular tourist destinations such as **Niseko** in Hokkaido Prefecture are attracting tourists from all over the world and also feature several international luxury brand hotels.*

ビジネスホテル（リミテッドサービス型ホテル）
ビジネスホテルは、日本国内の各県のほとんど全ての主要都市にあります。
ビジネスホテルの数は、シティホテルよりも非常にたくさんあります。

シティホテル（フルサービス型ホテル）
ハイアットやマリオットなど国際的に有名な運営者が運営している**外資系
高級ホテル**は、主に、東京、横浜、大阪、京都、名古屋のような大都市に
あります。そのようなホテルは他の大都市にも進出してきています。
国内の運営者によって運営されているシティホテルは、各県のほとんどす
べての主要都市にあります。

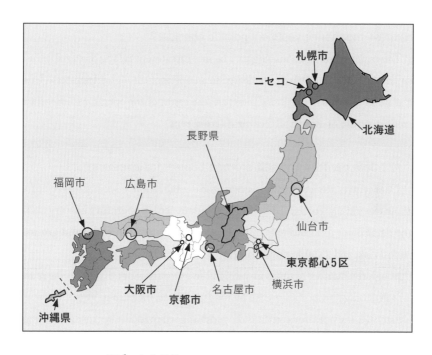

リゾートホテル
リゾートホテルは、日本中の有名な**観光地**にあります。特に、北
海道、沖縄県、長野県にはそのようなリゾートホテルが多くあ
ります。北海道の**ニセコ**などいくつかの人気観光地には、世界
各地から旅行者が訪れ、外資系高級ホテルも進出しています。

2-6 Other Properties (Nursing Homes, Data Centers, etc.)

Q : What kinds of **nursing care facilities** are there in Japan?

A : There are mainly two types of nursing care facilities available for investment. The first one is a paid **nursing home**.

The second one is a **serviced housing facility for the elderly** where each room is leased to elderly residents who can receive care services for additional fees.

Both facilities are master leased by the **operator** which operates the subject facility.

Q : What investment features are there for nursing care facilities and what is the most important investment point to consider?

A : The major feature of a nursing care facility investment is long term stable cash flow. Generally, the facility is master leased to an operator through **a long-term lease** such as 20 to 30 years in duration. Therefore, the credit of the operator is important. The rent structure of almost all facilities is **fixed rent**.

Q : Are **data centers** and **self-storage** popular for investors?

A : Data centers attract investors because the digitalization of society is expected to continue expanding. Foreign based funds and **data center operators** are very active in the data center fund business in Japan. They prefer location with **solid ground**, low **flood risk**, and a **stable power supply** to protect their data.

Although the number of funds investing in self-storage is not that large, the number of self-storage properties owned by funds has been increasing. When investing in self-storage, the operator's credit is the most important aspect because self-storage propertoes are operated and master leased by the operator.

Q : What is an operational asset?

A : Properties that are master leased to the operator are called **operational assets**.

2-6 その他不動産 （老人ホーム、データセンターなど）

Q：日本には、どのような種類の**介護施設**がありますか？

A：投資の対象としては主には2つの種類があります。

　1つ目は、有料**老人ホーム**です。

　2つ目は、**サービス付き高齢者向け住宅**で、各部屋は高齢者に賃貸され、高齢者は追加料金で介護サービスを受けることができます。

　いずれの施設も専門の**オペレーター**（施設運営者）により一括賃借されます。

Q：介護施設への投資の特徴は何ですか？また、介護施設に投資する場合に最も重要な点は何ですか？

A：介護施設への投資の主な特徴は長期安定的なキャッシュフローです。通常、介護施設はその施設を運営するオペレーターに20年から30年といった**長期賃貸借**で賃貸されます。それゆえ、オペレーターの信用度がとても重要となります。ほとんどの施設の賃料体系は**固定賃料**です。

Q：**データセンター**や**トランクルーム**は投資家に人気がありますか？

A：データセンターに関しては、デジタル社会の進展が見込まれることが投資家を惹きつけています。外資系ファンドや**DC運営者**が活発に日本でのデータセンターファンドビジネスに関して活動しています。データ保護のため、**硬い地盤**や**水害リスク**が少ない立地、また、**安定的な電力供給**を確保できる立地が好まれます。

　トランクルームに関するファンドは日本ではまだ多くはありませんが、都心部ではファンドに保有されるトランクルームも多くなってきました。トランクルームへの投資に際しては、運営者の信用力が最も大事です。なぜなら、トランクルームはその運営者により運営され長期で賃貸されるからです。

Q：オペレーショナルアセットとは何ですか？

A：運営者により一括賃貸される不動産を**オペレーショナルアセット**と呼びます。

Characteristics of Non-Operational Assets: Tenants and users are the same.

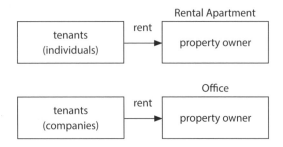

Characteristics of Operational Assets: Tenants and users are different.

Users and major considerations

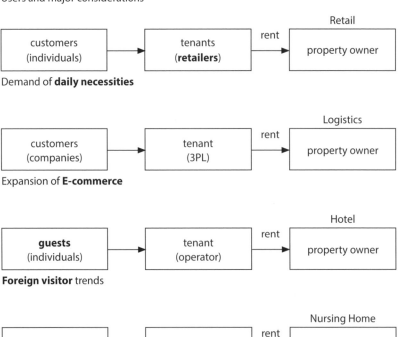

ノンオペレーショナルアセットの特徴：テナントと利用者が同じ

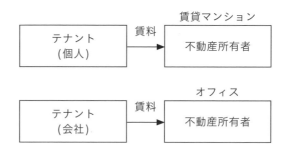

賃貸マンション

| テナント
(個人) | 賃料 → | 不動産所有者 |

オフィス

| テナント
(会社) | 賃料 → | 不動産所有者 |

オペレーショナルアセットの特徴：テナントと利用者が違う

利用者と主な留意事項

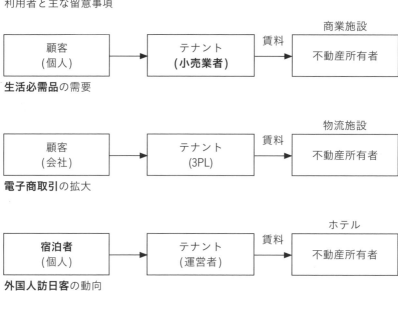

商業施設

| 顧客
(個人) | → | テナント
(小売業者) | 賃料 → | 不動産所有者 |

生活必需品の需要

物流施設

| 顧客
(会社) | → | テナント
(3PL) | 賃料 → | 不動産所有者 |

電子商取引の拡大

ホテル

| **宿泊者**
(個人) | → | テナント
(運営者) | 賃料 → | 不動産所有者 |

外国人訪日客の動向

老人ホーム

| 入居者
(高齢者) | → | テナント
(運営者) | 賃料 → | 不動産所有者 |

高齢化社会の進展

2-7 Overview of Japan and Greater Tokyo

Q : How many islands are there in Japan?

A : Japan is made up of 4 main islands including **Hokkaido, Honshu, Shikoku** and **Kyushu**. In addition, there are about 7,000 small islands in Japan.

Q : How many prefectures are there in Japan?

A : Japan is made up of 47 prefectures. As explained on page 40, although most of the prefectures are called "ken" in Japanese, four prefectures are not called "ken".

Q : What is the difference between a prefecture and a city?

A : There are mainly three layers in the Japanese political system. The first one is the national government. The second one is the local government of each **prefecture** including Tokyo Metropolis, Osaka Prefecture, Kyoto Prefecture, and Hokkaido Prefecture. The third one is the local government of each **city**, **town**, and **village**. So, a city is under a prefecture, but several cities called **government-ordinance designated cities** have almost the same power as a prefecture.

Q : What is the Greater Tokyo Area?

A : According to the National Capital Region Development Law, the "Greater Tokyo Area" includes Tokyo Metropolis and the neighboring seven prefectures. Outside of this law, there is no other official definition available to define this area.

In many cases, the **Greater Tokyo Area** refers to **Tokyo Metropolis** and three surrounding prefectures known as **Kanagawa Prefecture, Chiba Prefecture**, and **Saitama Prefecture**.

As of October 1st, 2020, the total population in Japan was about 126.15 million.

The Greater Tokyo Area makes up almost one third of this population. Many people commute from surrounding prefectures to Tokyo Metropolis (this area therefore makes up one huge economic block, which attracts many real estate investors).

2-7 日本と首都圏の概要

Q：日本には、いくつの島がありますか？

A：日本は、4つの主要な島、**北海道**、**本州**、**四国**、そして、**九州**から構成されています。加えて、約7千の小さな島が日本にはあります。

Q：日本には、いくつの県がありますか？

A：日本は、47の都道府県から構成されています。しかし、41ページで説明したように、ほとんどの都道府県が、日本語で「県」と呼ばれるのに対して、4つの都道府県は「県」とは呼ばれません。

Q：県と市の違いは何ですか？

A：日本には主に3つの統治機構があります。1つ目は国。2つ目は、東京都、大阪**府**、京都**府**、北海**道**を含む各県。3つ目は各**市**町村です。ですから、市は県の下にあります。しかし、**政令指定都市**と呼ばれるいくつかの市は、県と同じような自治能力を持ちます。

Q：首都圏とは何ですか？

A：首都圏整備法では、首都圏とは、東京都と周辺の7県のことを指します。しかし、この法律以外には、首都圏に対する明確な定義はありません。

　多くの場合、**首都圏（東京圏）**とは、東京都と周辺の3県（**神奈川県**、**千葉県**、**埼玉県**）のことを言います。

　2020年10月1日時点で、日本の総人口は約1億2615万人です。

　首都圏には、約3分の1の人口が集中しています。多くの人が周辺の県から東京都に通勤しており、首都圏は一体の巨大な経済圏を構成しています。このことが、多くの不動産投資家がこのエリアに投資を行う理由となっています。

Overview of Japan and Greater Tokyo

(Source: 2020 National Census)

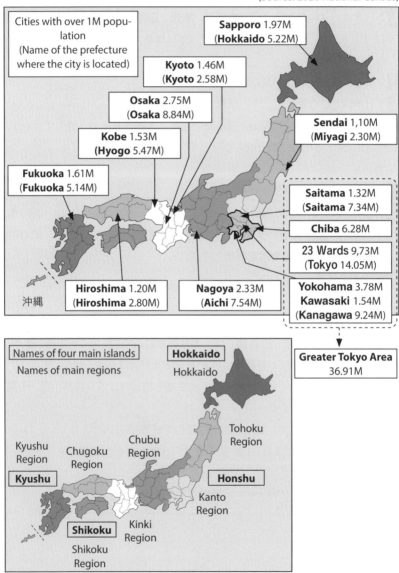

Cities with over 1M population
(Name of the prefecture where the city is located)

Sapporo 1.97M
(**Hokkaido** 5.22M)

Kyoto 1.46M
(**Kyoto** 2.58M)

Osaka 2.75M
(**Osaka** 8.84M)

Sendai 1,10M
(**Miyagi** 2.30M)

Kobe 1.53M
(**Hyogo** 5.47M)

Fukuoka 1.61M
(**Fukuoka** 5.14M)

Saitama 1.32M
(**Saitama** 7.34M)

Chiba 6.28M

23 Wards 9,73M
(**Tokyo** 14.05M)

Hiroshima 1.20M
(**Hiroshima** 2.80M)

沖縄

Nagoya 2.33M
(**Aichi** 7.54M)

Yokohama 3.78M
Kawasaki 1.54M
(**Kanagawa** 9.24M)

Greater Tokyo Area
36.91M

Names of four main islands
Names of main regions

Hokkaido
Hokkaido

Kyushu Region
Kyushu

Chugoku Region

Chubu Region

Tohoku Region

Honshu

Kanto Region

Shikoku
Shikoku Region

Kinki Region

日本と首都圏の概要

（参照：2020年国勢調査）

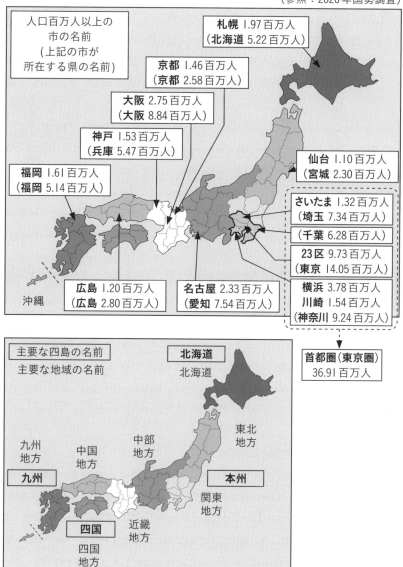

人口百万人以上の
市の名前
（上記の市が
所在する県の名前）

札幌 1.97百万人
（北海道 5.22百万人）

京都 1.46百万人
（京都 2.58百万人）

大阪 2.75百万人
（大阪 8.84百万人）

神戸 1.53百万人
（兵庫 5.47百万人）

福岡 1.61百万人
（福岡 5.14百万人）

仙台 1.10百万人
（宮城 2.30百万人）

さいたま 1.32百万人
（埼玉 7.34百万人）

（千葉 6.28百万人）

23区 9.73百万人
（東京 14.05百万人）

横浜 3.78百万人
川崎 1.54百万人
（神奈川 9.24百万人）

広島 1.20百万人
（広島 2.80百万人）

沖縄

名古屋 2.33百万人
（愛知 7.54百万人）

首都圏（東京圏）
36.91百万人

主要な四島の名前
主要な地域の名前

北海道
北海道

九州
地方

中国
地方

中部
地方

東北
地方

九州

本州

四国

近畿
地方

関東
地方

四国
地方

2-8 Overview of Tokyo Metropolis and Tokyo 23 Wards

Q : How can Tokyo Metropolis be divided?

A : Tokyo Metropolis is mainly divided into three areas. The first one is the area called the "**Tokyo 23 Wards**". The second one is called the "Tama Area" which is located in the west side of the Tokyo 23 Wards and has 26 cities, towns, and villages. The third one is called the "Islands Area" which are the Ogasawara and Izu Islands.

Q : What is the difference between "Ku" and "Shi" in Tokyo Metropolis?

A : "Ku" in Tokyo Metropolis has almost the same political power as that of "Shi" which is translated into "**city**" in English. That is why "Ku" in Tokyo Metropolis is officially translated into "city" in English. However, "Ku" is also used as just a small residential block in the cities designated by ordinances. Those "Ku" are translated into "**ward**" which is normally used as the translation for "Ku" in Tokyo Metropolis.

Q : How big are the Tokyo 23 Wards?

A : The area of the Tokyo 23 Wards is 621.98km^2, which is a little bit smaller than that of Singapore. But the population of the Tokyo 23 Wards is about 9.73 million, which is much larger than that of Singapore. Furthermore, its **daytime population** increases a lot because many people commute to work from other Greater Tokyo areas. For example, the population of Chiyoda Ward increases from about 67 thousand to about 904 thousand during the workday.

Q : What is the Yamanote Line?

A : The "**Yamanote Line**" is a famous **loop railway line** located in central Tokyo and its inner area is almost the same size as that of Manhattan, NY. Major stations such as Shinjuku, Shibuya, and Ikebukuro also have **terminal stations** of other lines to suburban areas of Tokyo, including Kanagawa, Saitama, and Chiba prefectures. Additionally, on the inner side of the Yamanote-line, there are 13 **subway** lines, many of which are also connected to the above lines in suburban areas.

2-8 東京都と東京23区の概要

Q：東京都はどのように区分することができますか？

A：東京都は主に3つの地域に分けることができます。1つ目は、**東京23区**と呼ばれる地域です。2つ目は、東京23区の西側に位置する多摩地域で、26の市町村があります。3つ目は、島しょ地域と呼ばれる地域で小笠原諸島と伊豆諸島のことです。

Q：東京都の区と市にはどのような違いがありますか？

A：東京都の区は、市と概ね同様の行政単位です。ですから、東京都の**区**は、公式には、cityと訳されています。しかし、区は、政令指定都市の中の行政区分でも用いられており、この場合にはwardと訳されています。このwardが東京都の区の訳としても通常用いられています。

Q：東京23区はどれくらいの大きさですか？

A：東京23区の面積は、621.98平方キロメートルで、シンガポールの面積よりも少し小さい大きさです。しかし、東京23区の人口は、973万人で、シンガポールの人口よりもはるかに多い人々が住んでいます。さらに、首都圏の他の地域から多くの人々が通勤してくるため、その**昼間人口**は大幅に増えます。例えば、千代田区の人口は、約6万7千人ですが、昼間には約90万4千人にもなります。

Q：山手線とは何ですか？

A：有名な「**山手線**」は、東京の都心に位置する**環状線**で、その内側の面積は、ニューヨークのマンハッタン島に匹敵します。新宿、渋谷、池袋といった主要な駅は、他の鉄道線の**ターミナル駅**にもなっており、神奈川県、埼玉県、千葉県を含む東京の郊外に向かう多くの鉄道が走っています。また、山手線の内側には、13の**地下鉄**が走っており、これらの多くも上記の郊外への鉄道と接続しています。

Overview of Tokyo's 23 Wards

(Source: 2020 National Census)

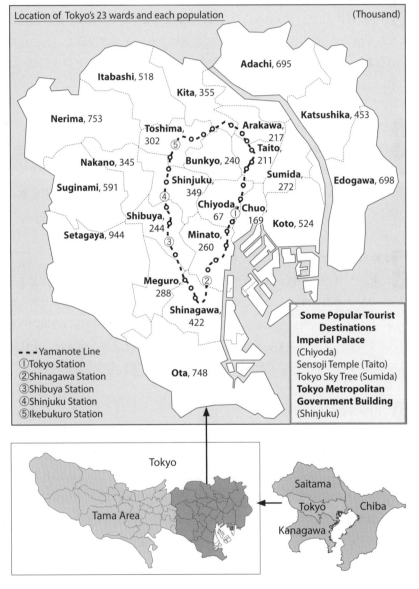

Location of Tokyo's 23 wards and each population (Thousand)

Adachi, 695

Itabashi, 518

Kita, 355

Nerima, 753

Katsushika, 453

Toshima, 302 ⑤

Arakawa, 217

Taito, 211

Nakano, 345

Bunkyo, 240

Suginami, 591

Shinjuku, 349 ④

Sumida, 272

Edogawa, 698

Suginami, 591

Chiyoda, 67

Chuo, 169

Shibuya, 244 ③

Koto, 524

Setagaya, 944

Minato, 260

Meguro, 288

②

Shinagawa, 422

Ota, 748

- - - Yamanote Line
① Tokyo Station
② Shinagawa Station
③ Shibuya Station
④ Shinjuku Station
⑤ Ikebukuro Station

Some Popular Tourist Destinations
Imperial Palace
(Chiyoda)
Sensoji Temple (Taito)
Tokyo Sky Tree (Sumida)
Tokyo Metropolitan Government Building
(Shinjuku)

Tokyo

Tama Area

Saitama

Tokyo

Chiba

Kanagawa

東京23区の概要

(参照：2020年国勢調査)

東京23区の位置と各区の人口 (単位:千人)

足立, 695
板橋, 584
北, 355
葛飾, 453
練馬, 753
荒川, 217
豊島 302 ⑤
文京, 240
台東, 211
墨田, 272
中野, 345
新宿, 349
江戸川, 698
杉並, 591
千代田 67
中央, 169 ①
④
渋谷 244
江東, 524
③
港, 260
世田谷, 944
目黒, 288
②
品川, 422
大田, 748

- - - 山手線
① 東京駅
② 品川駅
③ 渋谷駅
④ 新宿駅
⑤ 池袋駅

いくつかの観光名所
皇居（千代田）
浅草寺（台東）
東京スカイツリー（墨田）
東京都庁（新宿）

東京都
多摩地域

埼玉
東京
千葉
神奈川

2-9 Overview of Building MEP Systems

Q : Who is involved in constructing a building?

A : There are three major players involved, starting with the **clients** who want to construct a specific building, **architectural design firms** that are in charge of building design, and the **contractor** who constructs the building.

Q : What kind of role does an architectural design firm play?

A : An architectural design firm plays three major roles including **building design**, **building structure**, and **building facilities**.

Q : What kinds of building facilities are there?

A : There are a variety of types of building facilities.

The first one is **HVAC systems** such as ventilation fans, air conditioners, etc.

The second one is **electrical systems** such as lighting equipment.

The third one is **plumbing systems**, such as those in the kitchen, bathroom, and lavatory areas.

The fourth one is **gas equipment**.

The fifth one is security systems such as intercoms and security gates.

The sixth one is **fire prevention equipment** to prevent a fire from spreading.

The seventh one is elevators and escalators.

Q : How long does it take to complete a building?

A : Generally, it depends on how high the subject building will be built.

It takes about 3 months to create the design and get a **building permit**.

It usually takes about a month to complete one floor. So, if the building is 10 stories tall, it will take about 10 months to complete.

Additionally, it takes one to two months to complete all the building details.

Therefore, an additional four to five months should be added to the number of floors to calculate the total number of months required to complete the building.

建物設備の概要

Q：建物を建てるには、どのような関係者が関わりますか？

A：建物を建てたい**施主**、建物の設計を担う**設計会社**、実際に建物を建設する**施工会社**の3つが関わります。

Q：設計会社はどのような役割を担いますか？

A：設計会社は主に3つの役割を担います。**建物の意匠（デザイン）、建物の構造、建物の設備**です。

Q：建物の設備にはどのようなものがありますか？

A：様々な設備があります。

　1つ目は、換気扇やエアコンなどの**空調設備**です。

　2つ目は、照明器具などの**電気設備**です。

　3つ目は、**給排水設備**です。台所、浴室、便所などが例として挙げられます。

　4つ目は、**ガス設備**です。

　5つ目は、警備設備です。インターホンやセキュリティゲートなどが挙げられます。

　6つ目は、**消防設備**です。火災を防ぐためのものです。

　7つ目は、エレベーターやエスカレーター設備です。

Q：建物の建設にはどのくらいの期間がかかりますか？

A：通常は、建物の高さによります。

　建物の設計や**建築確認**におおむね3か月を要します。

　また、1つの階を建てるのに約1か月かかります。ですから、10階建てのビルの場合には、約10か月要します。

　加えて、建物全体の完成には1～2か月かかります。

　したがって、全体としては、建物の階数プラス4～5か月を要します。

Illustrated Real Estate Terminologies

Overview of Building Mechanical, Electrical and Plumbing Systems

*Modern buildings cannot function without **HVAC (Heat, Ventilation and Air Conditioning) systems, electrical systems, plumbing systems**, and other equipment. The major systems and equipment for a building are as follows:*

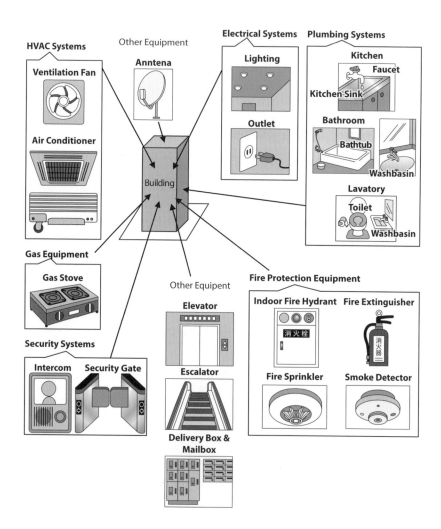

建物設備の概要

現代の建物は、**空調設備**、**電気設備**、**給排水設備**などの設備がなければ、機能しません。主要な建物設備には、以下のような設備があります。

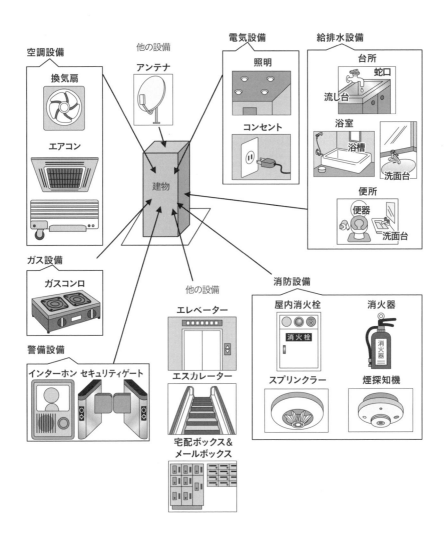

2-10 Overview of Room Layouts in Rental Apartments

Q : How are roon layouts of residential properties classified in Japan?

A : The definition of a **room layout** in Japan is different from that in other countries. Below are the major differences between western countries and Japan.

Studio includes 1K and 1R.

1(One) Bedroom includes 1DK and 1LDK.

2(Two) Bedroom includes 2DK and 2LDK.

3(Three) Bedroom includes 3DK and 3LDK.

Q : What is the difference between 1K and 1R?

A : K means kitchen and R means room. 1K is one room with a separate kitchen. Even if it is small, the kitchen is separated from the room. On the other hand, 1R has no separation between the room and kitchen.

Q : What is the difference between DK and LDK?

A : DK means a dining room with a kitchen. LDK means a living and dining room with a kitchen.

Q : Who are the main users for each layout?

A : 1K, 1R, 1DK, and 1LDK are used mainly by single people. 1DK, 1LDK, 2DK, and 2LDK are used mainly by couples. 2DK, 2LDK, 3DK, and 3LDK are used mainly by couples with one child. 3DK, 3LDK, 4DK, and 4LDK are used mainly by couples with multiple children.

Q : Have room layouts been affected by **COVID-19**?

A : People now prefer larger spaces and more rooms than before COVID-19. Because more people are allowed to **work from home**, they spend more time at their residence. So, the number of rental apartments offering shared working space and conference space has been increasing.

2-10 賃貸マンションの間取りの概要

Q：日本の住宅は、間取りでどのように分類されますか？

A：日本の**間取り**の定義は、他国と違います。下記は、欧米と日本の主な違いです。

　ステューディオは、**ワンルームや1K**。

　1ベッドルームは、**1DKや1LDK**。

　2ベッドルームは、**2DKや2LDK**。

　3ベッドルームは、**3DKや3LDK**。

Q：1Kと1Rの違いは何ですか？

A：Kは台所を意味します。Rは部屋のことです。1Kは、1部屋と独立した台所があります。一方で、1Rは、部屋と台所の仕切りがありません。

Q：DKとLDKの違いは何ですか？

A：DKは食堂と台所を意味します。LDKは居間、食堂、台所を意味します。

Q：各々の間取りは誰に使われていますか？

A：1K、1R、1DK、そして1LDKは主に1人によって使用されます。1DK、1LDK、2DK、2LDKは、主にカップルによって使用されます。2DK、2LDK、3DK、3LDKは、主にカップルと1人の子供によって使用されます。3DK、3LDK、4DK、4LDKは、主にカップルと2人以上の子供によって使用されます。

Q：**コロナ**による間取りへの影響はありましたか？

A：人々は、より広いスペースや多くの間取りを求めるようになっています。より多くの人が**在宅勤務をする**ようになったため、家にいる時間が増えているのです。共同作業場や共同会議室を備えた賃貸マンションの数も、分譲マンションほどではありませんが、増えています。

Overview of Room Layouts in Rental Apartments and Condominiums

Rental apartments and *condominiums* are very popular places for people in Japan to live. The following terminologies help to explain the *room layouts* in Japan.

Types of Floor Plans

"1K" means 1 room and a kitchen. Unlike "1R" which has no separation between a kitchen and a room, 1K has separation between a kitchen and a room.

"1DK" means one room and a dining room with a kitchen.

"1LDK" means one room and a living & dining room with a kitchen.

"2DK" means two rooms and a dining room with a kitchen.

"2LDK" means two rooms and a living & dining room with a kitchen.

"3LDK" means three rooms and a living & dining room with a kitchen.

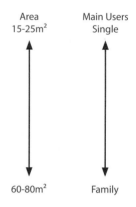

Area	Main Users
15-25m²	Single
↕	↕
60-80m²	Family

Layout Example: 1K

Entrance	MB
Kitchen	Lavatory
	Bathroom
	Closet
Room	
Balcony	

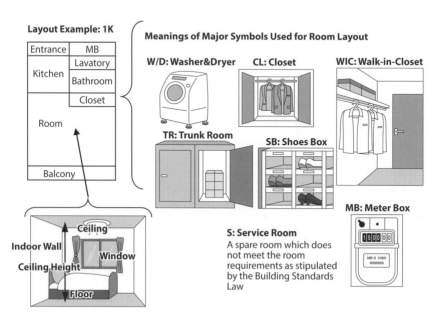

Meanings of Major Symbols Used for Room Layout

W/D: Washer&Dryer **CL: Closet** **WIC: Walk-in-Closet**

TR: Trunk Room **SB: Shoes Box**

MB: Meter Box

S: Service Room
A spare room which does not meet the room requirements as stipulated by the Building Standards Law

Indoor Wall / Ceiling / Ceiling Height / Window / Floor

賃貸マンションと分譲マンションの間取りの概要
日本人にとって、賃貸マンションと分譲マンションは、代表的な住む場所となっています。以下の用語は、それらの**間取り**を理解するのに役立ちます。

間取りのタイプ

「IK」とは、1部屋とキッチンがあるタイプです。部屋と台所に仕切りがない「ワンルーム」と異なり、IKはキッチンが部屋から独立しています。

「IDK」とは、1部屋とダイニングキッチンがあるタイプです。

「ILDK」とは、1部屋とリビングダイニングキッチンがあるタイプです。

「2DK」とは、2部屋とダイニングキッチンがあるタイプです。

「2LDK」とは、2部屋とリビングダイニングキッチンがあるタイプです。

「3LDK」とは、3部屋とリビングダイニングキッチンがあるタイプです。

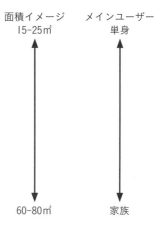

面積イメージ 15-25㎡ / メインユーザー 単身
60-80㎡ / 家族

間取りの例: IK

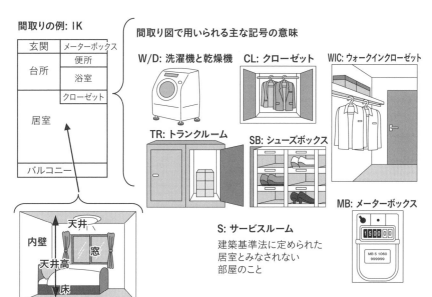

間取り図で用いられる主な記号の意味

W/D: 洗濯機と乾燥機　CL: クローゼット　WIC: ウォークインクローゼット
TR: トランクルーム　SB: シューズボックス　MB: メーターボックス
S: サービスルーム
建築基準法に定められた居室とみなされない部屋のこと

Column | Why do foreign investors like Japanese real estate?

Foreign investors are attracted to the Japanese real estate market for its stability, low cost of debt financing, and clear legal ownership structures. Japan also provides an attractive choice for diversifying their global real estate holdings.

Japan has historically provided very **stable income**, or **investment yield**, which investors can feel confident and secure receiving. Some of the best choices for stable income producing assets in Japan are residential rental buildings and large retail buildings that are operated under a master lease from a credible operator. Vacancy rates for residential buildings in Tokyo have historically remained at around 5%, which is one of the lowest rates in the world, providing a consistent stream of rental income to the owner. Large retail buildings that operate under a master lease take away the risk of vacancy as the rental income is guaranteed by the operator and the owner can consistently receive the same rent each month, regardless of the performance of the retail tenants.

Japan also continues to provide the lowest cost for debt finance in the world, which increases the total return for investors when they use debt finance to purchase and hold their investment properties. This is also referred to as the **yield spread**, and Japan offers the most attractive spread compared to all other major real estate markets.

The investment structures and legal ownership in Japan are very transparent and mature. Institutional investors feel very safe and secure when they purchase and own real estate in Japan, which includes full legal rights over both the land and buildings that they acquire. In other foreign markets, sometimes land cannot be purchased by a foreign investor and is required to be leased from the home country.

The Japanese real estate market is one of the largest in the world and will continue to attract foreign investors in the years to come.

コラム なぜ海外投資家は日本の不動産に投資するのか？

　海外投資家が日本の不動産を好む理由としては、安定性、低金利のローン、そして透明性の高い所有権制度が挙げられます。また、日本への投資は、不動産の国際分散投資においても魅力的な選択肢となっています。

　日本での不動産投資は歴史的に、非常に**安定的なインカム収入**、つまり、**投資利回り**を提供してきており、投資家は自信をもって投資することができます。安定的な収益をあげられる投資対象としては、賃貸マンションへの投資や信用度の高い運営者が一括借りしている商業施設が挙げられます。東京の賃貸マンションの空室率はおおむね5％で世界的に見ても最も低い水準です。これが投資家に安定的なリターンをもたらす要因となっています。運営者による一括借りの大規模な商業施設では、運営者が賃料を保証することで個別テナントの状況に関わらず安定的な賃料を毎月得ることができます。
　また、日本では、世界的に見て最も安いデット資金を調達することができます。これにより投資家は投資リターンをあげることができます。これは、イールドギャップ（**金利差**）という言葉として投資家の間で用いられている用語ですが、他の主要国と比べても日本は最も魅力的なイールドギャップがある国となっています。

　投資ストラクチャーや所有権の法制度も日本は透明性が高く成熟しています。機関投資家は、土地と建物の完全な法的な権利を取得することができるため、投資の安全性を感じることができます。他の国では、海外投資家は土地を取得できない、また、借りて利用しなければならないなどの制限があるからです。

　日本の不動産市場は、世界でも最も巨大な市場の一つであり、今後も海外投資家にとって魅力的な市場であるでしょう。

Chapter 3

Basic Structures of Real Estate Investment in Japan and the Rest of the World

第3章

日本と世界における
不動産投資ストラクチャー
の概要

3-1 Why do investors around the world invest in real estate?

Q : Why do investors choose real estate as an investment?

A : The main reason for choosing to invest in **real estate** is because it provides lots of different ways to make money. Real estate provides steady **rental income** from the tenants who lease the building and real estate can also go up in value over time and produce a big **capital gain** when it is sold.

The other reason people like real estate is because they follow the proverb, "don't put all your eggs in one basket." Investing money only in stocks increases investment risk. **Diversification**, which means investing in a variety of assets, is the key to modern investment strategies. Real estate is usually considered less risky than **stocks** and a bit riskier than **bonds**.

Real estate is also a very good **hedge against inflation**, so when the price of goods goes up, real estate rents usually go up as well and the investor can benefit.

Q : What is the rental income from real estate?

A : Owning **rental property** can provide stable income which is provided by **rent** from the tenants. This income is similar to **dividends** from stocks or **interest** from bonds.

Q : What is a capital gain?

A : Real estate investors have the opportunity for a capital gain when they sell the property. This happens when the **sales price** is higher than the original **purchase price**. However, if the sales price is lower than the original purchase price, investors can incur a **capital loss**.

Q : Can investors invest in an **owner-occupied property**?

A : Yes, investors can purchase the property and then lease it back to the current owners. From the current owner's point of view, they sell the property and then lease it back from the purchaser, or investor. This is called a **sale and lease back**.

3-1 なぜ、世界中の投資家が不動産に投資しているのか?

Q：なぜ、投資家は不動産に投資するのですか?

A：**不動産**に投資する最大の理由は、様々な収益を上げることができるからです。建物を賃借しているテナントから安定的な**賃料収入**を得ることができ、また、価値の上昇で、売却により大きな**キャピタルゲイン（売却益）**を得ることも可能です。

他の理由としては、「1つのかごに卵を入れるな」という格言に従っていることです。1社の株式だけに投資することはリスクを高めることになります。様々な資産に投資するという**分散投資**は、現在の投資戦略において重要となっています。不動産のリスクは、通常、**株式**より低く、**債券**よりは高いとされています。

また、不動産は物価上昇に合わせて賃料も上昇するため、**インフレヘッジ**にも向いています。

Q：不動産からの賃料収入とは何ですか?

A：**賃貸不動産**を保有することで、テナントからの**賃料**という安定的な収入が得られます。これは、株式からの**配当**や債券からの**利払い**と同様のものです。

Q：不動産のキャピタルゲインとは何ですか?

A：不動産の投資家には、賃貸不動産の売却により、将来、キャピタルゲイン（売却益）が得られる可能性があります。キャピタルゲインは、**売却価格が取得価格**よりも高い場合に得られます。但し、逆の場合には、**キャピタルロス（売却損）**が発生します。

Q：投資家は所有者が使用している**自社不動産**に投資できますか?

A：はい。その不動産を取得した後に現在の所有者に賃貸することで、賃料収入が得られます。現在の所有者からすると、保有不動産を売却した後に買主、つまり、投資家から賃借することであり、これを、**セール＆リースバック**と呼びます。

Diversification

Investors prefer to make an investment portfolio that is made up of multiple assets, such as stocks, bonds, and alternative assets including real estate, in order to reduce their risk. Many investors invest in those assets not only in their home country but also in other countries.

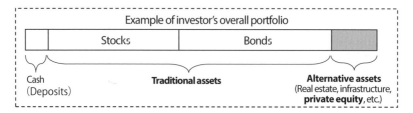

Income gain

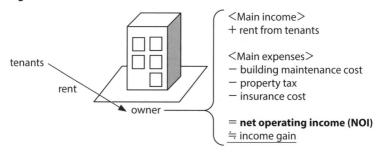

<Main income>
+ rent from tenants

<Main expenses>
− building maintenance cost
− property tax
− insurance cost

= **net operating income (NOI)**
≒ income gain

Capital gain

step 1
property acquisition

step 2
property sale

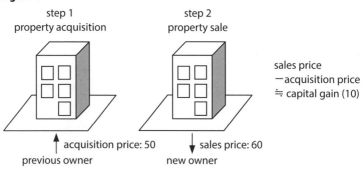

sales price
−acquisition price
≒ capital gain (10)

acquisition price: 50
previous owner

sales price: 60
new owner

分散投資

投資家は、リスクを軽減するために、株式、債券、そして不動産などの代替資産といった様々な資産から成る投資ポートフォリオを作ることを好みます。多くの投資家は、自国だけでなく他国にも投資を行っています。

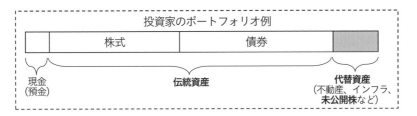

投資家のポートフォリオ例

現金（預金） ／ 伝統資産 ／ 代替資産（不動産、インフラ、**未公開株**など）

インカムゲイン

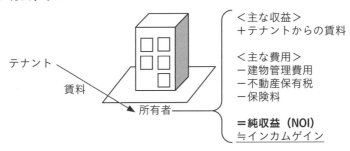

テナント
賃料
所有者

＜主な収益＞
＋テナントからの賃料

＜主な費用＞
－建物管理費用
－不動産保有税
－保険料

＝純収益（NOI）
≒インカムゲイン

キャピタルゲイン

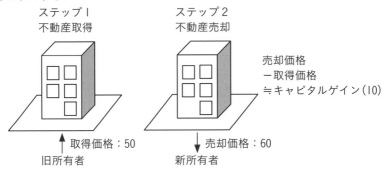

ステップ1
不動産取得

ステップ2
不動産売却

売却価格
－取得価格
≒キャピタルゲイン（10）

↑取得価格：50
旧所有者

↓売却価格：60
新所有者

3-2 Who are real estate investors globally?

Q : Who are real estate investors?

A : They are usually divided into two types: **retail investors** and **institutional investors**. Retail investors are usually individuals while institutional investors represent professional investors such as **insurance companies, banks, pension funds** and **mutual funds. Sovereign wealth funds** known as **SWFs** are also major institutional investors. **High net worth individuals (HNWIs)** or **Ultra HNWIs** sometimes invest large amounts of money into real estate directly or through a **family office** they set up and hire professionals to manage their funds.

Q : How do retail investors invest in real estate?

A : There are two main ways for individuals to invest in real estate: **direct real estate investment** and **indirect real estate investment**. Direct investment means the individual directly owns the real estate and leases it out to tenants. Indirect investment means that an individual invests in shares or units of a real estate investment fund like a **REIT** or a mutual fund that invests in various REITs.

Q : How do institutional investors invest in real estate?

A : Like retail investors, institutional investors can invest in real estate through direct investment or indirect investment. In terms of indirect investment, they invest in listed shares (units) such as REITs, and they also invest in unlisted **private real estate funds**. These unlisted private funds are usually not available to retail investors because the minimum investment amount is typically many millions of dollars.

Q : How do institutional investors raise money to invest in real estate?

A : Institutional investors raise money from many individuals and then invest it as a pool of capital. Insurance companies collect money as **insurance premiums**. Banks collect money as **deposits**. Pension funds collect money as reserves for future **pension payments**. Mutual funds collect individuals' investment money.

3-2 誰が、不動産に投資しているのか？

Q：誰が、不動産に投資しているのですか？

A：投資家は、大きくは2つのタイプ、**一般投資家**と**機関投資家**に分けることができます。一般投資家とは通常、個人投資家を意味します。また、機関投資家とは、プロ投資家のことで、**保険会社**、**銀行**、**年金基金**、**投資信託**などが挙げられます。SWFの名で知られる**政府系ファンド**も代表的な機関投資家です。**富裕層**や**超富裕層**も、直接、もしくは、自らの資金を運用するために専門家を雇って設立した**ファミリーオフィス**を通じて機関投資家と同様の多額の金額を不動産に投資することがあります。

Q：個人投資家はどのように不動産に投資するのですか？

A：大きくは2つの投資の方法、**直接不動産投資**と**間接不動産投資**があります。直接投資とは、個人投資家が、自ら直接不動産を保有してテナントに賃貸する方法です。間接投資とは、個人投資家が、REIT（リート／**不動産投資信託**）や、様々なREITに投資する投資信託といった不動産投資ファンドの株式や投資口を保有する方法です。

Q：機関投資家はどのように不動産に投資するのですか？

A：個人投資家と同様に、機関投資家も、直接投資もしくは間接投資により、不動産に投資することができます。間接投資に関しては、機関投資家は、REITのような上場株式（投資口）への投資だけではなく、非上場の**私募不動産ファンド**への投資も行っています。これらの非上場の私募ファンドは、最低投資額が数億円になるため、個人投資家は、通常、投資することができません。

Q：機関投資家はどうやって不動産に投資する資金を調達するのですか？

A：機関投資家は、多くの個人から資金を集めて、それらの資金をまとめて投資しています。保険会社は個人から**保険料**を徴収しています。銀行は個人から**預金**でお金を集めています。年金基金は将来の**年金支払い**の積立金として個人からお金が集まります。投資信託は、個人の投資資金を集めます。

Direct real estate investment

The investor owns the real estate and the title wholly and directly.

Indirect real estate investment

*The investor indirectly owns the real estate through owning all or parts of the **shares** (**units**, **beneficiary certificates**) issued by the SPC, which is usually a company or a trustee and managed by the asset management company. The asset management company is also regarded as an institutional investor.*

investor

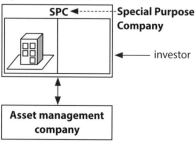

Major institutional investors

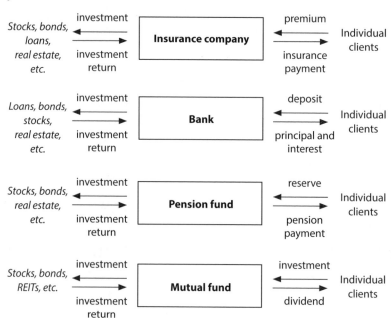

直接不動産投資

投資家は、直接、完全に、不動産、そしてその権利を保有します。

間接不動産投資

*投資家は、通常、会社や受託者のようなSPCにより発行される**株式（投資口、受益証券）**の全部もしくは一部を保有することで間接的に不動産を保有します。また、このSPCは資産運用会社により運営されます。資産運用会社は、機関投資家でもあります。*

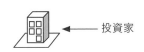

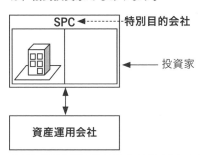

代表的な機関投資家

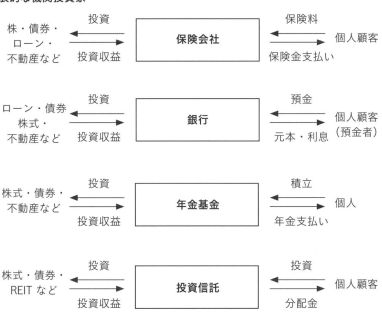

3-3 | What is a REIT?

Q : What is a REIT?

A : The word **REIT** is an abbreviation of the words **Real Estate Investment Trust**.

Investing in REITs is one of the most popular **indirect real estate investment** options for both retail and institutional investors around the world. By meeting some requirements, REITs may not have to pay **corporate taxes**. To be precise, REITs can minimize corporate tax payments to almost zero by meeting specific requirements. So, the investors have almost the same investment benefits as investors who choose to own real estate directly. But unlike direct investment, which requires investors to prepare a large sum of money up front, REITs allow investors to purchase smaller units of well-diversified real estate portfolios, which are much more affordable.

Usually, REITs are listed on the **stock exchange** of their home country, so investors can purchase and sell their shares or units at anytime. While REITs have high **liquidity**, they can also have high **volatility** in their share prices much like typical stocks do.

Q : What kinds of REITs are there in the world?

A : There are mainly two different kinds of REITs available to investors, which are defined by how they are managed: **self-management** or **external management**.

Self-management REITs can be found in the US, UK, and France, and these companies look and act much more like a regular **listed real estate company** that has a focus on stable rental income. These companies usually directly own and manage the real estate themselves.

External management REITs can be found in Singapore, Australia, and Japan, and they act much more like **listed mutual funds**. In Singapore and Australia, the entity that owns the real estate is called a **trust**, or a **trustee**. In Japan, the owner of the real estate is called an **investment corporation**. The investment management of the real estate is then entrusted to third party **asset management companies**.

3-3 REITとは何か？

Q：REITとは何ですか？

A：REIT（リート）は、**不動産投資信託**の略称です。

　REITへの投資は、世界中の個人投資家や機関投資家にとって、最も人気のある**間接不動産投資**の一手法です。REITは、一定の要件を満たすことで、**法人税**を支払わなくてすみます。正確に言うと、一定の要件を満たすことで、法人税の支払いをほぼゼロにまで極小化できるのです。したがって、投資家は、直接不動産に投資したのと同じような投資効果を得ることができます。また、多額の金額を要する直接投資と異なり、REITに投資することで投資家は、小額で分散された不動産ポートフォリオに投資することが可能となります。

　通常、REITは、各国の**証券取引所**に上場しています。したがって、投資家は、いつでもその株式や投資口を売買することができます。このような高い**流動性**がある一方で、株式のような**価格変動の大きさ**は、直接不動産投資を望む投資家には好まれません。

Q：どのようなタイプのREITがありますか？

A：どのように運用されるかによって、大きくは、**内部運用型**と**外部運用型**という2つのタイプがあります。

　内部運用型REITの例には、米国、英国、フランスのREITが挙げられます。これらのREITは、安定的な賃貸収入を得ることに特化している通常の**上場不動産会社**のようなものです。これらのREITは、直接不動産を保有し、自ら運用します。

　外部運用型REITの例には、シンガポール、豪州、日本のREITが挙げられ、**上場投資信託**に似ています。シンガポールと豪州では、不動産を保有する器として**信託**（つまり**受託者**）が用いられます。日本では、**投資法人**と呼ばれる会社が用いられます。そして、不動産投資運用は、外部の**資産運用会社**に委託されます。

Real estate operating company (REOC)

REOCs are **publicly traded real estate companies** that can invest in **income producing properties** as well as **real estate development**. Additionally, they can retain earnings and reinvest them in real estate. However, they must pay **corporate tax**, and their investors receive a dividend after deducting **retained earnings** and corporate tax.

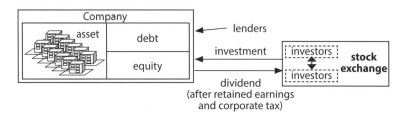

Real estate investment trust (REIT) — self-management type

This type of REIT acts like a publicly traded real estate company that focuses on investing in income producing properties. But they must pay almost all their earnings to their investors as dividends. Therefore, they can be exempt from corporate tax and investors can receive their dividends before the deduction of retained earnings and corporate tax.

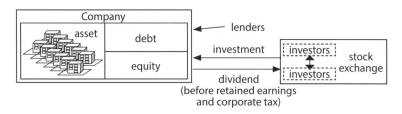

Real estate investment trust (REIT) — external management type

This type of REIT acts like **publicly traded mutual funds** which must entrust their management to an **asset management company**. Their other characteristics are almost the same as those of the self-management type REITs.

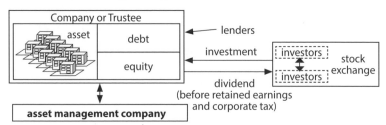

不動産会社

*REOCとは、**上場不動産会社**のことで、**収益不動産**だけでなく、**不動産開発**にも投資が可能です。加えて、利益を留保して、それを不動産に再投資することができます。しかしながら、**法人税**を支払わなければなりません。つまり、投資家は、**内部留保**後、法人税支払い後の配当を受け取ることになります。*

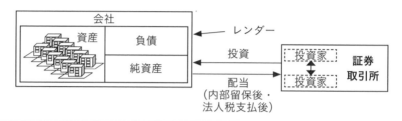

不動産投資信託（リート）－内部運用型

このタイプのREITは、収益不動産への投資に特化した上場不動産会社のようなものです。しかし、REITは、利益のほとんど全てを投資家に配当として支払わなければなりません。それゆえ、法人税の免除を受けることができます。つまり、投資家は、内部留保前、法人税支払い前の配当を受け取ることができます。

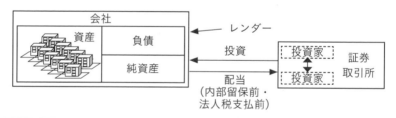

不動産投資信託（リート）－外部運用型

*このタイプのREITは、その運用を**資産運用会社**に委ねなければならない**上場投資信託**のようなものです。その他の特徴は、内部運用型のREITとほぼ同様です。*

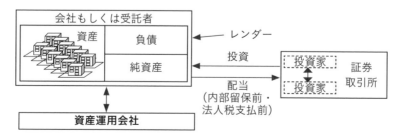

3-4 What are some other types of real estate funds?

Q : What is a **Private Real Estate Fund**?

A : A private real estate fund is an indirect form of real estate investment, but is not listed on any stock exchange, so the shares or units cannot be freely traded like REIT shares. This type of fund is usually used by **institutional investors** because the minimum investment requirements are usually quite large. Like REITs, private funds can avoid paying **corporate tax** on their profits by meeting certain requirements so they can enjoy the same tax benefits as direct investment.

Q : What kinds of private real estate funds are there?

A : There are mainly two types of private funds: **closed-end funds** and **open-end funds**.

Closed-end funds have an investment timeline determined when the fund is launched. During the term of the investment, investors are not allowed to take money out or add new money to the fund. It is a set schedule, usually running for 3, 5 or 7 years for institutional investors. In Japan, a **TMK** or **TK-GK** structure is usually used for closed-end funds.

An open-end fund structure does not have a set investment timeline, and investors can take money out and add new money into the fund freely. Because open-end funds are not listed on a stock exchange, if too many investors ask for their money back at the same time, the fund would not be able to return all the money immediately because they would first need to sell the real estate in the fund. This is called low **liquidity** and is a drawback for open-end fund structures. In Japan, the **private REIT** represents this structure.

Q : Are there any popular unlisted real estate funds for **retail investors**?

A : There are some non-listed **open-ended real estate funds** available to retail investors in parts of Europe and the US. Like listed REITs, the minimum investment amounts are small, and they have attracted many retail investors.

3-4 REIT以外にどのような不動産ファンドがあるのか?

Q：**私募不動産ファンド**とは何ですか?

A：私募不動産ファンドは、間接不動産投資の一手段ですが、証券取引所には上場しておらず、REITのようにその株式や投資口を自由に売買することはできません。このタイプのファンドは、投資に必要な金額が大きく、通常、**機関投資家**により活用されています。REITと同様に、一定の要件を満たすことで**法人税**の支払いを回避できるため、投資家は、直接不動産投資と同様の効果を得ることができます。

Q：私募不動産ファンドにはどのようなタイプがありますか?

A：主に、**クローズドエンドファンド**と**オープンエンドファンド**という2種類のファンドがあります。

前者は、有期限のファンドです。その期間、投資家は資金をファンドから回収することができず、また、ファンドに新たな資金を投資することもできません。通常、3年、5年、7年などの期間で、機関投資家に活用されています。日本においては、**TMK**ストラクチャーや**TK-GK**ストラクチャーが、このクローズドエンドファンドのタイプで用いられます。

後者は、無期限のファンドです。投資家は、いつでも、ファンドから資金を回収することができ、また、ファンドに新たな投資をすることも可能です。しかし、証券取引所には上場していないため、解約が多いとすぐには資金を返還できず、不動産も売らざるを得ません。この**流動性**の低さが、このタイプのファンドの欠点です。日本では、**私募REIT**がこのタイプで用いられています。

Q：**個人投資家**が投資できる非上場の不動産ファンドはありますか?

A：米国や欧州の一部では、個人投資家も投資可能な**オープンエンド型不動産ファンド**が複数あります。REITと同様、投資に必要な金額が小額であるため、多くの個人投資家をひきつけています。

Closed-end fund

*Closed-end funds do not buy back the units they issue. That is, the funds do not allow investors to cancel / terminate the investment agreement before the end of the fund term. So, like the **TK-GK** structure and the **TMK** structure, the underlying real estate needs to first be sold in order to return the investor's initial investment. **J-REITs**, on the other hand, are listed on the stock exchange, so investors can sell their units on a daily basis.*

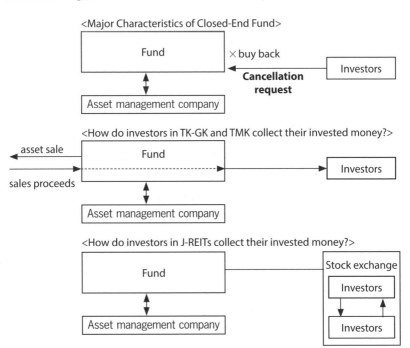

Open-end fund

*Open-end funds can buy back the units they issue. General mutual funds are good examples of open-end funds. In Japan, a **private REIT** structure is a type of open-end fund. But unlike mutual funds, cancellation requests are restricted due to the low liquidity of real estate.*

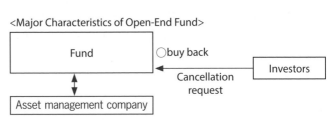

クローズドエンドファンド

クローズドエンドファンドは、発行した投資口の買戻しはしません。つまり、ファンド期限までに、投資家は解約することができません。したがって、*TK-GK* や *TMK* ストラクチャーのように、投資家は、不動産を売却して初めて投資資金を回収することができます。一方、*J-REIT*は、証券取引所に上場しているため、日々投資口を売却することができます。

〈クローズドエンドファンドの主要な特徴〉

〈TK-GK や TMK において投資家はどのように投資資金を回収するか？〉

〈J-REIT において投資家はどのように投資資金を回収するか？〉

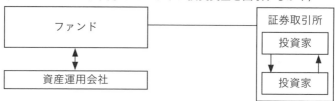

オープンエンドファンド

オープンエンドファンドは、発行した投資口の買戻しを行うファンドです。一般的な投資信託が、オープンエンドファンドの典型的な例です。日本では、*私募REIT*が、オープンエンドファンドです。しかし、投資信託と異なり、私募REITは、不動産の流動性が低いため、解約請求は制限されています。

〈オープンエンドファンドの主要な特徴〉

3-5 Real Estate Investment Structure in Japan 1: TK-GK

Q : What is a TK?

A : A **TK**, or **Tokumei Kumiai**, is a business partnership between two parties called the **TK investor** and the **TK operator**, and the contract between them is called the **TK agreement**. A TK is governed by Japanese **Commercial Law**. It is similar to a limited partnership but is actually a **silent partnership**. There can be more than one investor in this structure, but each investor is required to have a separate TK agreement with the TK operator.

Q : What is a GK?

A : A **GK**, or **Godo Kaisha**, is a special kind of Japanese corporation that is governed under Japanese **Corporate Law**. In a TK-GK structure, the GK plays the role of the TK operator and conducts the **TK business**, or real estate investment business, and distributes its profit to the TK investors based on the TK agreement. The **Financial Instruments and Exchange Law** (**FIEL**) also states that a GK must appoint a licensed **asset management company** to manage the business.

Q : Why is a TK-GK structure used for real estate investment?

A : The TK-GK structure limits the liability of the investors and avoids **double taxation** of profits as long as the relationship between the TK operator and the TK investors is maintained as a silent partnership. In this structure, the investors must maintain a silent, or passive position. If the investors break this rule or become very active in the investment management of the real estate, the TK could be reclassified as a **general partnership**, and lose its **limited liability** status, and be required to pay corporate taxes.

Another key point in the TK-GK structure is that real estate must be entrusted to a Japanese **trust bank** and be purchased in the form of **trust beneficiary interests** (**TBI**) by the GK to avoid regulation by the **Real Estate Specified Joint Business Law**, explained in Chapter 3-8.

3-5 日本の不動産投資ストラクチャー1: TK-GK

Q：TKとは何を意味するのですか？

A：TKとは、**匿名組合**の略称で、**匿名組合員**と**営業者**と呼ばれる2者間の組合です。両者の契約は**匿名組合契約**と呼ばれます。匿名組合は、**商法**により規定されています。それはリミテッドパートナーシップに類似していますが、実際には**サイレントパートナーシップ**を意味します。匿名組合は、複数の投資家による投資が可能なストラクチャーですが、それぞれの投資家が、別々の匿名組合契約を営業者と締結しなければなりません。

Q：GKとは何を意味するのですか？

A：GKとは、**合同会社**の略称で、日本の**会社法**で規定されている会社形態の1つです。TK-GKストラクチャーにおいては、合同会社は、匿名組合契約に基づき、**匿名組合事業**、つまり、不動産投資事業を行い、その利益を匿名組合員に分配する営業者の役割を担います。また、**金融商品取引法**に従い、合同会社はその事業運営を、免許のある**資産運用会社**に委託しなければなりません。

Q：なぜ、TK-GKストラクチャーが不動産投資に用いられるのですか？

A：このストラクチャーは、営業者と匿名組合員（投資家）の関係が匿名組合である限りにおいては、投資家の有限責任と、**二重課税**を回避することができます。すなわち、このストラクチャーにおいては、投資家は、サイレントであること、つまり、消極的な立場であることを求められます。もし、投資家が、このルールを破り、不動産の投資運用に積極的に関与した場合には、匿名組合が一般的な組合（**任意組合**）とみなされ、投資家は**有限責任**を確保できず、法人税を支払う必要があります。

また、このストラクチャーにおいて他の重要な点は、不動産を**信託銀行**に信託して、**信託受益権**の形態で、合同会社が取得しなければならないことです。そうしなければ、本章3-8節で説明する**不動産特定共同事業法**の規制を受けることになります。

Silent partnership in Japan

A **silent partnership** in Japan is similar to a **limited partnership** in the US. The **TK operator** is like a **general partner** who conducts business **(TK business)** for the partnership and bears unlimited liability for the business. On the other hand, a **TK investor** is like a **limited partner,** who just invests money into the business conducted by a general partner and bears **limited liability** for the business. Additionally, the TK investor cannot actively get involved in the TK business.

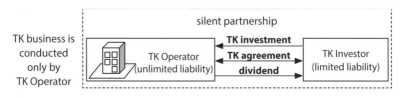

General partnership in Japan

A **general partnership** (NK, or Nin'i Kumiai) in Japan is similar to an association of partners that conduct business together. So, although the partners can appoint one of them as the representative operator, they equally bear **unlimited liability**.

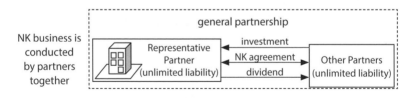

TK-GK structure

TK investors do not actually own the shares of the GK; they own the shares of the TK business which gives them the right to the profits of the business. The shares of the GK are generally owned by a **bankruptcy remote entity** called an Ippan Shadan Hojin (ISH).

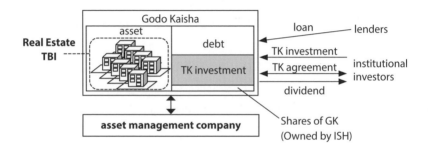

匿名組合

日本の**匿名組合**は、米国の**リミテッドパートナーシップ**に似ています。**匿名組合の営業者**は、匿名組合の事業（**匿名組合事業**）を行い、その事業の全責任を負う**ジェネラルパートナー**と言えます。一方、**匿名組合員**は、ジェネラルパートナーが行う事業に単に出資し、その事業の**有限責任**を負うだけの**リミテッドパートナー**と言えます。また、匿名組合員は匿名組合事業に積極的な関与はできません。

匿名組合事業は
営業者によって
のみ行われる

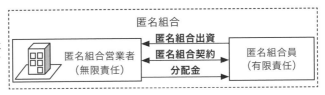

任意組合

日本の**任意組合**は、共同事業者が何かの活動（ビジネスを含む）を一緒にやるための単なる共同体です。したがって、共同事業者は、共同事業者の誰かを事業の代表者とすることができますが、皆が**無限責任**を負います。

組合事業は
組合員全員で
行われる

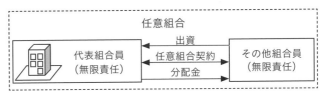

TK-GK ストラクチャー

匿名組合員が投資するのは、合同会社の持分（≒株式）ではなく、匿名組合事業の持分です。同事業の持分を持つことで匿名組合員は、同事業の利益を得る権利を持ちます。合同会社の持分は、通常、一般社団法人と呼ばれる**倒産隔離のための器**に保有されます。

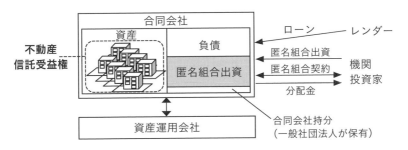

3-6 Real Estate Investment Structure in Japan 2: TMK

Q : What does TMK mean?

A : **TMK** is an abbreviation of the Japanese words **Tokutei Mokuteki Kaisha** and is a kind of **special purpose company**, or **SPC** which is governed by the **Asset Liquidation Law**. Like a TK-GK, a TMK is used for the purpose of investing in real estate in Japan and the structure provides limited liability to the investors and avoids double taxation by meeting certain requirements.

Q : How do investors use a TMK structure?

A : A TMK can purchase real estate in Japan by raising money through issuing shares to investors. These shares are called **preferred shares**.

A TMK can also borrow money from a bank or other institution in order to buy real estate. In terms of debt finance, a TMK usually has to issue bonds, called **specified bonds**, in order to meet one of the requirements that give the investors tax benefits.

Like the TK-GK structure, the TMK usually uses an asset management company to manage the business.

Q : What are the main differences between a TK-GK and a TMK?

A : A TMK is considered a more complicated structure to set-up and manage compared to the TK-GK structure, but a TMK allows the investors to take an active role in the investment, whereas the TK-GK structure requires the investors to be passive.

The TMK structure is governed by a strict Asset Liquidation Law which requires that the TMK itself register with the **local financial bureau** governed by the **FSA** - a financial watchdog in Japan. A TMK also has to prepare and file an **Asset Liquidation Plan** (**ALP**) which details how to raise equity and debt, what kinds of assets are to be acquired, and how to manage and dispose of them. The TMK must operate in accordance with the ALP.

3-6 日本の不動産投資ストラクチャー2： TMK

Q：TMKとは何を意味するのですか？

A：TMKとは日本語の**特定目的会社**の略称です。特定目的会社とは、「**資産の流動化に関する法律（資産流動化法）**」に定められている**特別目的会社**のことです。TK-GKと同様に、TMKは、日本での不動産投資に用いられます。TMKストラクチャーでは、投資家は、有限責任を確保し、一定の要件を満たすことで二重課税を回避することができます。

Q：投資家はTMKを用いてどのように不動産に投資するのですか？

A：TMKは、投資家に証券を発行して資金を調達し、不動産を取得することができます。この証券は**優先出資証券**と呼ばれます。

　TMKはまた、不動産を取得するために、銀行や他の金融機関から資金を借りることができます。また、デット資金に関しては、二重課税を回避するための1つの要件を満たすために、TMKは通常、**特定社債**と呼ばれる社債を発行する必要があります。

　TK-GKストラクチャーと同様、TMKは通常その運営を運用会社に委ねています。

Q：TK-GKストラクチャーとTMKストラクチャーの主な違いは何ですか？

A：TMKは、TK-GKストラクチャーと比べて、その組成や運用が複雑だとみなされています。しかし、TK-GKの投資家が「消極的な投資家」である必要があるのに対して、TMKの投資家はTMKの事業に積極的に関与することができます。

　TMKは、資産の流動化に関する法律により規制されており、投資家は、金融監視機関である**金融庁**が管轄する**地方財務局**にTMKの登録を行う必要があります。TMKはまた、どのように資金を調達するか、どのような資産を取得するか、そして、どのようにその資産を運用・処分していくかを詳細に記載した「**資産流動化計画**」を作成し、届出しなければなりません。TMKは、この資産流動化計画に従って運営を行う必要があります。

TMK structure

*The relationship between specified shares and preferred shares is similar to **ordinary shares** and preferred shares of a Kabushiki Kaisha* (KK). Specified shares are usually owned by a **bankruptcy remote entity** such as the Japanese Ippan Shadan Hojin (ISH).*

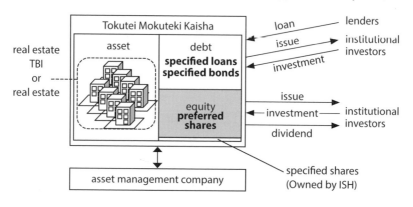

Major requirements for foreign investors to avoid double taxation

Requirement 1: More than 50% of the preferred shares must be underwritten by a Japanese entity. So, foreign investors usually set up a Japanese SPC or a Japanese branch of the overseas SPC.

Requirement 2: Some of the specified bonds must be underwritten by one or more **qualified institutional investors (QIIs)**, as defined by the **Special Taxation Measures Law**. So, Japanese banks, which provide loans to the TMK, usually underwrite the bonds as well.

<Typical finance structure of TMK for foreign investors>

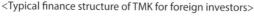
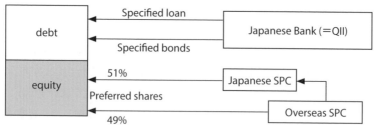

---

* **Kabushiki Kaisha**   In Japan, Kabushiki Kaisha is usually called Kabushiki Gaisha.

TMKストラクチャー

特定出資と優先出資証券との関係は、株式会社*の**普通株**と優先株との関係に類似しています。特定出資は、通常、一般社団法人のような**倒産隔離のための器**が保有します。

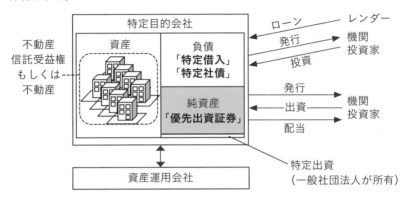

海外投資家が二重課税を回避するための主な要件

要件①：50%超の優先出資証券が国内の主体によって引受けられること。したがって、海外投資家は、通常、日本のSPCを設立するか、海外SPCの支店を設立します。

要件②：特定社債が1つもしくは複数の**適格機関投資家**（**租税特別措置法**により定義）のみによって引受けられること。したがって、通常、TMKにローンを提供する銀行が、当該社債も引受けています。

〈海外投資家によるTMKの典型的な資金調達ストラクチャー〉

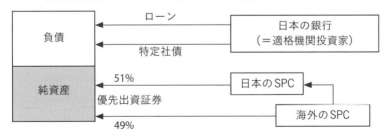

＊**株式会社**　ビジネスでは、株式会社（かぶしきがいしゃ）は、しばしば株式会社（かぶしきかいしゃ。省略するとKK）と呼ばれます。

3-7 Real Estate Investment Structure in Japan 3: REIT

Q : What does J-REIT mean in Japan?

A : **J-REIT** stands for **Japanese Real Estate Investment Trust**. J-REITs started in 2001, and there are 60 J-REITs listed on the **Tokyo Stock Exchange (TSE)** as of March 31st, 2023. Their **market capitalization** is about 1.5 trillion yen. There are also unlisted REITs, which are called **Private REITs** and are only used by **institutional investors**. The REIT structure in Japan is governed by the **Investment Trust and Investment Corporation Law** and an **investment corporation** is used to own and manage the real estate or real estate TBI on behalf of the investors.

Q : Who are the sponsors of J-REITs?

A : The major shareholder of an **asset management company** that manages an investment corporation is called a "sponsor". Major sponsors are usually real estate companies that develop properties to be injected into the REITs. Each REIT adopts several measures, such as **same boat investment** requirements, to deal with the **conflict of interest** between the sponsor and investors and secure **alignment of interest** with investors.

Q : What are the main differences between a J-REIT, a TK-GK, and a TMK?

A : All three structures allow investors to achieve **limited liability** and avoid **double taxation**. But J-REITs are different because they are listed and used by both retail and institutional investors. Because J-REITs are widely distributed to **retail investors**, they are strictly regulated by the Japanese **FSA** and have many more disclosure requirements than the TMK and TK-GK structures. Because J-REITs are listed, J-REITs can provide much more **liquidity** to investors compared to a TMK or TK-GK. However, the **volatility** of their unit price is their main drawback. Private REITs are established for investors seeking the lower volatility of real estate as compared to stocks. Additionally, investment corporations of J-REITs have been subject to **merger and acquisition** activities.

3-7 日本の不動産投資ストラクチャー３：REIT

Q：J-REITとは何を意味するのですか？

A：J-REITとは、**日本の不動産投資信託**を意味します。J-REITは、2001年に創設され、2023年3月末時点で、**東京証券取引所に60銘柄が上場**しています。**時価総額は約15兆円**です。一方、上場しておらず、**機関投資家**だけを対象とするREITは、通常、**私募REIT**と呼ばれています。日本のREITストラクチャーは、**投資信託及び投資法人に関する法律（投信法）**が規制しています。投資家のために不動産や不動産信託受益権を保有・運用するSPCには**投資法人**が用いられます。

Q：J-REITのスポンサーとは何ですか？

A：投資法人を運営する**資産運用会社**の主な株主をスポンサーと呼びます。主なスポンサーは、REITに組み込める物件を開発している不動産会社です。各REITは、スポンサーと投資家との**利益相反**に対応し、投資家との**利益の一致**を確保するために、**セームボート投資**のような対策を採用しています。

Q：TK-GKやTMKと、J-REITとの主な違いは何ですか？

A：どのストラクチャーも、投資家は**有限責任**であり、**二重課税**の回避も可能です。しかし、J-REITは、TK-GKやTMKと異なり、上場し、機関投資家だけでなく、個人投資家も対象にしているという点が異なります。また、J-REITは、**個人投資家**に広く流通しているので、**金融庁**による規制が厳しく、要求される情報開示事項もTMKやGKと比べて多くなっています。

　J-REITは上場しており、TMKやTK-GKと比べ、格段に**流動性**があります。一方で、J-REITの投資口価格における**価格変動の大きさ**は、大きな短所です。私募REITは、株式よりも不動産の価格変動の低さを好む機関投資家のために組成されています。また、J-REITの投資法人は、**合併・買収**の対象ともなってきました。

REIT structure

*Ownership shares of Investment Corporations, which are called **investment units**, are owned by retail investors and institutional investors in a J-REIT and only by institutional investors in a Private REIT*

J-REIT

Retail and institutional investors can buy and sell the units issued by the investment corporation anytime through a stock exchange.

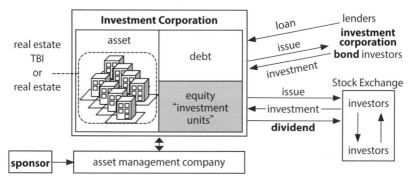

J-REITs focus on **ESG investment**. They actively acquire **environmental certifications** like CASBEE (similar to LEED in the US and BREEAM in the UK) through installing **LED lighting**, **solar panels**, etc., which leads to **GHG(greenhouse gas)** emissions reduction.

Private REIT

Investors can ask the investment corporation to purchase back their units or sell their units to other investors.

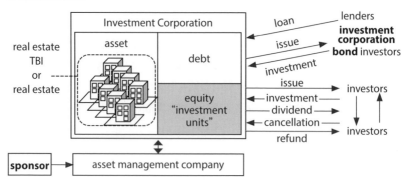

REITストラクチャー

投資法人の所有権、つまり、投資口（投資証券）は、J-REITでは機関投資家と個人投資家が、私募REITでは機関投資家のみが保有しています。

J-REIT

個人投資家を含む投資家は、証券取引所を通じて、株式のように、投資口をいつでも売ったり、買ったりすることが可能です。

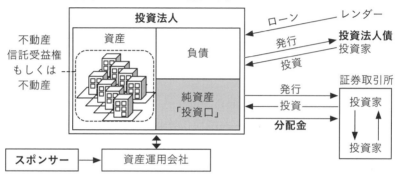

J-REITは**ESG投資**に力を入れています。**温室効果ガス**を減らすことになる**LED照明**や**太陽光パネル**の設置などを通じて、積極的にCASBEE（米国のLEED、英国のBREEAMに類似）のような**環境認証**を取得しています。

私募REIT

投資家が資金を回収する方法としては、投資法人に払戻しを要求するか、他の投資家を見つける方法があります。

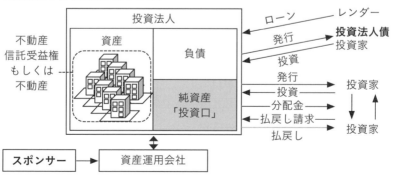

3-8 Other Real Estate Investment Structures in Japan

Q : Is it possible for foreign investors to directly invest in real estate in Japan without having to use an investment vehicle like a TMK or TK-GK?

A : Yes, foreign individuals or foreign companies are allowed to legally and directly own real estate in Japan. Some foreign investors have investment regulations in their home countries that do not allow them to use other vehicles like a TMK, or TK-GK and therefore need to directly hold the **title** to the real estate they purchase. However, **direct real estate investment** in Japan does not offer the same tax incentives as the TMK and TK-GK structures, so it is not commonly used.

Q : Why do some foreign investors prefer to invest in real estate directry?

A : When a TMK or TK-GK structure is used, the legal owner of the real estate is actually the investment vehicle or a trust bank and not the investors themselves. That is why some investors, such as high net worth individuals, prefer to own and register propeties by using an overseas SPC.

Q : What is the **Real Estate Specified Joint Business Structure**?

A : This structure is governed by the **Real Estate Specified Joint Business Law**. This structure is usually used for retail investors in Japan who wish to invest in real estate through a real estate company that owns and manages real estate directly.

Like a TK-GK structure, this structure can also use a **silent partnership** structure between the investors and the real estate company. But unlike a TK-GK structure, the real estate company is required to obtain a **qualified real estate specified joint business operator** license from the **MLIT**.

One of the biggest reasons why a GK, within a TK-GK structure, invests in only **real estate trust beneficiary interest (TBI)** instead of **fee simple estate** is because the GK does not qualify for the required license from the MLIT.

Currently, if an asset management company holds the required license, it may use a TK-GK structure to invest in fee simple real estate.

日本における他の不動産投資ストラクチャー

Q：海外投資家が、TMKやTK-GKなどの投資ビークルを用いずに、直接日本の不動産に投資することは可能ですか？

A：はい。海外の個人や海外の会社は、法的に、日本の不動産を直接保有することができます。いくつかの海外投資家は、自国の投資規制により、TMKやTK-GKといった他のビークルを使用することができず、直接、不動産の**所有権**を保有する必要があります。しかし、日本における**直接不動産投資**は、TMKやTK-GKストラクチャーで可能な税の優遇措置を得ることができず、あまり、用いられていません。

Q：なぜ、いくつかの海外投資家は、直接不動産投資を好むのですか？

A：TMKやTK-GKストラクチャーを用いた場合、不動産の所有者は、それらの投資ビークルもしくは信託銀行となり、投資家自身ではありません。それゆえ、超富裕層などいくつかの投資家は対象不動産を直接自ら保有し登記するのを好むのです。

Q：**不動産特定共同事業スキーム**とは何ですか？

A：このスキームは、**不動産特定共同事業法**により規制されています。通常、日本の個人投資家が、対象不動産を直接保有し運営している不動産会社を通じて、当該不動産への投資をするために用いられています。

　TK-GKストラクチャーと同様に、このスキームも投資家と不動産会社との間で**匿名組合**を用いることができます。しかし、TK-GKストラクチャーと異なり、不動産会社は**国土交通省**から、**不動産特定共同事業者**の免許を得なければなりません。

　このことが、TK-GKストラクチャーで、GKが、**現物不動産**ではなく、**不動産信託受益権**に投資する主な理由の1つとなっています。当該GKでは、必要な免許を国土交通省から得られないからです。

　なお、現在では、もし、資産運用会社が不動産特定共同事業法の免許を持っていれば、TK-GKストラクチャーで現物不動産に投資することも可能です。

Illustrated Real Estate Terminologies

Typical Investment Structures by Overseas Investors

There are generally three types of investment options for overseas investors to invest in Japanese properties. The first one is to invest in one or more properties directly. Investing through a KK as their subsidiary is included in this type. The second one is to invest in one or more properties through a TK-GK or TMK structure. The third one is to invest in a real estate portfolio through a J-REIT.

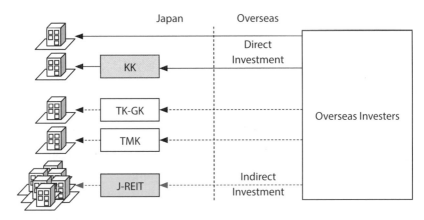

Real Estate Specified Joint Business Structure

A typical example of this structure is for a **real estate operating company** to raise money from **retail investors** and then invest it in real estate on behalf of those investors. The **Real Estate Specified Joint Business Law** requires the company, which plays a **TK operator** role, to obtain a license based on this law. To obtain this license, the company is required to be a **licensed real estate agent company**.

The company may also become a **TK investor** by itself in order to mitigate the risk for retail investors, who can contribute their money to the TK operator as **preferred TK investors**.

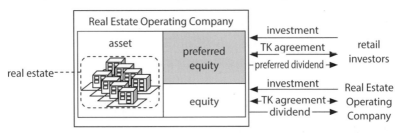

The structure allows the company to make an NK agreement (explained on pege 120) with retail investors who would like to co-own the subject property to have the same tax effect as a property owner.

海外投資家による代表的な投資ストラクチャー

海外投資家が日本の不動産に投資するには主には3つの方法があります。1つ目は、単独もしくは複数の不動産に直接投資することです。子会社としての株式会社を通じた投資も含みます。2つ目は、単独もしくは複数の不動産にTK-GKやTMKを通じて投資することです。3つ目の方法はJ-REITなどを通じた不動産ポートフォリオへの投資です。

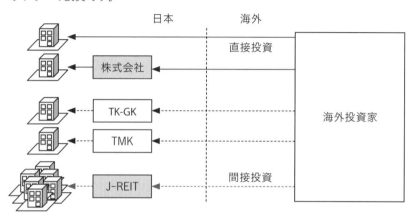

不動産特定共同事業スキーム

*典型的なスキームは、**不動産会社**が**個人投資家**から資金を集め、不動産に直接投資する際に用いられます。**不動産特定共同事業法**は、匿名組合の営業者となるこの不動産会社に、同法に基づく免許を得ることを求めています。この免許を得るためには、当該会社は、**宅地建物取引業者**であることが求められます。*

*この不動産会社は、自ら**匿名組合員**ともなることも可能です。個人投資家を**優先匿名組合員**とすることで、個人投資家のリスクを軽減するためにこのような仕組みが採用されることがあります。*

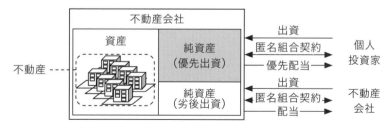

このスキームで不動産会社は、121ページで説明した任意組合契約を個人投資家と結ぶことも可能です。これらの個人投資家は、不動産所有者と同様の税効果を得るため、対象不動産を共有したいのです。

3-9 What is a Trust Beneficiary Interest on Real Estate in Japan?

Q : What is the trust scheme in Japan?

A : The trust scheme is the relationship between a trustor, a trustee, and a beneficiary. A **trustor**, which is an individual or a company, entrusts its assets to a trustee. A **trustee** then becomes the **legal owner** of the assets, or **entrusted assets**, on behalf of a beneficiary. The **beneficiary** then has the right to receive the economic benefit from these assets. This right is called the **trust beneficiary interest (TBI)**.

In Japan, **trust banks** or **trust companies** that register with or get a license from the **FSA** based on the **Trust Business Law**, play the role of trustee. Japanese trust banks are allowed to conduct trustee business under the **Act on Provision of Trust Business by Financial Institutions**.

Q : Why is the TBI structure used for real estate transactions in Japan?

A : When real estate is transformed into TBI, it becomes securitized and easier to use as a financial product for investors. In order for real estate to become TBI, the trust bank first conducts detailed **due diligence** on the property, as they will be assuming the role of the new legal owner as well as providing a **fiduciary duty** to the beneficiary. As a result, the property that can be converted into TBI is regarded as an **investment grade property**.

After a property is entrusted, the trust bank continues its fiduciary role and holds the deposits of the tenants and collects the rent and other income from the property. This makes the cash management process for real estate much easier for investors and lenders.

Trust banks charge an **initial trust set up fee** and an **annual trust running fee** in compensation for their above services.

When properties are entrusted and converted into TBI, there are also tax acquisition incentives that drastically reduce the costs of purchasing real estate in Japan.

Additionally, the TK-GK structure is required to use TBI instead of **fee simple estate** to avoid regulation by the **Real Estate Specified Joint Business Law**.

3-9 不動産信託受益権とは何か?

Q：信託スキームとは何ですか?

A：信託スキームは、委託者、受託者、受益者という3者からなる関係です。**委託者**とは、受託者に保有資産を信託する個人や会社のことを言います。**受託者**とは、受益者のために**信託財産の法律上の所有者**となるもののことです。**受益者**は、信託財産からの経済的利益を受ける権利を持ちます。この経済的利益を受ける権利を**信託受益権**と呼んでいます。

　日本では、**信託銀行や信託業法**に基づき**金融庁の登録もしくは免許を受けた信託会社**が受託者の役割を務めます。日本の信託銀行は、**金融機関の信託業務の兼営等に関する法律**により、信託受託業務を営むことができます。

Q：なぜ、不動産取引において信託受益権が用いられるのですか?

A：不動産を信託受益権にすることで、有価証券とみなされ、金融商品として投資家が扱いやすくなります。信託銀行は、受益権化するために、対象不動産の詳細なデューデリジェンスを行います。信託銀行は、法律上の所有者として当該不動産の責任者となり、また、受益者に対する**受託者責任**も負うためです。結果、信託受益権になり得る不動産は、**投資適格物件**だとみなされています。

　受託後は、信託銀行は当該不動産の法律上の所有者となり、また、受益者への忠実義務を負いながら、テナントから敷金を保管し、賃料や他の収入を収受します。したがって、投資家やレンダーには、資金管理も容易になるというメリットがあります。

　これらのサービス提供の対価として、信託銀行は、**当初信託報酬**や**期中信託報酬**を求めます。

　対象不動産が受託され、信託受益権として取引される場合、不動産取得に係る税率が軽減され、大幅に取得コストが削減できるというメリットもあります。

　加えて、TK-GKストラクチャーの場合には、**不動産特定共同事業法**の規制があるため、**現物不動産**ではなく、信託受益権を用いなければなりません。

Trust Scheme

The trust scheme needs three parties, but it doesn't necessarily need three independent parties. As in pattern 2, a trustor can also be a beneficiary.

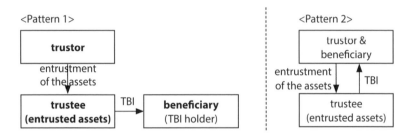

Overview of the Real Estate Trust Beneficiary Interest Scheme

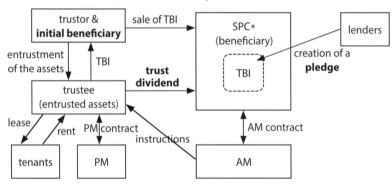

Overview of Tax merits of TBI∗

- *Real estate acquisition tax*, the rate of which is 3% to 4% of the *tax assessed value* of a property, is not imposed on TBI acquisitions.
- When real estate is converted into TBI, the rate of the *registration tax* for ownership transfer is 0.3% of the tax assessed value of the land and 0.4% of the tax assessed value of the building compared to 1.5% and 2% respectively, for the ownership transfer of *fee simple real estate*.
- Once real estate is converted into TBI, the rate of registration tax for TBI ownership transfer is only JPY1,000 per *land registry* and *building registry* to be reregistered.

∗ **SPC**   GK(TK-GK), TMK, and Investment Corporation (REIT)
∗ ⋯**of TBI**   The above tax rates are based on the related tax laws as of April 2023. The rates could change according to the law amendment.

基本的な信託スキーム

信託スキームは、3者が必要です。しかし、必ずしも、3人、3社が別々に必要というわけではありません。パターン2のように、委託者は受益者を兼ねることができます。

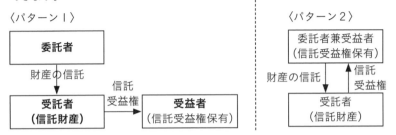

〈パターン1〉

委託者 →（財産の信託）→ 受託者（信託財産）→（信託受益権）→ 受益者（信託受益権保有）

〈パターン2〉

委託者兼受益者（信託受益権保有）→（財産の信託）→ 受託者（信託財産）→（信託受益権）→ 委託者兼受益者

不動産信託受益権スキームの概要

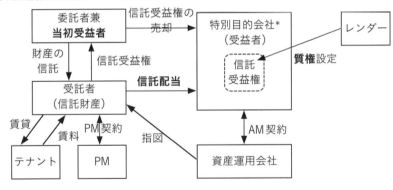

委託者兼 **当初受益者** →（信託受益権の売却）→ 特別目的会社*（受益者）←（質権設定）← レンダー

財産の信託 / 信託受益権

受託者（信託財産）→（**信託配当**）→ 信託受益権

賃貸 / 賃料 / PM契約 / 指図

テナント / PM / **AM契約** / 資産運用会社

信託受益権の税メリット概要*

- **課税標準額**に対して3%から4%が課せられる**不動産取得税**は、信託受益権の取得に関しては課せられません。
- 不動産を信託受益権にする際に必要となる所有権移転登記に係る**登録免許税**は、土地の課税標準額に対して0.3%、建物の課税標準額に対して0.4%です。しかし、**現物不動産**の所有権移転に関しては、それぞれ、1.5%、2%が課せられます。
- いったん、不動産が信託受益権になると、信託受益権の移動に係る登録免許税は、**土地登記簿**、**建物登記簿**ごとに千円しか、課せられません。

* **特別目的会社**　合同会社(TK-GK)、特定目的会社、及び投資法人(REIT)などのことです。
* …**税メリット概要**　上記の税率は2023年4月時点の関連法律に基づくものです。法律改正で変更になる可能性があります。

3-10 What are some other real estate investment considerations in Japan?

Q : Is it normal for real estate investors to borrow money from lenders?

A : Yes, many investors use loans to increase their **investment returns**. For many years, the **interest rates** in Japan have been very low, and the **yield spread** between the **yield on income producing properties** compared to **Japanese government bonds (JGBs)** has been larger than that of other countries, which continues to attract foreign investors to real estate in Japan.

Q : **Are there any considerations when foreign investors ask for loans?**

A : The main clients of almost all Japanese **lenders** are Japanese companies. So, they are not used to dealing with foreign clients in English. It is necessary for foreign investors to determine whether or not the lenders can deal with the loan execution process in English. Additionally, it is not commonplace for Japanese banks to provide loans to foreign real estate vehicles. So, when foreign investors want to directly invest in real estate in Japan and use leverage, it is also necessary for them to determine which lenders can support it.

Q : What is the **Financial Instruments and Exchange Law (FIEL)** ?

A : The FIEL mainly governs players who deal with **financial products** such as **securities**. Regarding the real estate investment business, the law defines "**investment securities (investment units** of REIT)" and "**preferred shares** and **specified bonds** (TMK)" as securities. Importantly, the law also defines "**TK investment**" and "**TBI**" as **deemed securities** and regulates them.

So, to deal with **real estate TBI**, the **real estate agent company** is required to be both a **licensed real estate agent company** and a **type II financial instruments business operator.**

An **asset management company** is required to obtain a license as an **investment management business** or **investment advisory business.**

日本での不動産投資において他に考慮すべきことは何か?

Q：日本では、不動産投資において、通常、借入を実施しますか?

A：はい、多くの投資家が、**投資利回り**を上げるために借入れを利用します。長年にわたり、日本の**金利**は非常に低く、**不動産利回り**と**国債利回り**との**イールドギャップ**（**金利差**）が他国と比べて非常に大きいことが、海外投資家にとっては日本への不動産投資を行うひとつの動機となっています。

Q：海外投資家がローンを利用するときに考慮すべき点は何ですか?

A：ほとんど全ての日本の**レンダー**の主な顧客は日本の会社です。したがって、英語で海外の顧客に対応することには慣れていません。海外投資家にとっては、彼らが英語でローン実行までのプロセスを完遂できるかどうか確認しておく必要があります。

　加えて、海外の不動産投資ビークルへのローン提供も通常は行われていません。したがって、海外投資家が直接、日本の不動産に投資し、かつ、ローンを利用して投資利回りを上げたい場合には、日本のレンダーが対応できるかどうかの確認が必要です。

Q：**金融商品取引法**とは何ですか?

A：金融商品取引法は、主に**有価証券**などの**金融商品**を扱うプレイヤーを規制しています。不動産投資に関しては、REITの投資口である**投資証券**やTMKの**優先出資証券**、**特定社債**などが有価証券と定義されています。重要なのは、**匿名組合出資**や**信託受益権**が、**みなし有価証券**とされ、規制の対象になっていることです。

　したがって、**不動産信託受益権**を扱うには、**不動産仲介会社**は、**宅地建物取引業者**であるとともに、**第二種金融商品取引業者**の登録を行う必要があります。

　資産運用会社（アセットマネジメント会社）に関しては、同法に基づき、**投資運用業**もしくは**投資助言業**の登録を得る必要があります。

Leverage

The financial term "leverage" usually means using debt. Leverage makes it possible for equity investors to acquire real estate using only a small amount of their own money.

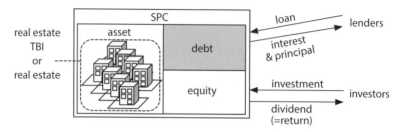

Leverage effect

*By utilizing leverage, equity investors can enhance their **return on investment** (ROI) as long as the **property yield** is higher than the **interest rate** and the asset value is higher than the debt amount. However, the fluctuation of ROI is higher compared with no debt, which means leverage makes equity investments riskier. These effects are called the "leverage effect".*

Loan to value ratio

*Loan to value ratio **(LTV)** means the ratio of the loan amount to the **purchase price (LTP)**, **appraisal value**, or **total acquisition cost (LTC)** of the subject real estate. The ratio is also called the **gearing ratio**.*

Difference between "Investment Management" and "Investment Advisory"

*An asset management company that has an investment management license can make investment decisions to buy and sell properties on behalf of investors. This type of business is often called a **discretionary investment management business**.*

Investment management business

<e.g.>
AM for REIT
AM for TMK
AM for TK-GK

Investment advisory business

<e.g.>
AM for TMK
AM for TK-GK (Certain procedures are required for a GK. Validity check of silent partnership structure is also required)

レバレッジ

レバレッジとは、借入を用いることです。借入を用いることで、エクイティ投資家は、小額の投資で対象不動産を取得することが可能になります。

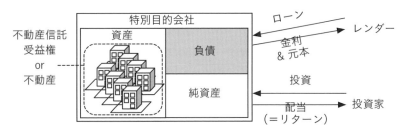

レバレッジ効果

レバレッジを利用することで、エクイティ投資家は、**投資利回り**を上げることができます（但し、**不動産利回り**が**借入金利**よりも高いこと、また、不動産価格が借入額よりも高いことが条件です）。しかし、投資利回りの変動は借入を用いない場合に比べて高くなります。つまり、レバレッジの利用により、リスクの高い投資となります。これらの効果をレバレッジ効果と呼んでいます。

負債比率

負債比率とは、**購入価格に対する借入額の比率**、**鑑定評価額**に対する借入額の比率、もしくは、**総取得コストに対する借入額の比率**のことを言います。この比率は、また、**ギアリング・レシオ**とも呼ばれます。

「投資運用業」と「投資助言業」との違い

投資運用業の登録をしている資産運用会社は、投資家のために、不動産の売買に関する投資判断を行うことができます。このタイプのビジネスは、しばしば、**投資一任業**と呼ばれます。

投資運用業

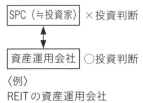

〈例〉
REIT の資産運用会社
TMK の資産運用会社
TK-GK の資産運用会社

投資助言業

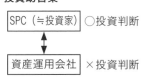

〈例〉
TMK の資産運用会社
TK-GK の資産運用会社（合同会社に一定の手続きが必要。匿名組合性の確認も必要）

Column | Do foreign investors like the investment structures in Japan?

When foreign investors first come to Japan, they usually talk with legal and tax advisors and study the three options available to own real estate: the TK-GK, the TMK, and direct ownership. Foreign investors look at the structures from three perspectives: the first is their **tax liability**, the second is the **ownership structure**, and the third is the operational structure.

For tax liability, the direct scheme is the least attractive structure when considering acquisition taxes. To reduce the tax liability, the TK-GK or TMK/TBI structures are much more attractive and tax efficient.

For the ownership structure, foreign investors who wish to have more control prefer the TMK structure, as they can own the **voting rights** shares of the TMK and play an active role in the management of the property. The TK-GK structure does not allow the investor to own the voting right shares of the GK, and the investors need to maintain a passive position, which limits their day-to-day involvement in the property.

For the operations structure, the TK-GK is the easiest to set up and run, as the structure is very simple and the **withholding tax** rate is usually set at about 20%. The TMK structure is much more complicated and requires several entities to be created for the structure to work well, but this could ultimately lower the effective tax rate below 20% through **tax treaties** between Japan and several other developed countries.

Overall, the TMK remains the most popular structure for foreign investors, even though the operational aspects are more complicated to set up and manage. Foreign investors usually do not favor the passive requirement of the TK-GK structure as they prefer to play a more active role in the investment of the property, and they also prefer the tax advantages the TMK structure can provide.

Investment structuring and options in Japan may continue to evolve and change and foreign investors are regularly discussing this with their tax and legal counterparties to ensure they are using the best possible investment vehicles to optimize tax liability and provide maximum management control.

コラム 海外投資家は日本の投資ストラクチャーを気に入っているか？

　海外投資家は、最初に来日した際、法律や税の専門家と、不動産を保有する3つの選択肢について話し合うことになります。具体的には、TK-GK、TMK、そして、直接保有です。海外投資家は、それらのストラクチャーを3つの観点から検証します。まず、**税負担**、そして、**所有形態**、最後に、運営形態です。

　税負担に関しては、取得にかかる税金を考慮すると、直接保有が最も税負担が高くなります。その税負担を軽減するために、信託受益権を組み合わせたTK-GKやTMKがより魅力的な選択肢であり税効率の高いストラクチャーとなります。

　所有形態に関しては、より関与を深めたい海外投資家にとっては、**議決権**の保有が可能で、積極的に不動産投資運用に関与できるTMKが好ましいと言えます。TK-GKストラクチャーでは、GKの議決権を持つことはできず、また、投資家には消極的な立場が求められるため、日々の不動産運用に関与することは制限されます。

　運営形態に関しては、TK-GKストラクチャーは設立が容易で、その後の運営も簡単です。また、**源泉徴収税**は通常は約20％で固定されています。TMKストラクチャーはTK-GKと比べると相当複雑で、海外投資家にとっては複数のSPCが必要となります。しかし、日本といくつかの国の**租税条約**により、最終的に源泉徴収税を20％未満とすることができる場合もあります。

　設立などの運営形態に関しての煩雑さはあるものの、全般的には、TMKが海外投資家にとっては最も人気のあるストラクチャーです。海外投資家は、TK-GKのように消極的な役割を求められることを通常好まず、TMKを通じて運用に積極的に関与できることを求めます。また、TMKストラクチャーを活用した税制メリットもTMKが好まれる点です。

　日本での投資ストラクチャーやその選択肢については、おそらく、今後も改善され、海外投資家は、定期的に、税や法律の専門家と、どのような投資形態が最も税効率がよく、最も運用に関与できるのかを検討していくことになるでしょう。

Chapter 4

Real Estate Investment Process in Japan

日本における不動産投資プロセスの概要

4-1 Sourcing Route

Q : How do investors find real estate that's for sale in Japan?

A : The most popular way to find **real estate for sale** in Japan is through the use of brokers. They usually provide two kinds of opportunities: a **bid** or a **private treaty**. They make a variety of suggestions to property owners to become the **seller's agent** or the **exclusive seller's agent**. Direct transactions without the use of brokers are rare in Japan.

Q : What kinds of real estate brokers are there in Japan?

A : **Real estate agent companies** include trust banks and affiliates of major publicly listed real estate companies. Foreign real estate agent companies are also active.

Trust banks have the most information regarding properties for sale and so are one of the most powerful brokers. Over time, trust banks involved in the real estate brokerage business and finance business have developed close relationships with large companies that hold vast amounts of real estate as well as major real estate developers.

Affiliates of major listed real estate companies also have very good information on properties for sale, and they continue to expand their customer base with corporations and investors. **Foreign real estate agent companies** also have access to properties for sale and specialize in serving foreign investors who need services in English under global service standards.

Q : What kinds of services do **real estate brokers** offer in Japan?

A : They introduce properties for sale to a buyer and also provide viewing inspections. If the prospective buyer is interested in the property, the broker will help negotiate with the seller and also provide all property information to the buyer. Before signing a PSA, brokers are required to provide the **Property Disclosure Statement of Important Issues** and explain this document to the buyer. Brokers also assist and manage the closing procedure and all closing documentation.

Q：投資家はどのように売却物件を探すのですか？

A：**売却物件**を探索する最も一般的な方法は、仲介業者の活用です。仲介業者は、通常、**入札**か**相対取引**という2つの機会を提供してくれます。**売主側仲介業者**、もしくは**売主側の単独仲介業者**となるために仲介業者は様々な提案を不動産保有者に行っています。仲介業者なしの相対取引は日本では稀です。

Q：日本にはどのような不動産仲介業者がありますか？

A：**不動産仲介会社**には、信託銀行や大手上場不動産会社の関連会社があります。外資系不動産仲介会社も、日本で活発に活動しています。

　信託銀行は、最も多くの不動産売却情報を持っており、最も有力な仲介業者の1つです。長年にわたって不動産仲介や融資ビジネスに携わっている信託銀行は、多くの不動産を保有している大企業や主要な不動産開発会社と、親密な関係を築いています。

　大手上場不動産会社の関連会社も、多くの不動産売却情報を持っており、さらに、法人客や投資家にも、ビジネスを広げようとしています。**外資系不動産仲介会社**も、不動産売却情報へのアクセスが可能です。彼らは、グローバル標準かつ英語でのサービスを求める外資系投資家へのサービスに強みがあります。

Q：　日本では**不動産仲介業者**はどのような役務を提供しますか？

A：不動産仲介会社は、売却物件を買主に紹介します。買主が興味を持った物件については買主を案内します。もし買主が特定の物件に強い関心を持てば、売主と交渉を行い、対象物件の情報を全て買主に提供します。契約締結の前には、**重要事項説明書**を提示して、その内容を買主に説明する必要があります。さらに、仲介会社は、物件引渡しやそのための資料作成のサポートや調整も行います。

Basic process of real estate investment in Japan: Step 1

*The first step to invest in real estate in Japan is to find real estate that is for sale. The most popular way is to use **real estate brokers.***

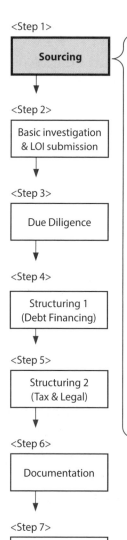

<Step 1>

Sourcing

<Step 2>

Basic investigation & LOI submission

<Step 3>

Due Diligence

<Step 4>

Structuring 1 (Debt Financing)

<Step 5>

Structuring 2 (Tax & Legal)

<Step 6>

Documentation

<Step 7>

Closing

<Basic information on the property for sale>
- **Property name**
- **Type of ownership**
- **Fee simple estate** or **TBI**
- **Location (address, distance from the nearest station, location map,** etc.)
- **Land area**
- **Gross floor area (GFA)**
- **Building completion date (building age)**
- **Building structure (Steel-reinforced concrete structure, reinforced concrete structure, steel structure)**
- **Number of floors** or **number of sories (e.g., Ten stories above ground and two below)**
- **Standard floor area (for office buildings)**
- **Number of rooms (for rental apartments)**
- **Floor plan (for rental apartments)**
- **Picture of the building**
- **Construction company**
- **Net rentable area (NRA) / Net lettable area (NLA)**
- **Single tenant** or **multiple tenants**
- **Occupancy rate (vacancy rate)**
- **Asking price**
- **Actual gross yield, actual NOI yield**, etc.
- Other important information **(Boundary dispute, encroachment, illegal building, legal nonconforming building, lawsuit to evict the tenant,** etc.)

<Major reasons for real estate sale>
Sellers have a variety of reasons to sell their properties. However, companies always consider the **unrealized profit and loss** of the subject property. That is the difference between its **book value** and **estimated sales price** because most companies adopt **Japanese Generally Accepted Accounting Principles (JGAAP)** where the asset value of properties is calculated based on their acquisition cost.

日本における基本的な不動産投資のプロセス：ステップ1
日本での不動産投資の最初のステップは、売却不動産情報を探索することです。
*最も一般的な方法は、**不動産仲介業者**を活用することです。*

＜ステップ1＞

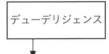

ソーシング

＜ステップ2＞

基礎調査
& LOI提出

＜ステップ3＞

デューデリジェンス

＜ステップ4＞

ストラクチャリング1
（デット資金調達）

＜ステップ5＞

ストラクチャリング2
（税務＆法務）

＜ステップ6＞

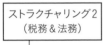

ドキュメンテーション

＜ステップ7＞

クロージング

＜売却物件の基本的な情報＞
・物件名
・所有形態
・現物不動産か信託受益権か
・位置（住所、最寄駅からの距離、位置図などを含む）
・土地面積
・延床面積
・建物竣工年月日（築年数）
・建物構造
　（鉄骨鉄筋コンクリート（SRC）造、鉄筋コンクリート
　（RC）造、鉄骨（S）造）
・建物階数
　（例：地上10階地下2階建）
・基準階面積（オフィスビルの場合）
・戸数（賃貸マンションの場合）
・間取り図（賃貸マンションの場合）
・建物写真
・建設会社
・賃貸可能面積
・単独テナントか複数テナントか
・稼働率（空室率）
・希望売却価格
・現況表面利回り、現況NOI利回りなど
・その他重要情報
　**（境界紛争、越境、違法建築物、既存不適格建築物、
　テナント明渡訴訟など）**

＜不動産売却の主な理由＞
売主は保有不動産を売却する様々な理由を持っています。しかし、会社は常に対象不動産の**含み損益**、つまり、**簿価**と**推定売却価格**との差額を考慮に入れています。多くの会社は、不動産価値が取得コストを基準として計算される**日本の会計基準**を採用しているからです。

Basic Investigation & LOI Submission

Q : Once investors are interested in purchasing a property, what is the next step?

A : The next step is to sign a **Non-Disclosure Agreement**, also called an "**NDA**," on the subject property with the owner. The purpose of this agreement is to keep the information the owner gives to the prospective buyer private and protected.

Q : What kinds of documents are disclosed after the NDA has been signed?

A : The documents and agreements required to create a cash flow analysis are disclosed to the prospective buyer. Some examples of these documents might include PM reports, **rent rolls**, and documents related to property tax.

Q : Why is a PM report important?

A : The **PM report,** provided by property management companies, is usually generated on a monthly basis and details the performance of the property. The PM report includes the status of the tenants, money that is received, and payments that are made. It also explains any special charges and details past repairs. The PM report also lists any **delinquent tenants, cancellation notice,** and/or issues that have occurred during the month.

Q : Once a buyer gets serious about purchasing the property, what is the next step?

A : The next step is for the buyer to submit a **letter of intent (LOI)**. The LOI includes the buyer's proposed purchase price and the buyer's conditions to purchase the property. The LOI has an **expiration date** usually ranging from 1 to 4 weeks. If the seller agrees with the terms in the LOI, they countersign the LOI or draft the **letter of acceptance (LOA)**. At this point, the buyer secures **preferential negotiation rights** and 1 to 3 months of exclusive due diligence can begin. This term is also called the "**exclusive negotiation period.**"

4-2 基礎調査と購入意向表明書の提示

Q：ある不動産の購入を検討したいと思った場合、次のステップは何ですか？

A：次のステップは、物件所有者と、対象不動産に係る**秘密保持契約**に署名することです。秘密保持契約の目的は、購入希望者が、所有者から提供される情報を外部に漏らさないようにすることです。

Q：秘密保持契約に署名した後、どんな書面が開示されますか？

A：キャッシュフロー分析を行うのに必要な書類や契約書が開示されます。例えば、PMレポート、**レントロール**、不動産保有税に係る書類などです。

Q：なぜ、PMレポートが重要なのですか？

A：**PMレポート**は、プロパティマネジメント会社が月次で作成する対象不動産についての運営状況をまとめた報告書です。レポートには、テナントの状況、入金状況、出金状況が記載されます。また、その他の特別な費用や修繕内容が記載されます。さらに、**延滞テナント**や**解約予告**、当該月に発生した問題なども記載されます。

Q：購入者が真剣に買いたいと思った場合、次のステップは何ですか？

A：次のステップは、**LOI（購入意向表明書）**を提示することです。LOIには、購入希望価格や物件を取得するための条件が記載されます。LOIの**有効期限**は、通常1週間から4週間です。もし売主がLOIの内容に満足すれば、売主は、LOIに連署するか、**売渡承諾書**を作成します。この時点で買主は、**優先交渉権**を獲得し、1ヶ月から3ヶ月の間、排他的なデューデリジェンスを実施することができます。この期間は、**独占交渉期間**とも呼ばれます。

Basic process of real estate investment in Japan: Step 2

The second step to investing in real estate in Japan is to conduct a basic investigation of the **subject property**. *If buyers get seriously interested in purchasing the property, they submit an* **LOI** *to conduct exclusive* **due diligence** *on the property.*

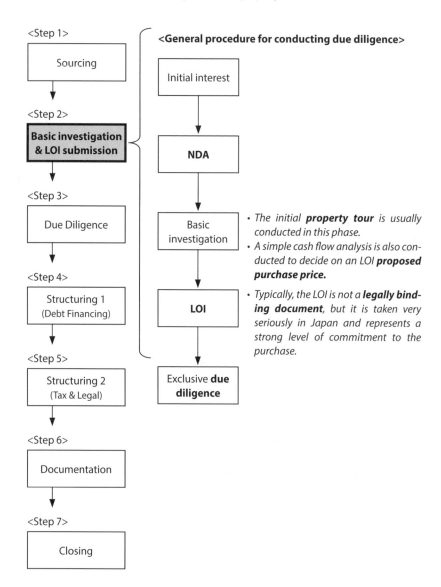

<Step 1>
Sourcing

<Step 2>
Basic investigation & LOI submission

<Step 3>
Due Diligence

<Step 4>
Structuring 1
(Debt Financing)

<Step 5>
Structuring 2
(Tax & Legal)

<Step 6>
Documentation

<Step 7>
Closing

<General procedure for conducting due diligence>

Initial interest

NDA

Basic investigation

LOI

Exclusive **due diligence**

- *The initial* **property tour** *is usually conducted in this phase.*
- *A simple cash flow analysis is also conducted to decide on an LOI* **proposed purchase price.**
- *Typically, the LOI is not a* **legally binding document**, *but it is taken very seriously in Japan and represents a strong level of commitment to the purchase.*

日本における基本的な不動産投資のプロセス：ステップ2

日本での不動産投資の2つめのステップは、対象不動産の基礎的な調査を行うことです。もし、買い手が、**対象不動産**の取得に真剣になれば、排他的な**デューデリジェンス**を実施するために*LOI*を提示します。

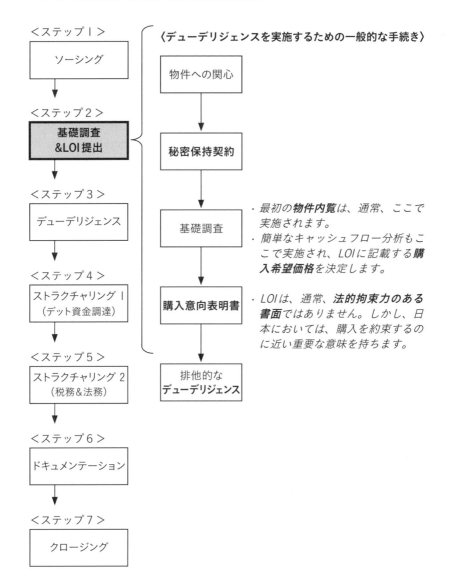

4-3 Due Diligence 1 — Cash Flow Analysis 1

Q : What kinds of income are generated from income producing properties?

A : A property will usually generate some or all of the following types of income: **rental income**, **CAM income** (explained below), **utility income**, **parking income**, and **other income** (illustrated on page 156).

Q : What is important when evaluating rental income?

A : Because rental income accounts for the majority of total income, it is critical to determine if the **existing rent** is higher or lower than the **market rent**. The difference between them is called the **rent gap**. For **rent revision**, **fixed term leases** help landlords raise rent through **tenant replacement**, while **ordinary leases** require them to negotiate with existing tenants. Additionally, **free-rent periods** should be considered when calculating actual rent. **Asking rent** is the rent offered by a landlord.

Q : What is CAM income?

A : The space in a building is usually divided into two types. The first is the area the tenant will use exclusively, such as their office space and meeting rooms. The second type are the **common areas** in the building that all the tenants share, such as the elevators, lobby, and stairways. These areas need to be maintained, cleaned, and well managed to ensure the building continues to operate smoothly. The cost to take care of these spaces is usually divided among the tenants in the building and is called the **common area maintenance charge (CAM)**. For the owner, this is referred to as CAM income.

Q : Are there any special types of income generated by a rental apartment?

A : Yes, residential properties may generate **key money** and **renewal fees**. But recently, tenants have become increasingly unwilling to accept these fees as necessary and this trend should be considered when determining the potential total income of the property.

4-3 デューデリジェンス 1 ― CF分析1

Q：収益不動産からの収益にはどのようなものがありますか？

A：不動産は、次のような種類の収入を生み出します。具体的には、**賃料収入**、**共益費収入**（下記参照）、**水道光熱費収入**、**駐車場収入**、**その他収入**（157ページに例示）などです。

Q：賃料収入を評価するときに重要なことは何ですか？

A：賃料収入は、総収入の大半を占めるため、**現行賃料**が**市場賃料（相場賃料）**よりも高いか低いかを確認することが非常に重要です。現行賃料と市場賃料の差を**賃料ギャップ（レントギャップ）**と呼んでいます。賃料改定に関しては、**定借**であれば**テナント入替**により賃料を上げやすいですが、**普通借**の場合は現行テナントとの交渉が必要です。加えて、実質賃料を把握するには**フリーレント期間**の考慮も必要です。**募集賃料**とは家主が提示する賃料のことです。

Q：共益費収入とは何ですか？

A：建物の床部分は、通常、2つの部分に分けられます。1つ目は、テナントが独占的に使用するオフィススペースや会議室です。2つ目は、全てのテナントが共同して使用するエレベーター、ロビー、階段などの**共用部分**です。これらの部分は、ビルを円滑に運営するために、保守清掃・管理が必要です。これらの費用は、建物のテナントにより分担され、**共益費**と呼ばれます。所有者の立場からすると、共益費収入となります。

Q：賃貸マンションに特有の収入はありますか？

A：はい、賃貸マンションには**礼金**と**更新料**があります。しかし、近年はテナントは、これらの費用を賃貸借契約の一部として認めない傾向が強まっており、総収入を計算するときには十分な検証が必要です。

Illustrated Real Estate Terminologies

Basic process of real estate investment in Japan: Step 3
The third step to investing in real estate in Japan is to conduct due diligence. **Cash flow analysis** *is a primary aspect of the due diligence process.*

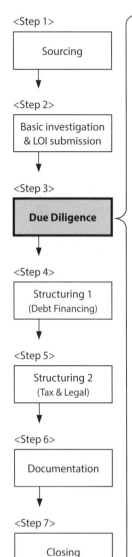

<Step 1>

Sourcing

<Step 2>

Basic investigation & LOI submission

<Step 3>

Due Diligence

<Step 4>

Structuring 1 (Debt Financing)

<Step 5>

Structuring 2 (Tax & Legal)

<Step 6>

Documentation

<Step 7>

Closing

<How to project "total income">

+**Rental income** (assuming full occupancy)
+**CAM income** (assuming full occupancy)
+**Utility income**
+**Parking income** (assuming full occupancy)
+**Other income**
Total = **Potential gross income (PGI)**
−**Vacancy loss** (Rental Income)
−Vacancy loss (CAM Income)
−Vacancy loss (Parking Income)
Total = **Effective gross income (EGI)**

<Examples of other income>
- **Storage room income**
- **Advertising facilities (e.g., billboard)income**
- **Vending machine income**
- **Cancellation penalty income**
- **Key money income** (residential)
  In Greater Tokyo, when a residential tenant signs a new lease, they are often required to pay the owner "key money," which is usually equivalent to 1-2 months of rent. This money is not a **deposit** *and will not be returned, but it has been and remains a very common custom in this area. (Key money customs should be considered because they vary according to each area in Japan).*
- **Renewal fee income** (residential)
  Renewal fees are usually paid when the tenant decides to renew their residential lease contract, which is typically a 2-year period in Japan. This fee is normally equivalent to one-month's rent.

<What is Tsubo?>
Japanese real estate players normally use the **monthly rent per tsubo** *(1 square meter equals approx. 0.3025 tsubo) to analyze the rent gap. It is calculated by dividing the monthly rent by the net rentable area. CAM income is usually regarded as a part of the rental income.*

日本における基本的な不動産投資のプロセス：ステップ3

日本での不動産投資の３つめのステップは、デューデリジェンスを行うことです。**キャッシュフロー分析**は、デューデリジェンスプロセスの重要な部分です。

＜ステップ１＞

ソーシング

＜ステップ２＞

基礎調査
＆ LOI 提出

＜ステップ３＞

デューデリジェンス

＜ステップ４＞

ストラクチャリング１
（デット資金調達）

＜ステップ５＞

ストラクチャリング２
（税務＆法務）

＜ステップ６＞

ドキュメンテーション

＜ステップ７＞

クロージング

〈総収入の計算方法〉

＋賃料収入（満室想定）
＋共益費収入（満室想定）
＋水道光熱費収入
＋駐車場収入（満室想定）
＋その他収入
合計 ＝ 潜在総収入
－空室損失（賃料収入）
－空室損失（共益費収入）
－空室損失（駐車場収入）
合計 ＝ 有効総収入

〈その他収入の例〉

- トランクルーム収入
- 広告施設（看板など）収入
- 自動販売機収入
- 解約違約金収入
- 礼金収入（住宅の場合）

　首都圏においては、賃貸マンションのテナントは契約の際、賃料の１ヶ月から２か月分の礼金を所有者に支払うことを求められます。これは**敷金**ではなく、返還されません。このエリアでは、一般的な慣習となっています。（礼金の慣習は、地域により異なるため、留意が必要です）。

- 更新料収入（住宅の場合）

　更新料は、テナントが、賃貸借契約を更新する際に支払われるものです。日本では、住宅の賃貸借契約は、通常、２年間です。更新料は、通常、１か月分の賃料相当です。

＜坪とは何か？＞

　日本の不動産プレイヤーは、賃料ギャップを把握するために、通常、**坪当たり月額賃料**（1㎡≒0.3025坪）を用います。これは、月額賃料を賃貸可能面積で割ることで計算されます。共益費収入は、通常、賃料の一部とみなされます。

Due Diligence 2 — Cash Flow Analysis 2

4-4

Q : What kinds of expenses are involved in managing an income producing property.

A : Some of the basic costs include **maintenance costs, utility expenses, minor repair costs, property management fees, leasing costs, property taxes, insurance premiums,** and **other expenses** (illustrated on page 160).

Q : What are some of the most important expenses in evaluating a property?

A : It is important to clearly understand all expenses, as they lower the level of profit. However, property taxes such as **fixed asset tax** and **city planning tax** are particularly important expense items because they strongly impact the cash flow of a property. Also, these expenses cannot be controlled or modified because they are set by the local governments.

Q : How is property tax calculated?

A : Taxes vary depending on the type of building, the age the building, and the **land and building tax assessed value** as determined by the local government. These taxes are re-calculated every 3 years when the local government assigns a tax value (called "**fixed asset tax value**") to the land and buildings. The fixed asset tax is levied not only on land and buildings but also on **depreciable assets**, while the city planning tax is levied on land and buildings.

Q : What is the difference between **Net Operating Income (NOI)** and **Net Cash Flow (NCF)**?

A : NOI is calculated as **effective gross income (EGI)** minus the total expenses. NCF is calculated as NOI minus **CAPEX**. In Japan, leasing costs are usually calculated as part of expenses.

4-4 デューデリジェンス 2 ― CF分析2

Q：収益不動産を運営するのに必要な費用にはどのようなものがありますか？

A：基本的な費用としては、**維持管理費**、**水道光熱費**、**修繕費**、プロパティマネジメントフィー、**テナント募集費用**、**不動産保有税**、**損害保険料**、その他費用（161ページに例示）があります。

Q：不動産を評価する上で最も留意が必要な費用は何ですか？

A：費用は、収益レベルを下げるものですので、不動産に係る全ての費用を明確に理解することが重要です。しかし、**固定資産税**と**都市計画税**といった不動産保有税は非常に重要な費用項目です。なぜなら、その額が不動産のキャッシュフローに大きな影響を及ぼし、また、その額は地方公共団体により定められコントロールできないからです。

Q：不動産保有税はどのように計算されますか？

A：それらの税額は、建物の種類、建物の築年数、及び、地方公共団体が定める**土地建物課税標準額**により、変わります。固定資産税と都市計画税は、地方公共団体が3年ごとに定める土地と建物の**固定資産税評価額**に基づいて、再計算されます。固定資産税は、土地と建物だけでなく、**償却資産**にも課せられます。一方、都市計画税は、土地と建物に課せられます。

Q：**NOI**（**純収益**）と**NCF**（**ネットキャッシュフロー**）との違いは何ですか？

A：NOIは、**有効総収入**から総費用を差し引いて求められます。NCFは、NOIから**資本的支出**を差し引いて求められます。日本では、テナント募集費用は、費用の一部として計算されます。

Basic process of real estate investment in Japan: Step 3

The third step to investing in real estate in Japan is to conduct due diligence. Cash flow analysis is a primary aspect of the due diligence process.

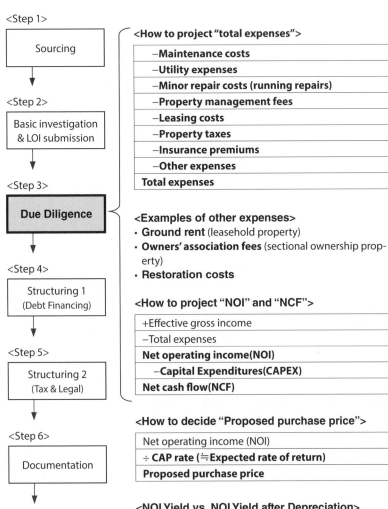

<Step 1>

Sourcing

<Step 2>

Basic investigation & LOI submission

<Step 3>

Due Diligence

<Step 4>

Structuring 1
(Debt Financing)

<Step 5>

Structuring 2
(Tax & Legal)

<Step 6>

Documentation

<Step 7>

Closing

<How to project "total expenses">

−Maintenance costs
−Utility expenses
−Minor repair costs (running repairs)
−Property management fees
−Leasing costs
−Property taxes
−Insurance premiums
−Other expenses
Total expenses

<Examples of other expenses>
- **Ground rent** (leasehold property)
- **Owners' association fees** (sectional ownership property)
- **Restoration costs**

<How to project "NOI" and "NCF">

+Effective gross income
−Total expenses
Net operating income(NOI)
−Capital Expenditures(CAPEX)
Net cash flow(NCF)

<How to decide "Proposed purchase price">

Net operating income (NOI)
÷ **CAP rate (≒Expected rate of return)**
Proposed purchase price

<NOI Yield vs. NOI Yield after Depreciation>

NOI	NOI − Depreciation
÷Purchase Price	÷Purchase Price
NOI Yield	**NOI Yield after Depreciation**

日本における基本的な不動産投資のプロセス：ステップ3

日本での不動産投資の3つめのステップは、デューデリジェンスを行うことです。
キャッシュフロー分析は、デューデリジェンスプロセスの重要な部分です。

＜ステップ1＞

ソーシング

↓

＜ステップ2＞

基礎調査
＆LOI提出

↓

＜ステップ3＞

デューデリジェンス

↓

＜ステップ4＞

ストラクチャリング1
（デット資金調達）

↓

＜ステップ5＞

ストラクチャリング2
（税務＆法務）

↓

＜ステップ6＞

ドキュメンテーション

↓

＜ステップ7＞

クロージング

〈総費用の計算方法〉

－維持管理費（建物管理費）
－水道光熱費
－修繕費
－プロパティマネジメントフィー
－テナント募集費用
－不動産保有税（公租公課）
－損害保険料
－その他費用
総費用

〈その他費用の例〉

・**地代**（借地物件の場合）
・**管理組合費**（区分所有物件の場合）
・**原状回復費**

〈NOI及びNCFの計算方法〉

＋有効総収入
－総費用
純収益（NOI）
－資本的支出
ネットキャッシュフロー（NCF）

〈購入希望価格の決め方〉

純収益（NOI）
÷還元利回り（≒期待利回り）
購入希望価格

<NOI利回りと償却後NOI利回りとの違い>

NOI	NOI－減価償却費
÷購入価格	÷購入価格
NOI利回り	**償却後NOI利回り**

4-5 Due Diligence 3 — Engineering Report

Q : What is an **Engineering Report**?

A : This report mainly details the technical inspection of the building and its condition before purchase. **ER** stands for Engineering Report.

Q : What kinds of details are included in an Engineering Report?

A : The key parts of the report include "the **building condition** survey report," "the **building environment risk** assessment survey report," "the **soil contamination** risk assessment report," and "the **earthquake risk** assessment report." The building condition survey report includes a **legal compliance** section to make sure there are no illegal aspects to the building. These reports require not only **site inspection** but also a lot of documents, such as the **completion drawing, structural calculation report, statutory inspection reports**, etc. If **earthquake reinforcement work** has been conducted, related documents are also needed.

Q : Who can prepare an Engineering Report?

A : In Japan, no specific qualification is needed to prepare an ER. But the major players in the ER market are **general contractors**, affiliates of major **non-life insurance companies**, independent firms, and foreign affiliated firms specializing in ER. These companies are members of "BELCA" the Building and Equipment Long-life Cycle Association, which adheres to self-imposed guidelines.

Q : Why is an Engineering Report required?

A : The **Real Estate Appraisal Standards** in Japan require **licensed real estate appraisers** to make use of the ER to forecast future cash flows and determine the cap rate and discount rate. One example of this is **CAPEX**.

Additionally, other parties engaged in acquiring real estate, such as asset management companies, lenders, and trust banks acting as **trustees**, also make use of the ER to understand the risk of the subject property.

デューデリジェンス3
──エンジニアリングレポート

Q：**エンジニアリングレポート**とは何ですか？

A：エンジニアリングレポートは、取得前に、主に建物とその状態の技術的なチェックを行うものです。**ER**はエンジニアリングレポートの略称です。

Q：エンジニアリングレポートにはどのような報告書が含まれますか？

A：レポートの重要な部分は、「**建物状況調査報告書**」、「**建物環境リスク調査報告書**」、「**土壌汚染調査報告書**」、「**地震リスク**調査報告書」で構成されます。建物状況調査報告書には、建物に違法箇所がないかどうかを確認する**遵法性**の調査が含まれます。これらの報告書の作成には、**現地調査**だけでなく、**竣工図**、**構造計算書**、**法定点検報告書**など、多くの書類が必要となります。もし、**耐震補強工事**が実施されていれば、その関係書類も必要になります。

Q：誰がエンジニアリングレポートを作成できるのですか？

A：日本では、エンジニアリングレポートを作成するのに特別な資格は必要ありません。主要なプレイヤーは、**ゼネコン**、主要な**損害保険会社**の関連会社、独立系会社、外資系会社などがあります。これらの会社は、自主規制ガイドラインを定めているBELCA：公益社団法人ロングライフビル推進協会の会員となっています。

Q：なぜ、エンジニアリングレポートが求められるのですか？

A：日本の**不動産鑑定評価基準**は、**不動産鑑定士**に、キャッシュフローを予測したり、キャップレートや割引率を決めるために、エンジニアリングレポートの結果を活用することを求めています。1つの例が、**資本的支出**です。

　また、投資不動産取得に係る他の会社、例えば、アセットマネジメント会社、レンダー、**受託者**としての信託銀行なども、対象不動産のリスクを把握するために、エンジニアリングレポートを活用しています。

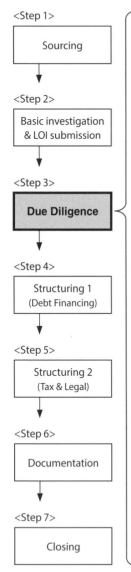

Basic process of real estate investment in Japan: Step 3
*The third step to investing in real estate in Japan is to conduct due diligence. **ER** plays an important role in helping investors estimate the physical risk of the subject property.*

<Step 1>
Sourcing

<Step 2>
Basic investigation & LOI submission

<Step 3>
Due Diligence

<Step 4>
Structuring 1
(Debt Financing)

<Step 5>
Structuring 2
(Tax & Legal)

<Step 6>
Documentation

<Step 7>
Closing

<General contents of the ER>

Investigation report		Item
Building condition survey		Location overview
		Building overview
		M&E system overview
		Renovation / renewal history and plans
		Structural overview
		Compliance with the law
		Emergency repair / renewal expenses
		Short-term repair / renewal expenses
		Long-term repair / renewal expenses
		Replacement cost
Building environment survey	Phase 1	Asbestos
		PCBs
		Others
Soil pollution risk assessment	Phase 1	Soil survey
Earthquake risk assessment (PML)		Simple analysis
		Detailed analysis

(Based on the BELCA Guideline for making the ER report on RE investment and transaction)

<Earthquake Risk>
*Because Japan is prone to earthquakes, the **Probable Maximum Loss(PML)** percentage is an important figure. The PML estimates are found in the earthquake risk assessment report and estimate the potential damage to the building in the event of a strong earthquake. Usually, investors will feel comfortable with a PML of 15% or below. When PML is in excess of 20%, lenders sometimes require **earthquake insurance** to be applied for.*

<Earthquake Resistance>
*Buildings constructed after 1981 have been subject to the amendments made to the **Building Standards Law** and are required to observe **new earthquake resistance standards**. The previous standards are called **former earthquake resistance standards**.*

日本における基本的な不動産投資のプロセス：ステップ３
日本での不動産投資の３つめのステップは、対象不動産のデューデリジェンスを
行うことです。**エンジニアリングレポート**は、投資家が、対象不動産の物理的な
リスクを把握するために重要な役割を果たします。

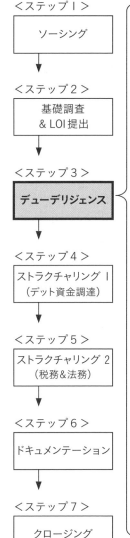

＜ステップ１＞

ソーシング

＜ステップ２＞

基礎調査
＆ LOI 提出

＜ステップ３＞

デューデリジェンス

＜ステップ４＞

ストラクチャリング１
（デット資金調達）

＜ステップ５＞

ストラクチャリング２
（税務＆法務）

＜ステップ６＞

ドキュメンテーション

＜ステップ７＞

クロージング

〈標準的なエンジニアリングレポートの内容〉

調査報告書		調査項目
建物状況調査		立地調査概要
		建築概要調査
		設備概要調査
		更新・改修履歴
		及び更新改修計画の調査
		構造概要調査、設計基準
		遵法性
		緊急を要する修繕更新費用
		短期修繕更新費用
		長期修繕更新費用
		再調達価格の算定
建物環境リスク評価	フェーズ１	アスベスト
		PCB
		その他の項目
土壌汚染リスク評価	フェーズ１	土壌汚染の可能性
地震リスク評価（PML）		簡易分析（統計的な方法）
		詳細分析（解析的な方法）

（ BELCA「不動産投資・取引におけるエンジニアリング・レポー
ト作成に係るガイドライン」参照））

〈地震リスク〉
　日本は非常に地震が多いので、**予想最大損失率(PML)**
は重要な数値です。PML は、地震リスク評価報告書の
中に記載されます。PML は、大地震が発生した場合に
予測される建物の損失割合を示したものです。通常、
PML が 15％以下の場合には、何も問題となりません。
PML が 20％を超えた場合には、レンダーに**地震保険**の
付保を求められる場合もあります。

〈耐震性〉
　建築基準法が改正された 1981 年以降に建設された建
物は、**新耐震基準**を満たしています。それ以前の基準
は**旧耐震基準**と呼ばれています。

4-6 Due Diligence 4 — Real Estate Appraisal Report

Q : What is a **Real Estate Appraisal Report**?

A : This report assigns a **market value** to a property (both land and buildings).

Q : Who can provide a Real Estate Appraisal Report?

A : In Japan, only a licensed **real estate appraiser** can provide this report. The **MLIT** governs the licensing process and administers the exam.

Q : How does a real estate appraiser value a property?

A : In Japan, appraisers must follow the **Japanese Real Estate Appraisal Standards** as set by the MLIT. The standards provide three valuation approaches: **Income Approach**, **Market Approach**, and **Cost Approach**. Regarding income producing properties, such as those purchased by TK-GKs, TMKs, and REITs, appraisers must also follow the **Guidelines Regarding Appraisal of Securitized Properties**, which are established by the Japan Association of Real Estate Appraisal.

Q : What is the Income Approach?

A : An appraiser has two methods in the Income Approach: the **Discounted Cash Flow (DCF) Method** and the **Direct Capitalization Method**. The DCF method assumes the present value by looking at the total investment span of the property and its estimated annual cash flows, which are then divided by a **discount rate**. The direct capitalization method assumes the current value of the property by looking at the stabilized annual cash flows divided by the **capitalization rate (CAP rate)**. Appraisers must use the engineering report (ER) to estimate the cash flow of the property and determine the discount rate and CAP rate.

Q : What are comps?

A : **Comps** is the abbreviation of "comparables" used in the Market Approach.

Q：**不動産鑑定評価書**とは何ですか？

A：不動産鑑定評価書は、不動産（土地と建物）の**市場価値**を示すものです。

Q：不動産鑑定評価書は誰が作成できますか？

A：日本では、資格を持つ**不動産鑑定士**だけが作成することができます。この資格に関わっているのは**国土交通省**で、同省が試験も実施しています。

Q：不動産鑑定士はどのように対象不動産を評価するのですか？

A：不動産鑑定士は、国土交通省が定める**不動産鑑定評価基準**に従わなければなりません。鑑定評価基準は、**収益還元法、取引事例比較法、原価法**という3つの手法を定めています。TK-GK、TMK、REITにより取得される収益不動産に関しては、公益社団法人日本不動産鑑定士協会連合会が定める**証券化対象不動産の鑑定評価に関する実務指針**にも従わなければなりません。

Q：収益還元法について詳しく教えてもらえますか？

A：収益還元法には、**DCF法**と**直接還元法**の2つがあります。DCF法は、毎年の予想キャッシュフローを**割引率**で割り戻してそれぞれの現在価値を算出し、それらを足し上げることで求めます。直接還元法は、標準的な年間のキャッシュフローを**還元利回り（キャップレート）**で割って求めます。不動産鑑定士は、これらのキャッシュフロー、還元利回り、割引率の算定にあたっては、エンジニアリングレポートを参照しなければなりません。

Q：コンプスとは何ですか？

A：取引事例比較法で用いられる**取引事例**のことです。

Basic process of real estate investment in Japan: Step 3

*The third step to investing in real estate in Japan is to conduct due diligence. The **Appraisal Report** plays an important role in helping investors determine the **market value** of the subject property.*

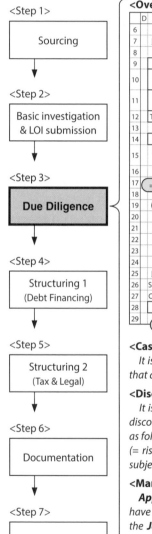

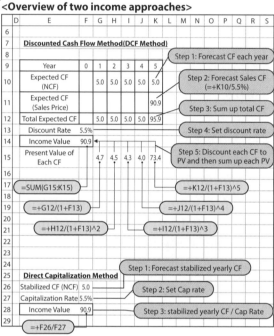

<Cash Flow>

It is very important for appraisers to estimate the cash flows that are generated from the subject property appropriately.

<Discount Rate and Cap Rate>

It is also very important for appraisers to set an appropriate discount rate and cap rate. The basic idea behind these rates is as follows: **Risk free rate** (=10 year **JGB** yield) + **risk premium** (= risk premium of general real estate + risk premium of the subject property).

<Market Value>

Appraisal value is considered market value. Although there have not been official comments, the **market value** based on the **Japanese real estate appraisal standards** is the same concept as the market value based on the **International Valuation Standards (IVS)**.

日本における基本的な不動産投資のプロセス：ステップ3

日本での不動産投資の3つめのステップは、対象不動産のデューデリジェンスを行うことです。**鑑定評価書**は、投資家が、対象不動産の**市場価値**を把握するために重要な役割を果たします。

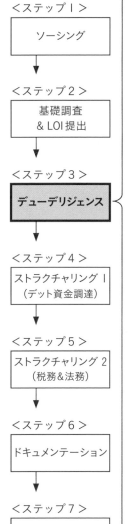

- ＜ステップ１＞ ソーシング
- ＜ステップ２＞ 基礎調査 & LOI 提出
- ＜ステップ３＞ **デューデリジェンス**
- ＜ステップ４＞ ストラクチャリング１（デット資金調達）
- ＜ステップ５＞ ストラクチャリング２（税務&法務）
- ＜ステップ６＞ ドキュメンテーション
- ＜ステップ７＞ クロージング

〈2つの収益還元法の概要〉

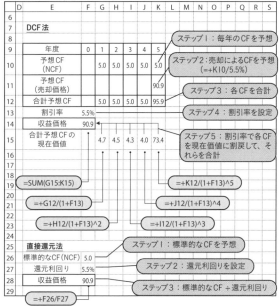

〈キャッシュフロー〉

　対象不動産から生み出されるキャッシュフローを予測することが、鑑定士にとって、非常に重要です。

〈割引率とキャップレート〉

　適切な割引率とキャップレートを定めることもまた、鑑定士にとって、非常に重要です。これらの率の基本的な考え方は次のとおりです。**リスクフリーレート**（10年もの**日本国債の利回り**）＋**リスクプレミアム**（不動産一般のリスクプレミアムと対象不動産のリスクプレミアム）。

〈市場価値〉

　鑑定評価額は市場価値とみなされます。正式な見解はでていませんが、日本の**不動産鑑定評価基準**に基づく正常価格は、**国際評価基準**が定める市場価値の概念と同様です。

4-7 Structuring 1 — Debt Financing

Q : Is financing of real estate investment vehicles in Japan possible?

A : Yes, loans can be given to investment vehicles in Japan such as TMK and TK-GK structures.

Q : Why do investors use debt financing?

A : Many investors try to increase their **investment return** by utilizing the **low interest rate** environment in Japan.

Q : Who are the major lenders in Japan?

A : The primary players involved in financing are Japanese banks, Japanese **leasing companies**, life insurance companies, and foreign banks active in Japan.

Q : How do lenders decide their interest rates?

A : The interest rate is determined by the **base rate** plus the **spread**. The base rate represents the basic funding cost of lenders. The spread and the **upfront fees** act as profit for lenders.

Q : What is the procedure for providing loans?

A : After conducting basic due diligence, lenders offer borrowers a **term sheet** outlining tentative loan conditions, including **loan amount**, **LTV**, upfront loan fee, base rate (**floating rate** or **fixed rate**), spread, **principal repayment method (bullet repayment** or **amortization)**, **covenants**, **cash reserve**, **loan execution conditions** (**CP: conditions precedent**), etc. Investors then review the term sheet, and further negotiation on loan terms usually takes place. Covenant refers to the **special agreement** the borrower must observe, such as the maximum LTV, minimum **DSCR (Debt Service Coverage Ratio)**, necessary reporting to the lender, etc. If the borrower breaches the covenant, the lender can take several measures. One example is to force the borrower to suspend its dividend to investors.

ストラクチャリング 1 — デットファイナンス

Q：日本の投資ビークルでローンの調達は可能ですか？

A：はい、TMK や GK など日本の投資ビークルでのローン調達は可能です。

Q：なぜ、投資家はデットファイナンスを利用するのですか？

A：多くの投資家が、日本の**低金利**の状況を活用して、**投資利回り**を上げようとしています。

Q：誰が主要なレンダーですか？

A：ローン資金提供に関与している主なプレイヤーには、銀行、**リース会社**、生命保険会社、外資系銀行があります。

Q：レンダーはどのように金利を決めるのですか？

A：金利は、**ベースレート（基準金利）＋スプレッド（利ざや）**で決まります。ベースレートはレンダーの資金調達コストのようなものです。スプレッドはレンダーの儲けです。**貸付手数料**もレンダーの儲けです。

Q：ローンを提供する手続きはどのようになっていますか？

A：基礎的な調査を実施した後、レンダーは、借主に対して、**タームシート**と呼ばれるローンの仮条件を記したものを提供します。内容としては、**ローン金額**、**LTV（負債比率）**、貸付手数料、基準金利（**変動金利**もしくは**固定金利**）、スプレッド、**元金返済方法（期限一括返済**もしくは**分割返済**）、**コベナンツ**、**積立金**、**貸付実行前提条件**などがあります。投資家は、このタームシートを吟味し、ローン条件について更なる交渉を実施していきます。コベナンツとは、借主が守らなければならない**特約事項**を意味します。例えば、最大LTV、最小限の**元利返済金カバー率**、レンダーへの必要報告事項などです。もし借主がコベナンツに違反すれば、レンダーは、借主の投資家への配当を一時停止するなど、いくつかの措置をとることができます。

Basic process of real estate investment in Japan: Step 4

*The fourth step is to consider debt financing. Many investors prefer to utilize debt financing in order to enhance their **investment returns**.*

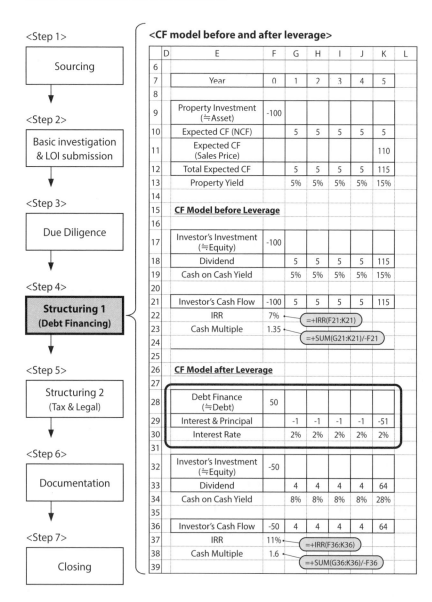

<Step 1>

Sourcing

<Step 2>

Basic investigation & LOI submission

<Step 3>

Due Diligence

<Step 4>

Structuring 1 (Debt Financing)

<Step 5>

Structuring 2 (Tax & Legal)

<Step 6>

Documentation

<Step 7>

Closing

<CF model before and after leverage>

	D	E	F	G	H	I	J	K	L
6									
7		Year	0	1	2	3	4	5	
8									
9		Property Investment (≒Asset)	-100						
10		Expected CF (NCF)		5	5	5	5	5	
11		Expected CF (Sales Price)						110	
12		Total Expected CF		5	5	5	5	115	
13		Property Yield		5%	5%	5%	5%	15%	
14									
15		**CF Model before Leverage**							
16									
17		Investor's Investment (≒Equity)	-100						
18		Dividend		5	5	5	5	115	
19		Cash on Cash Yield		5%	5%	5%	5%	15%	
20									
21		Investor's Cash Flow	-100	5	5	5	5	115	
22		IRR	7%	=+IRR(F21:K21)					
23		Cash Multiple	1.35						
24				=+SUM(G21:K21)/-F21					
25									
26		**CF Model after Leverage**							
27									
28		Debt Finance (≒Debt)	50						
29		Interest & Principal		-1	-1	-1	-1	-51	
30		Interest Rate		2%	2%	2%	2%	2%	
31									
32		Investor's Investment (≒Equity)	-50						
33		Dividend		4	4	4	4	64	
34		Cash on Cash Yield		8%	8%	8%	8%	28%	
35									
36		Investor's Cash Flow	-50	4	4	4	4	64	
37		IRR	11%	=+IRR(F36:K36)					
38		Cash Multiple	1.6						
39				=+SUM(G36:K36)/-F36					

日本における基本的な不動産投資のプロセス：ステップ4

日本での不動産投資の４つめのステップは、デット資金を調達することです。多くの投資家が、**投資利回り**を上げるために、デット資金を活用することを好みます。

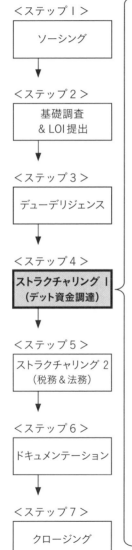

<ステップ１>

ソーシング

<ステップ２>

基礎調査
＆LOI提出

<ステップ３>

デューデリジェンス

<ステップ４>

ストラクチャリング１
（デット資金調達）

<ステップ５>

ストラクチャリング２
（税務＆法務）

<ステップ６>

ドキュメンテーション

<ステップ７>

クロージング

〈借入前及び後のCFモデル〉

	D	E	F	G	H	I	J	K	L
6									
7		年度	0	1	2	3	4	5	
8									
9		不動産投資額 （≒アセット）	-100						
10		予想CF（NCF）		5	5	5	5		
11		予想CF（売却価格）						110	
12		合計予想CF		5	5	5	5	115	
13		不動産利回り		5%	5%	5%	5%	15%	
14									
15		**借入しない場合のCFモデル**							
16									
17		投資家の出資額 （≒エクイティ）	-100						
18		配当		5	5	5	5	115	
19		キャッシュオンキャッシュ		5%	5%	5%	5%	15%	
20									
21		投資家CF	-100	5	5	5	5	115	
22		IRR	7%	=+IRR(F21:K21)					
23		キャッシュマルチプル	1.35	=+SUM(G21:K21)/-F21					
24									
25									
26		**借入した場合のCFモデル**							
27									
28		借入による 資金調達額 （≒デット）	50						
29		元利返済		-1	-1	-1	-1	-51	
30		金利		2%	2%	2%	2%	2%	
31									
32		投資家の出資額 （≒エクイティ）	-50						
33		配当		4	4	4	4	64	
34		キャッシュオンキャッシュ		8%	8%	8%	8%	28%	
35									
36		投資家CF	-50	4	4	4	4	64	
37		IRR	11%	=+IRR(F36:K36)					
38		キャッシュマルチプル	1.6	=+SUM(G36:K36)/-F36					
39									

4-8 Structuring 2 — Tax & Legal

Q : What are the major tax issues for investors in TK-GK and TMK structures?

A : The most important issue is how to avoid **double taxation** between the SPC level and the investor level. As general Japanese corporations, TMKs and GKs are obliged to pay **corporate taxes** based on their **taxable income**. Therefore, satisfying the necessary criteria for TMK and GK structures in order to avoid corporate tax liability is very important.

Q : Are there any other tax issues, especially for foreign investors?

A : In terms of foreign investors, the potential for double taxation by Japan as well as the offshore nation remains an important consideration. To reduce overall tax costs, investors must carefully consider the rate of the **withholding tax** and the tax specifics of the **tax treaty** between Japan and the country of origin of the foreign vehicle.

Q : What are the major legal issues in the TK-GK and TMK structures?

A : The most important issue is how to achieve **bankruptcy remoteness**. Typically, lenders seek to minimize the **bankruptcy risks** of a TMK or GK structure before providing loans to these SPCs. As an example, the lender may require the voting right shares of the TMK or GK to be held by a bankruptcy remote SPC, such as **ISH** called Ippan Shaddan Hojin, etc.

Q : Who deals with the above tax and legal issues.

A : A skilled **tax attorney** from a **tax firm** can assist investors with the development of effective tax structures. A skilled **lawyer** from a specialized **law firm** also plays a critical role in successfully dealing with real estate legal issues.

Investors and lenders usually require a **tax opinion report** from a tax firm and a **legal opinion report** from a law firm to confirm how the subject investment structure deals with tax and legal issues.

4-8 ストラクチャリング 2 ── 税務&法務

Q：TK-GKやTMKにおいて、主な税務上の問題には何がありますか？

A：最も重要な問題は、いかにSPCレベルと投資家レベルでの**二重課税**を回避するかです。TMKやGKは、**課税所得**に対して**法人税**等を支払う義務がある日本の会社です。したがって、一定の要件を満たして、TMKやGKの法人税を回避することが非常に重要になります。

Q：海外投資家に特有の税務上の問題はありますか？

A：海外投資家に関しては、日本レベルと海外レベルでの二重課税も大きな問題となります。全体の税負担を少なくするために、投資家は、**源泉徴収税**の税率や日本と外国との間における**租税条約**の内容に留意する必要があります。

Q：TK-GKやTMKにおいて、主な法律上の問題には何がありますか？

A：最も重要な問題は、いかに**倒産隔離**を達成するかです。一般的には、レンダーはTMKやGKにローンを提供するために、それらの**倒産リスク**を極小化することを求めます。例えば、TMKやGKの議決権持分は、**一般社団法人**など倒産隔離の図られたSPCにより保有されることが求められます。

Q：上記の税務上や法律上の問題を誰が対応しますか？

A：税効率の高いストラクチャーの構築には熟練した**税理士法人**の税理士によるサポートが必要ですし、法律上の問題を首尾よく処理するには、熟練した**法律事務所**の弁護士が重要な役割を果たします。

　投資家やレンダーは、通常、税務や法務に関して当該ストラクチャーがどのように対応しているかを確認するために、税理士法人からの**税務意見書**や法律事務所からの**法律意見書**を求めます。

Basic process of real estate investment in Japan: Step 5

*The fifth step to investing in real estate in Japan is dealing with tax and legal matters. AM and / or FM must consult with a **tax attorney** and a **lawyer** in order to increase their investors' total return.*

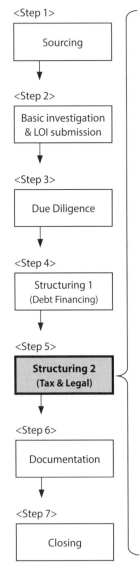

<Step 1>

Sourcing

<Step 2>

Basic investigation & LOI submission

<Step 3>

Due Diligence

<Step 4>

Structuring 1 (Debt Financing)

<Step 5>

Structuring 2 (Tax & Legal)

<Step 6>

Documentation

<Step 7>

Closing

<How to avoid double taxation>

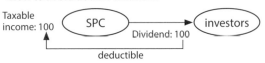

- If **taxable income** of the SPC is 100 and it pays out 100 as a dividend to investors, it may deduct 100 from its taxable income. In this case, the taxable income would be 0. So, the SPC does not need to pay corporate tax.
- A TMK may only receive this **tax incentive** by meeting the requirements stipulated by the **Special Taxation Measures Law**.
- A TK-GK may also receive this **tax break** if the relationship between the GK and its investors can be regarded as a **silent partnership (TK)**.

<How to minimize bankruptcy risk of the SPC>

- SPC's business must be restricted by its **articles of incorporation**.
- SPC's **voting right** shares must be held by a bankruptcy remote SPC like **Ippan Shadan Hojin (ISH)**.
- The voting right shares of the ISH must be held by an independent director (e.g. an independent accountant). So, the ISH is not governed by any related parties such as the AM, seller, etc. Since the ISH becomes the parent company of the SPC, the SPC is no longer governed by any related parties.
- Regarding the TMK, the ISH holds **specified sharess** (voting right shares) of the TMK.
- Regarding the TK-GK, the ISH does not hold the **TK investment**, but rather the voting right shares of the GK.
- Additional measures are also required to establish the **bankruptcy remoteness** of the SPC by the lenders.

日本における基本的な不動産投資のプロセス：ステップ5

日本での不動産投資の5つめのステップは、税務と法務を検討することです。AMやFMは、投資利回りを上げるために、**税理士**や**弁護士**と相談しなければなりません。

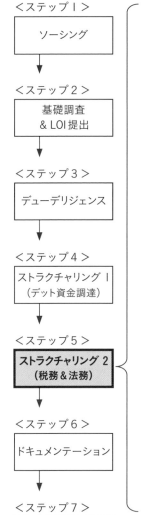

＜ステップ1＞

ソーシング

＜ステップ2＞

基礎調査
& LOI 提出

＜ステップ3＞

デューデリジェンス

＜ステップ4＞

ストラクチャリング 1
（デット資金調達）

＜ステップ5＞

ストラクチャリング 2
（税務＆法務）

＜ステップ6＞

ドキュメンテーション

＜ステップ7＞

クロージング

〈いかに二重課税を回避するか〉

- SPCの**課税所得**が100で、SPCがその100を配当として投資家に分配すれば、SPCは、その100を課税所得から控除することができます。そうすれば、課税所得がゼロになるため、SPCは実質的に法人税を支払わなくて済みます。
- TMKに関しては、**租税特別措置法**に記載されている一定の要件を満たせば、TMKは上記の**税の優遇措置**を享受できます。
- TK-GKに関しては、合同会社と投資家との関係が**匿名組合**である限り、上記の**税の優遇措置**を享受できます。

〈いかにSPCの倒産リスクを極小化するか〉

- SPCの事業は**定款**によって制限されなければいけません。
- SPCの**議決権**は、**一般社団法人**など倒産隔離された特別目的会社に保有されていなければなりません。
- 一般社団法人の議決権は、独立した会計士などにより保有されます。したがって、一般社団法人は、AMや売主などの関係者の関与を受けません。そして、当該一般社団法人が、SPCの親会社になることで、SPCも関係者の関与を受けないことになります。
- TMKに関しては、一般社団法人は、TMKの議決権持分である**特定出資**を保有します。
- TK-GKに関しては、一般社団法人は、**匿名組合出資**ではなく、合同会社の議決権持分（社員持分）を保有します。
- SPCの**倒産隔離**のために、上記以外のいくつかの措置が、レンダーから求められます。

4-9 | Documentation

Q : What kinds of contracts are involved in investing in real estate in Japan?

A : When a TMK acquires real estate in Japan, they must execute a **Real Estate Purchase and Sales Agreement (PSA)** with the seller. This agreement details the purchase and sales agreements and understandings between the parties, such as sales price, **penalty, compensation for damage**, etc.

Q : What kinds of contracts are involved in investing in TBI in Japan?

A : When real estate is purchased in a TK-GK structure or a TMK structure by using trust beneficiary interests (TBI), a **Trust Agreement** is needed between the trust bank and the seller in order for the seller to hold the primary real estate TBI. When real estate TBI is purchased by GK or TMK, the **Real Estate Trust Beneficiary Interest Purchase and Sales Agreement** is executed. Additionally, GK or TMK signs the Amendment Trust Agreement with the trust bank.

Q : What contracts are required when a loan is made?

A : The TMK, GK, or direct investor needs to conclude a **Loan Agreement** with the lender that details the payable interest rate as well as the other terms and conditions of the loan. Lenders also require further agreements regarding **security rights**, such as a **mortgage** or **pledge**, depending on the type of loan and property.

Q : What contracts are needed to manage the real estate?

A : In Japan, usually an **Asset Management Agreement** is needed with a licensed Asset Management Company that will manage the TMK or GK.

In terms of the day-to-day operation of the property, a **Property Management Agreement** must be concluded with a Property Management Company.

Additionally, an Accounting and Tax Service Agreement must be concluded with an accounting and tax firm specializing in accounting data processing, **tax returns**, and contract management on behalf of TMK or GK.

ドキュメンテーション

Q：不動産に投資する場合、どのような契約が必要ですか？

A：TMKが不動産を取得する場合、売主との**不動産売買契約書**が必要です。この契約書には、売買価格、**違約金**、**損害賠償**など、売主と買主の間の、売買に関する同意事項が記載されます。

Q：不動産信託受益権に投資する場合、どのような契約が必要ですか？

A：TK-GKストラクチャーやTMKストラクチャーが、信託受益権を用いて、不動産を取得する場合、売主が不動産信託受益権をまず保有するために、信託銀行と売主との**信託契約**が必要です。GKやTMKが不動産信託受益権を取得する場合には、**不動産信託受益権売買契約書**が締結されます。さらに、GKやTMKは、信託銀行と信託変更契約を締結します。

Q：ローンを調達する場合、どのような契約が必要ですか？

A：TMKやGKは、レンダーと**ローン契約**を締結する必要があります。ローン契約には金利や他のローン条件が記載されています。レンダーは、また、**抵当権**や**質権**のような**担保権**に関する契約書も求めます。

Q：不動産を管理するためにどのような契約が必要ですか？

A：TMKやGKを管理するために、ライセンスのあるアセットマネジメント会社との**アセットマネジメント契約**が必要となります。

日々の不動産管理に関しては、プロパティマネジメント会社との**プロパティマネジメント契約**が必要とされます。

また、TMKやGKの会計事務、**税務申告**、契約処理のために、会計税務事務所との事務委託契約が必要となります。

Basic process of real estate investment in Japan: Step 6

The sixth step in investing in real estate in Japan is executing the many forms of necessary documentation required in an indirect investment structure.

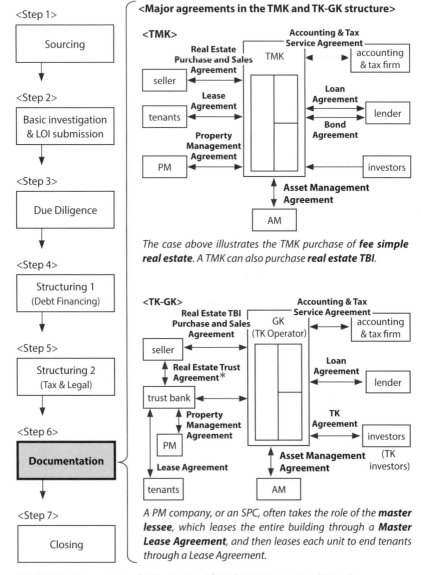

<Step 1>
Sourcing

<Step 2>
Basic investigation & LOI submission

<Step 3>
Due Diligence

<Step 4>
Structuring 1 (Debt Financing)

<Step 5>
Structuring 2 (Tax & Legal)

<Step 6>
Documentation

<Step 7>
Closing

<Major agreements in the TMK and TK-GK structure>

<TMK>

Accounting & Tax Service Agreement — accounting & tax firm

Real Estate Purchase and Sales Agreement — TMK — seller

Lease Agreement — tenants

Loan Agreement — lender

Bond Agreement

Property Management Agreement — PM

investors

Asset Management Agreement — AM

*The case above illustrates the TMK purchase of **fee simple real estate**. A TMK can also purchase **real estate TBI**.*

<TK-GK>

Accounting & Tax Service Agreement — accounting & tax firm

Real Estate TBI Purchase and Sales Agreement — GK (TK Operator) — seller

Real Estate Trust Agreement* — trust bank

Loan Agreement — lender

Property Management Agreement — PM

Lease Agreement — tenants

TK Agreement — investors (TK investors)

Asset Management Agreement — AM

*A PM company, or an SPC, often takes the role of the **master lessee**, which leases the entire building through a **Master Lease Agreement**, and then leases each unit to end tenants through a Lease Agreement.*

*Real Estate Trust Agreement is also called "**Trust Agreement for Real Estate Management and Disposal.**"

日本における基本的な不動産投資のプロセス：ステップ6

日本での不動産投資の6つめのステップは、ドキュメンテーションです。間接不動産投資においては、投資家は、多くの契約書や書類を求められます。

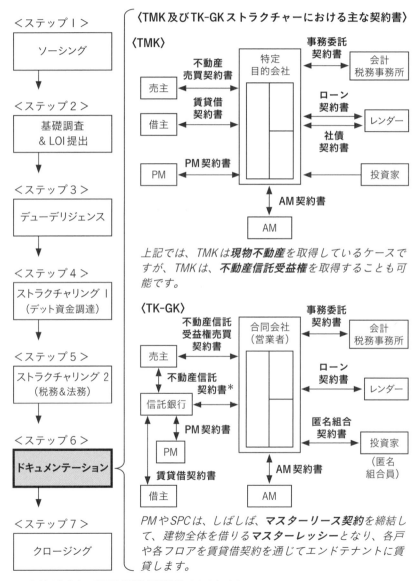

＜ステップ1＞
ソーシング

＜ステップ2＞
基礎調査
& LOI提出

＜ステップ3＞
デューデリジェンス

＜ステップ4＞
ストラクチャリング1
（デット資金調達）

＜ステップ5＞
ストラクチャリング2
（税務&法務）

＜ステップ6＞
ドキュメンテーション

＜ステップ7＞
クロージング

〈TMK及びTK-GKストラクチャーにおける主な契約書〉

〈TMK〉

事務委託契約書
不動産売買契約書
特定目的会社
会計税務事務所
売主
賃貸借契約書
ローン契約書
借主
社債契約書
レンダー
PM契約書
PM
投資家
AM契約書
AM

*上記では、TMKは**現物不動産**を取得しているケースですが、TMKは、**不動産信託受益権**を取得することも可能です。*

〈TK-GK〉

事務委託契約書
不動産信託受益権売買契約書
合同会社（営業者）
会計税務事務所
売主
不動産信託契約書*
ローン契約書
信託銀行
レンダー
PM契約書
匿名組合契約書
PM
投資家（匿名組合員）
賃貸借契約書
AM契約書
借主
AM

*PMやSPCは、しばしば、**マスターリース契約**を締結して、建物全体を借りる**マスターレッシー**となり、各戸や各フロアを賃貸借契約を通じてエンドテナントに賃貸します。*

*＊不動産信託契約書は、「**不動産管理処分信託契約**」とも呼ばれます。*

4-10 Closing

Q : How does an investor complete the purchase process?

A : The **closing** is officially completed once the seller has received payment and the buyer has recorded the official change of ownership in the real estate registry. A change in title ownership is recorded by a **judicial scrivener** and the procedure is carried out at the Legal Affairs Bureau in the district where the property is located.

In general, sellers, buyers, lenders, judicial scriveners, and brokerage companies meet at the same place on a **closing date**. A judicial scrivener confirms the necessary documents, including the **title deed** for the buyer. Once the seller confirms the payment, the judicial scrivener is asked to go to the Bureau to carry out the registry.

Q : When do investors and lenders inject money into an SPC so the entity can purchase real estate?

A : Typically, the lenders and investors will execute their agreements before injecting money into an SPC. After all agreements have been signed, money is usually injected into the SPC a few days before the closing date, initially by the investor and then by the lender on the closing date, in that order. The lender will not provide loans until the borrower has satisfied the **loan execution conditions (CP: conditions precedent)**, which include receipt of the equity investment from the investors.

Q : What is the difference between the closing of a TMK and a TK-GK?

A : TMK structures are generally more complicated than TK-GK structures because they are governed by the **Asset Liquidation Law**, which details the operation and set-up of the TMK entity.

Q : What is ALP?

A : When investors use a TMK, they are required to complete an **Asset Liquidation Plan (ALP)**, which details the real estate the TMK will purchase. The ALP is then submitted to the Local Financial Bureau of the FSA.

4-10 クロージング

Q：どのように投資家は不動産取得プロセスを完了させるのですか？

A：クロージング（**決済**）は、売主が売買代金を受け取り、買主が不動産登記簿で不動産所有権移転登記を行うことで完了します。所有権移転登記は、**司法書士**によって、対象不動産が属する法務局で手続きがなされます。

　通常は、**決済日**に、売主、買主、レンダー、司法書士、仲介会社は同じ場所に集まります。司法書士は**権利証**を含む登記必要書類を買主のために確認します。売主が売買代金の着金を確認したら、司法書士は登記手続きのために法務局に向かいます。

Q：SPCが不動産を取得できるように、投資家とレンダーからの資金提供はいつ実行されるのですか？

A：通常、レンダーと投資家は、SPCへの資金を提供する前に、契約を締結します。全ての必要な契約が締結された後、クロージングの数日前に、投資家からの資金が提供されます。そして、レンダーからの資金が決済日に提供されます。レンダーは**貸付実行前提条件**が充足されない限り、ローンを提供しません。貸付実行前提条件には、投資家からの資金受取も含まれます。

Q：TMKとTK-GKのクロージング手続きはどのように異なりますか？

A：TMKストラクチャーは、一般的に、TK-GKストラクチャーよりも複雑です。理由は、TMKは、**資産流動化法**の規制を受けているからです。資産流動化法には、TMKの設立や運営に関する詳細が定められています。

Q：資産流動化計画とは何ですか？

A：投資家がTMKストラクチャーを用いる場合には、金融庁の地方財務局に**資産流動化計画**の提出を求められます。資産流動化計画には、TMKが取得する不動産の詳細が記載されます。

Basic process of real estate investment in Japan: Step 7

The final step in investing in real estate in Japan is to conduct the closing. The TMK procedure is comparatively more complicated than that of the TK-GK structure.

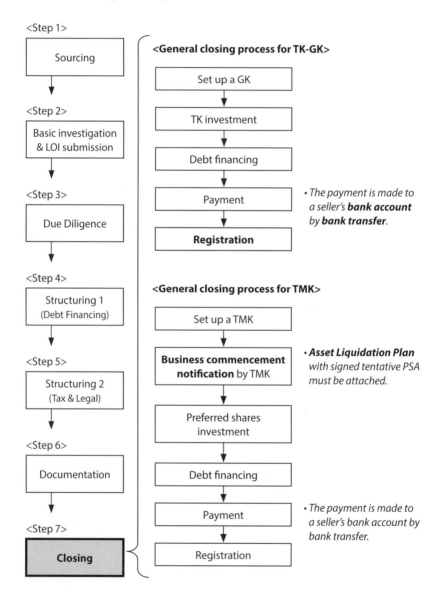

日本における基本的な不動産投資のプロセス：ステップ7
日本での不動産投資の最後のステップは、クロージング手続きです。TMKは、TK-GKよりも、より、クロージング手続きが複雑です。

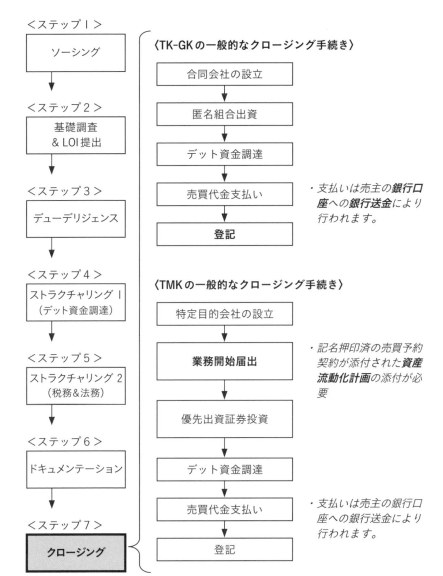

<ステップ1>
ソーシング

<ステップ2>
基礎調査
& LOI提出

<ステップ3>
デューデリジェンス

<ステップ4>
ストラクチャリング1
（デット資金調達）

<ステップ5>
ストラクチャリング2
（税務&法務）

<ステップ6>
ドキュメンテーション

<ステップ7>
クロージング

〈TK-GKの一般的なクロージング手続き〉

合同会社の設立

匿名組合出資

デット資金調達

売買代金支払い

登記

・支払いは売主の**銀行口座**への**銀行送金**により行われます。

〈TMKの一般的なクロージング手続き〉

特定目的会社の設立

業務開始届出

優先出資証券投資

デット資金調達

売買代金支払い

登記

・記名押印済の売買予約契約が添付された**資産流動化計画**の添付が必要

・支払いは売主の銀行口座への銀行送金により行われます。

When **foreign investors** make their first investments in Japan, some of the initial challenges they face are the **language barrier** and locating bilingual and bicultural service providers. The Japanese real estate market is still over 95% owned and operated by Japanese domestic companies, so locating bilingual vendors remains a challenge.

Foreign investors usually require bilingual and bicultural law firms to help with contract drafting and negotiation. The Purchase & Sales Agreement (**PSA**) needs to be provided in both the Japanese language and, usually, an English language translation. This requires additional translation costs and also adds additional time to the negotiation phase as each turn of the PSA document must be continually translated. When the PSA document is signed, usually the Japanese version is the binding contract document, and the English version serves only as an exhibit.

The investment structures available to foreign investors in Japan are essentially the TK-GK, the TMK, and **direct investment**. Foreign investors who wish to play an active role in their real estate investment management usually choose the TMK structure. Over the past decade, the TMK setup procedure and management process have fully developed, and most foreign investors are comfortable using this investment vehicle.

During the documentation phase, the biggest part of the negotiation is within the PSA where the seller and buyer both try to negotiate the most favorable terms. An area within the PSA, that is usually the most contested are the **Representations and Warranties**, whereby the purchaser is seeking protection from any unknown facts about the building, leases, and contracts and the seller is attempting to negotiate an **"as is"** sales condition. Usually both parties will make concessions during the negotiation, and the PSA will reflect a global standard amount for protection to both the buyer and seller.

コラム 海外投資家が投資する際に 支障となることは何か？

　海外投資家が、日本で最初の不動産投資を行うときに直面する課題は、**言葉の壁**で、海外と日本の両方の言語や文化を理解してくれるサービスの提供者を探すことです。日本の不動産は現在でも95％超は国内の会社により所有され運営されています。それゆえ、両方を提供できるプレイヤーの探索は課題です。

　海外投資家は、通常、両言語と両方の文化に精通した法律事務所に契約書のドラフトや交渉をサポートしてもらう必要があります。**売買契約書**は、日本語と英語訳が一緒に提供される必要があります。そのため、売買契約の交渉の都度翻訳が必要になり、追加の翻訳費用や時間が必要となります。売買契約が締結される際には、通常、日本語の契約書が正本となり、英語版の方は参考訳（別紙）として扱われることになります。

　日本において、海外投資家が選択するストラクチャーは、基本的には、TK-GK、TMK、**直接投資**のどれかです。不動産の投資運営に積極的に関与したい海外投資家は、通常、TMKを選択します。過去10年でTMKの設立や運営手続きは改善され、TMKを投資主体として活用することがほとんどの海外投資家にとっての選択肢となっています。

　ドキュメンテーションにおける最も大きな交渉箇所は、売買契約書における文言交渉です。売買契約書の中でも最も議論となるのが**表明保証**です。買主は建物、賃貸借、各種契約の知らない部分については保証を求めますが、売主は、「**現状有姿**」を売却条件とすることを好み、それを主張してきます。多くの場合、買主売主双方が交渉の過程で譲歩し、売買契約書はグローバル慣行に基づく表明保証が反映されることが多くなっています。

Chapter 5

Real Estate Businesses in Japan

第5章

日本の不動産ビジネス

5-1 Overview of Real Estate Businesses in Japan

Q : What kinds of real estate businesses are there in Japan?

A : There are a wide variety of major real estate businesses that include the **real estate development business, real estate leasing business, real estate management business, real estate brokerage business, real estate fund management business, real estate trust business**, and **real estate finance business**. Additionally, various real estate professionals are involved in the above real estate businesses.

Q : How are those businesses categorized?

A : They are mainly divided into three categories: real estate developers, real estate owners, and real estate financiers. Real estate developers buy land, construct a building, and then open the property for use. Real estate owners use the property themselves or lease it. Real estate financiers are mainly investors or lenders.

Q : Who are the major real estate owners?

A : There are mainly three types of owners: end users, real estate companies, and real estate funds. Some of the real estate companies have different main businesses. End user owners can include individuals, family offices, and various corporations.

Q : Could you explain how real estate funds own real estate?

A : It is difficult to say who the actual investors are within real estate funds, as this information is usually kept confidential.

But the legal owners of the real estate are often the **SPCs (Special Purpose Companies)** that are set up under a TMK structure. When the **TBI (trust beneficiary interests)** structure is used, the legal owner of the real estate would be the trust bank.

In both cases, a licensed **asset management company (AM)** is appointed to manage the real estate on behalf of the investors.

5-1 日本の不動産ビジネスの概要

Q：日本にはどのような不動産ビジネスがありますか？

A：様々な不動産ビジネスがあります。主なビジネスとしては、**不動産開発事業**、**不動産賃貸事業**、**不動産管理事業**、**不動産仲介事業**、**不動産ファンド運用事業**、**不動産信託事業**、そして、**不動産ファイナンス事業**があります。加えて、様々な不動産専門家がこれらの事業に関与しています。

Q：それらのビジネスはどのように分類できますか？

A：大きくは3つに分類することができます。不動産開発者（デベロッパー）、不動産所有者、そして、不動産への資金提供者です。不動産開発者は、土地を取得して、その土地に建物を建てて、不動産を利用できる状態にします。不動産所有者は、その不動産を自ら利用するか、テナントに利用してもらいます。不動産への資金提供者は、投資家かレンダーになります。

Q：主な不動産所有者は誰ですか？

A：大きくは、エンドユーザー、不動産会社、そして、不動産ファンドという3つのタイプに分けることができます。不動産会社には、不動産事業以外の事業を主要な事業としている会社もあります。また、エンドユーザーには、個人、個人事業主、そして、様々な会社があります。

Q：不動産ファンドがどのように不動産を所有しているのか説明してもらえますか？

A：通常は公にされない情報であるため実際の投資家が誰かを把握することは難しいです。

しかし、不動産の法律上の所有者は、しばしば、特定目的会社などの**特別目的会社**となることがあります。**信託受益権**が用いられるときには、法律上の不動産の所有者は信託銀行となります。

どちらのケースでも、ライセンスを持つ**資産運用会社**が指定され、投資家のために不動産を運用することになります。

Illustrated Real Estate Terminologies

Overview of Real Estate Businesses

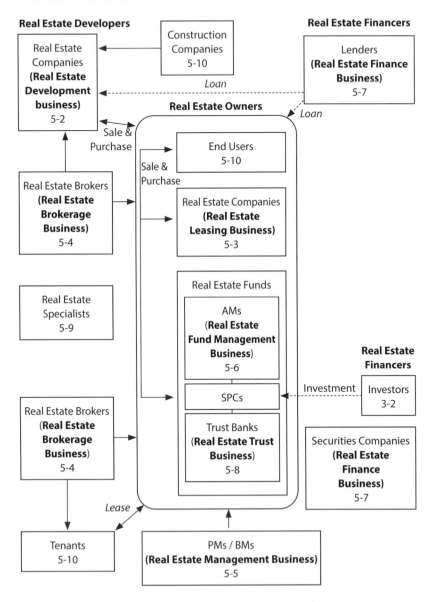

不動産ビジネスの概要

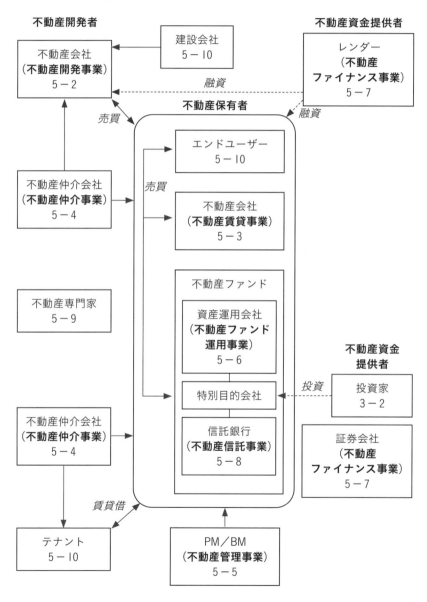

5-2 Real Estate Development Business

Q : What kinds of properties do **real estate developers** create?

A : There are a wide variety of properties that developers create in Japan such as large-scale **multi-use complexes** that include offices, retail stores, and hotels all combined into one project. Developers also build single office buildings, retail properties, condominiums, detached houses, and resort hotels.

Q : How do they make money from the **real estate development business**?

A : Developers can make a **development profit** when they sell the properties they develop for more money than it costs to develop them. The development cost includes the **building construction cost**. Developers sometimes keep the properties they build and lease them out to tenants, making money from the **rental income**.

Q : Who buys or leases the developed properties?

A : The end buyer or lessee really depends on the type of property that is developed. For example, condominium developers sell the condominium units they develop to individuals. Office developers lease office buildings to tenants, which are various companies. Developers can also sell an entire building to investors such as **J-REITs** or **Private Real Estate Funds**.

Q : What kinds of companies are involved in the development business?

A : There are three main types of real estate developers in Japan.

The first are **general real estate companies** which are active in the development business as well as the **real estate leasing business, real estate brokerage business,** and **real estate management business**. The second are **condominium specialized developers**. The third are companies that have other major businesses outside the real estate industry. Examples of such companies are **trading companies, railroad companies, general contractors, electric power companies**, etc.

5-2 不動産開発事業

Q：**デベロッパー**はどのような不動産を開発しているのですか？

A：デベロッパーが開発する不動産には様々な種類があります。例えば、オフィス、商業店舗、ホテルなどが一体となった大型の**複合施設**があります。また、デベロッパーは、単独のオフィスビルや商業施設、分譲マンション、戸建住宅、リゾートホテルなども開発しています。

Q：デベロッパーはどのように**不動産開発事業**から収益を得ているのですか？

A：デベロッパーは、開発に要した費用よりも高くその不動産を売れば、**開発利益**を得ることができます。その費用には**建築工事費**も含みます。また、**賃料収入**を得るために、開発した不動産を保有してテナントに貸すこともあります。

Q：開発した不動産は、誰に売却したり、賃貸したりしているのですか？

A：それは、どんな不動産を開発しているかによります。例えば、分譲マンションデベロッパーは、彼らが開発した分譲マンションを個人に売却しています。オフィスデベロッパーは、様々な企業にオフィスビルを賃貸しています。最近では、デベロッパーは、開発した不動産一棟全体を**J-REIT**や**私募ファンド**といった投資家にも売却しています。

Q：どのような会社が、開発事業を営んでいるのですか？

A：大きく分けると3つのタイプのデベロッパーがあります。

1つ目は、開発事業だけでなく、**不動産賃貸事業**、**不動産仲介事業**、そして、**不動産管理事業**も行う、**総合不動産会社**です。2つ目は、**分譲マンション専業デベロッパー**です。3つ目は、**商社**、**鉄道会社**、**ゼネコン**、**電力会社**など、他の主要なビジネスも営む会社です。

Basic business model of the real estate development business

*Developers sometimes buy land with an old building. In this case, they will tear down the old building and start the development of a new one. The **building demolition cost** is part for the consideration of the land purchase price.*

Case 1: Condominium Developer

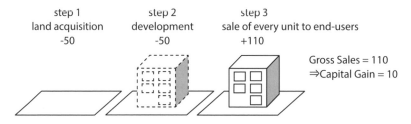

step 1
land acquisition
-50

step 2
development
-50

step 3
sale of every unit to end-users
+110

Gross Sales = 110
⇒Capital Gain = 10

Case 2: Commercial Property Developer (Sale)

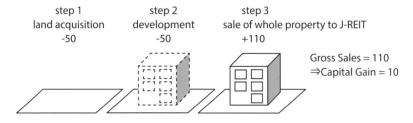

step 1
land acquisition
-50

step 2
development
-50

step 3
sale of whole property to J-REIT
+110

Gross Sales = 110
⇒Capital Gain = 10

Case 3: Commercial Property Developer (Lease)

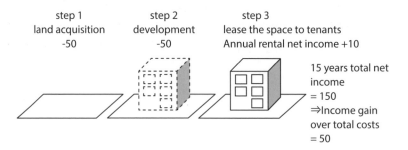

step 1
land acquisition
-50

step 2
development
-50

step 3
lease the space to tenants
Annual rental net income +10

15 years total net income
= 150
⇒Income gain over total costs
= 50

不動産開発事業の基本的なビジネスモデル

デベロッパーは、時には古い建物付きの土地を買います。その際には、当該建物を取り壊した後に開発を開始します。土地の取得価格を決めるために、**建物取壊費用**も考慮されます。

ケース１：分譲マンションデベロッパー

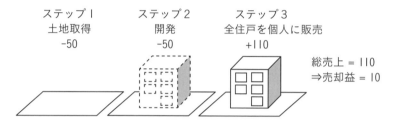

ケース２：商業用不動産デベロッパー（売却）

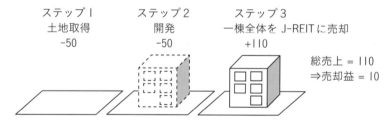

ケース３：商業用不動産デベロッパー（賃貸）

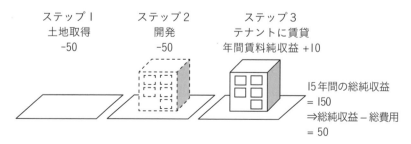

5-3　Real Estate Leasing Business

Q : What is the **real estate leasing business**?

A : This business focuses on the **rental income** that is collected from tenants who lease space in an office building, apartment, retail property, industrial property, or other types of real estate.

Q : Which companies are major players in the real estate leasing business?

A : **General real estate companies** deal in the real estate rental business as well as real estate development business. Most companies have focused on specific areas such as Marunouchi, Nihonbashi, Toranomon, Shibuya, etc., to create special characteristics to attract tenants. Some other major players in this business are **rental office building specialized companies**, where the rental income makes up a major portion of total sales.

Q : Do retail companies also deal in the real estate leasing business?

A : Large **retailers**, which operate large shopping centers or department stores, also deal in the real estate rental business by themselves or through their subsidiaries. They usually own the retail property and directly lease it to tenants, or they master-lease the property and then sublease parts of it to other retailers and receive rental income in return.

Q : Are REITs also active in the leasing business?

A : Listed REITs, which are called **J-REITs** in Japan, and **Private REITs** are also very active players in the real estate leasing business. Unlike other real estate companies, REITs do not have to pay **corporate tax** as long as they pay out almost all their rental income to investors as dividends. The details of REITs are described in Chapter 3.

5-3 不動産賃貸事業

Q：**不動産賃貸事業**とはどのようなビジネスなのですか？

A：不動産をテナントに貸して、テナントから**賃料収入**を得るビジネスです。対象不動産には、オフィスビル、賃貸マンション、商業施設、産業施設などがあります。

Q：どんな会社が不動産賃貸事業の主要なプレイヤーなのですか？

A：**総合不動産会社**は、不動産開発事業とともに不動産賃貸事業を手掛けています。多くの不動産会社は、丸の内、日本橋、虎ノ門、渋谷など特定のエリアに集中し、テナントにとって魅力のあるエリアにしようとしています。他にも、オフィスビルの賃料収入が売上のほとんどを占めている**オフィスビル賃貸専業会社**があります。

Q：小売業を営んでいる会社も、不動産賃貸事業に携わっているのですか？

A：大規模なショッピングセンターや百貨店などを運営する主要な**小売業者**も、また、自らもしくは子会社を通じて不動産賃貸事業を営んでいます。彼らは、商業施設全体を所有して他の小売業者に直接賃貸したり、商業施設全体を一括賃借した上で各店舗を他の小売業者に転貸して、賃料収入を得ています。

Q：REITも、積極的に賃貸事業を営んでいるのですか？

A：**J-REIT**と呼ばれる上場REITや**私募REIT**も、主要な不動産賃貸ビジネスプレイヤーです。他の不動産会社と異なり、REITは、ほとんど全ての賃料収益を投資家に配当として分配している限り、**法人税**を支払う必要がありません。REITの詳細については、第3章で説明しています。

Basic business model of the real estate rental business

Case 1: Development & Lease

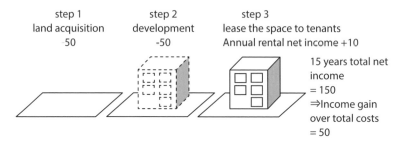

step 1
land acquisition
-50

step 2
development
-50

step 3
lease the space to tenants
Annual rental net income +10

15 years total net income
= 150
⇒Income gain over total costs
= 50

Case 2: Acquisition & Lease

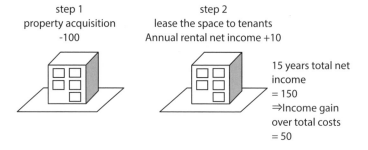

step 1
property acquisition
-100

step 2
lease the space to tenants
Annual rental net income +10

15 years total net income
= 150
⇒Income gain over total costs
= 50

Case 3: Master Lease

one or more **sub lessees** (one or more end tenants)

sublease

Master lessee

master lease

Owner of the property

rent A

rent B

There are mainly two types of master leases. In the **guaranteed rent type master lease**, usually rent A is larger than rent B. So, the master lessee can make a profit from the difference. The **rent-paying capacity** of the master lessee is important. On the other hand, in the **pass-through type master lease**, almost all rent A is paid to the property owner. In the above master lease scheme, sub lessees are called **end tenants**.

不動産賃貸事業の基本的なビジネスモデル

ケース1：開発＆賃貸

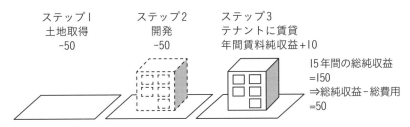

ステップ1
土地取得
-50

ステップ2
開発
-50

ステップ3
テナントに賃貸
年間賃料純収益+10

15年間の総純収益
=150
⇒総純収益 - 総費用
=50

ケース2：購入＆賃貸

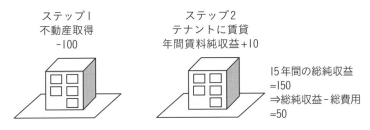

ステップ1
不動産取得
-100

ステップ2
テナントに賃貸
年間賃料純収益+10

15年間の総純収益
=150
⇒総純収益 - 総費用
=50

ケース3：マスターリース

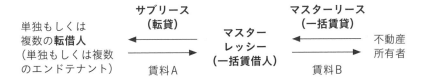

単独もしくは
複数の**転借人**
（単独もしくは複数
のエンドテナント）

サブリース
（転貸）
賃料A

マスター
レッシー
（一括賃借人）

マスターリース
（一括賃貸）
賃料B

不動産
所有者

マスターリースには主に2つのタイプがあります。**賃料保証型マスターリース**の場合、通常、賃料Aの方が賃料Bよりも大きいです。したがって、マスターレッシーは差額を利益とできます。マスターレッシーの**賃料支払能力**が重要となります。一方、**パススルー型マスターリース**では、賃料Aがほぼそのまま不動産所有者に払われます。なお、上記のようなマスターリーススキームでの転借人を**エンドテナント**と呼びます。

5-4 Real Estate Brokerage Business

Q : What is the **real estate brokerage business**?

A : There are mainly two types of real estate brokerage businesses in Japan.

The first is the business of receiving a **brokerage fee** for assisting someone or a company to purchase or sell a piece of real estate. A **real estate agent company** helps the seller find a buyer or a buyer find a good piece of property. In either case, the **broker** receives a brokerage fee, usually a percentage of the **sales price**, for their services. A broker introduces properties, organizes property viewings, provides detailed property information, and executes the transaction procedures.

Another kind of brokerage business is in the **leasing market**, where a broker will help a company, or a person find a property they would like to lease or help a property owner find a tenant. Once the broker finds such a space, or tenant, they receive a brokerage fee, usually based on the monthly rental amount.

It seems that real estate brokers in Japan have heavier responsibilities under the **Real Estate Brokerage Law** than brokers in other foreign countries. The law stipulates what brokers must do in a real estate transaction. To be able to handle TBI, the broker needs an additional license based on the **FIEL.**

Q : Who are the major players in the real estate brokerage business?

A : It depends on the type of business and the type of customer.

In terms of the brokerage business for real estate sale and purchase as it applies mainly to individuals (as opposed to companies), the major players in Japan are subsidiaries of **general real estate companies** and subsidiaries of trust banks.

The major players dealing with companies that wish to buy or sell real estate in Japan are **trust banks**, which have close relations with many domestic companies.

Other major players, especially for foreign investors, are global real estate service provider companies called **global real estate agents**.

In terms of the brokerage business for real estate leasing for both individuals and companies, there are several specialized real estate brokerage companies.

5-4 不動産仲介事業

Q：**不動産仲介事業**とはどのようなビジネスなのですか？

A：主に2つのタイプの不動産仲介ビジネスがあります。

1つは、不動産を売買したい会社や個人の仲介を行って**仲介手数料**を収受するビジネスです。この場合、**不動産仲介会社**は、不動産を売買したい個人や会社から、彼らのために買主や売主を探索します。どちらの場合でも、仲介会社は、**売買価格の数パーセントを仲介手数料として**得ます。仲介会社は、通常、買主や売主の不動産売買手続もサポートします。

もう1つは、**不動産賃貸市場**で仲介を行うタイプです。この場合、仲介会社は、不動産を賃借、もしくは、賃貸したい個人や会社から、彼らに物件やテナントを探索してあげることで、手数料を得ます。この手数料は、1か月分の賃料相当額です。

日本の不動産仲介会社は、**宅地建物取引業法**により、他国の仲介会社よりも重い責任を負っていると思われます。同法には、不動産取引にあたって、仲介会社が何をしなければいけないかが記載されています。信託受益権を扱うためには、仲介会社は、**金融商品取引法**に基づくライセンスも取得する必要があります。

Q：不動産仲介ビジネスの主要なプレイヤーは誰なのですか？

A：それは、ビジネスのタイプと顧客のタイプによります。

不動産売買仲介で主に個人客を対象にしている場合には、**総合不動産会社**や信託銀行の子会社が主要なプレイヤーです。

不動産売買を行う法人客を扱う主要なプレイヤーは、**信託銀行**です。信託銀行は、多くの企業と親密な関係を持っています。

特に海外投資家にとってのその他の主要なプレイヤーは、**グローバルエージェント**と呼ばれる世界的に不動産サービスを行っている会社です。

不動産賃貸仲介に関しては、個人客や法人客を対象にした専門の不動産仲介会社があります。

Basic business model of the real estate brokerage business

Case 1

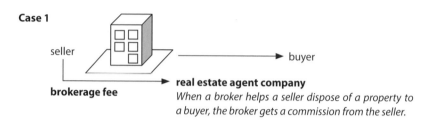

real estate agent company
When a broker helps a seller dispose of a property to a buyer, the broker gets a commission from the seller.

Case 2

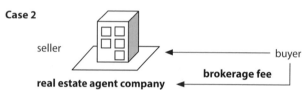

When a broker helps a buyer purchase a property from a seller, the broker gets a commission from the buyer.

Unlike in the US and Europe, in Japan it's not unusual for a broker to receive a commission from both the seller and the buyer. The maximum legal allowable commission is approx. 3% of the purchase price from each side. If the broker is getting paid from both the seller and the buyer, they could receive up to approx. 6% of the purchase price.

Case 3

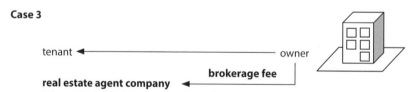

When a broker helps an owner lease their property to a tenant, the broker gets a commission from the owner.

Case 4

When a broker helps a tenant lease a property from the owner, the broker gets a commission from the tenant.

不動産仲介事業の基本的なビジネスモデル

ケース１

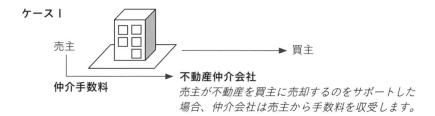

売主 ━━━━━━━━━━━━━━━━━━━━━━▶ 買主

仲介手数料 ━━━━▶ **不動産仲介会社**

売主が不動産を買主に売却するのをサポートした場合、仲介会社は売主から手数料を収受します。

ケース２

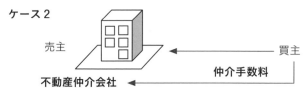

売主 ◀━━━━━━━━━━━━━━━━━━━ 買主

仲介手数料

不動産仲介会社

買主が不動産を売主から取得するのをサポートした場合、仲介会社は買主から手数料を収受します。

米国や欧州と異なり、日本では、売主、買主の両方に売買サポートを行った場合には、その両者から仲介手数料を収受するのが通常です。片側から収受できる手数料は約３％と法律で決められているので、この場合には、最大約６％の手数料を収受することができます。

ケース３

テナント ◀━━━━━━━━━━━━━━━━━━ 所有者

仲介手数料

不動産仲介会社 ◀━━━━━━━

所有者がテナントを探索するのをサポートした場合には、仲介会社は所有者から手数料を収受します。

ケース４

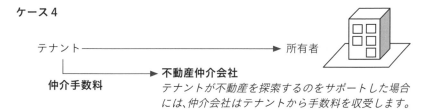

テナント ━━━━━━━━━━━━━━━━━━━━━▶ 所有者

━━━━▶ 不動産仲介会社

仲介手数料

テナントが不動産を探索するのをサポートした場合には、仲介会社はテナントから手数料を収受します。

5-5 Real Estate Management Business

Q : What is the **real estate management business**?

A : This is a business that manages real estate on behalf of the owner. Traditional real estate management businesses in Japan consist of the following two types:

The first type is the daily management services of a **condominium**, performed by a condominium management company. The services would include taking care of the property, performing repairs when needed, cleaning the **common areas**, providing security for the residents, and providing cash management of the **condominium owner's association** reserve fund.

The second type is building maintenance services for an office or retail building. These services include building cleaning, facility maintenance, building security, and other maintenance related duties. This type of business is carried out by **building maintenance companies** and called **building maintenance business.**

Q : Who are the major players in the real estate management business?

A : **General real estate companies** and **condominium developers** usually have subsidiaries that focus on the real estate management business. There are also independent real estate management companies that focus on this business.

Q : What is the **property management business**?

A : Basically, both **property management** and traditional real estate management are very similar, as they both provide daily management services to the owner of the property. However, the term property management is usually used when the investors are owning real estate in a **J-REIT** structure or a **private real estate fund** structure. In such a case the company that is providing the services is called the **property management company**. The services include **building maintenance, leasing management, construction management,** and monthly reporting (**PM reports**) on the income and expenses associated with the property. Many traditional real estate management companies have entered this business.

5-5 不動産管理事業

Q：**不動産管理事業**とはどのようなビジネスなのですか？

A：不動産所有者のために不動産管理を行うビジネスです。伝統的な日本の不動産管理ビジネスには、以下の２つのタイプがあります。

1つ目としては、分譲マンション管理会社が行う**分譲マンション**の日々の管理サービスです。このサービスには、対象不動産の点検、必要な修繕、**共用部分**の清掃、居住者のための警備、**管理組合**で積み立てている積立金の管理等があります。

もう1つは、オフィスビルや商業施設のための建物管理サービスです。この場合の建物管理には、清掃、設備保守、警備などが含まれます。このビジネスは、**建物管理会社**（ビルメンテナンス会社）により行われ、**建物管理事業**とも呼ばれます。

Q：不動産管理事業の主要なプレイヤーは誰なのですか？

A：**総合不動産会社**や**分譲マンションデベロッパー**は、通常、不動産管理事業を手掛ける子会社を持っています。そのほか、不動産管理事業だけに特化した独立系の不動産管理会社もあります。

Q：**プロパティマネジメント事業**とは何ですか？

A：基本的には、**プロパティマネジメント**と伝統的な不動産管理は同じで、両者とも、不動産所有者のための日々の不動産管理サービスを提供します。しかし、プロパティマネジメントという言葉は、特に、投資家が、**J-REIT**や**私募不動産ファンド**を通じて不動産に投資している際に用いられます。この場合に、不動産管理サービスを行う管理会社のことを**プロパティマネジメント会社**と呼びます。これらのサービスには、**建物管理**、**テナント管理**、**修繕管理**、そして、対象不動産に係る収支状況についての**PMレポート**と呼ばれる毎月のレポーティングサービスがあります。多くの伝統的な不動産管理会社が、この業務に参入しています。

Basic business model of the real estate management business

Case 1: Condominium Management Company

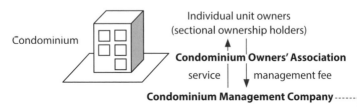

Every resident of the condominium is obliged to join the Condominium Owners' Association to jointly manage the condominium. The association usually enters into a management contract with a condominium management company which is generally a subsidiary of the developer of the condominium.

Case 2: Building Maintenance Company

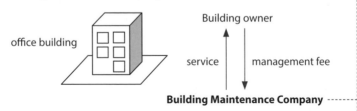

Case 3: Property Management Company

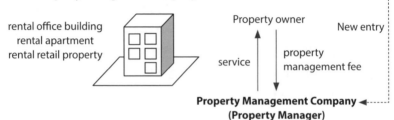

不動産管理事業の基本的なビジネスモデル

ケース１：分譲マンション管理会社

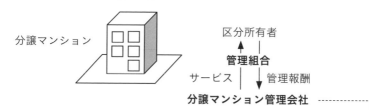

分譲マンションの区分所有者は、共同でマンション管理を行うため、管理組合に入る義務があります。管理組合は、通常、分譲マンション管理会社と管理契約を締結します。この管理会社は、一般的には、当該分譲マンションの開発会社の子会社です。

ケース２：建物管理会社

ケース３：プロパティマネジメント会社

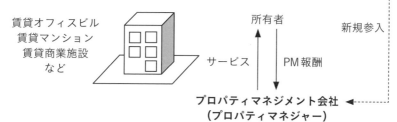

5-6 Real Estate Fund Management Business

Q : What is the **real estate fund management business**?

A : This type of business raises money from a sole investor or multiple investors for the purpose of investing in income producing properties. This business is conducted by **asset management companies**. They are also called **asset managers (AM)**, **fund management companies**, and **fund managers (FM)**. So, this business is also called "real estate asset management business." **AUM** is important for their business because it shows their **investment track record** to investors.

Asset management companies are required to acquire an **investment advisory business** license, or an **investment management business** license based on the FIEL.

Q : With whom does the asset management company make the contract?

A : The AM enters into an **asset management agreement** with the **SPC** used in the real estate fund. These SPCs are called Godo Kaisha in a TK-GK, Tokutei Mokuteki Kaisha in a TMK, and investment corporations in a REIT structure.

Q : What kinds of fees does the asset management company receive?

A : The AM receives an **acquisition fee** when acquiring a property, a **management fee** during the holding period, and a **disposition fee** when selling the property. **Performance fees** based on the performance of management and disposition are sometimes paid to the asset management company.

Q : Who are the major players in the real estate fund management business?

A : Many general real estate companies and other companies like trading companies, railroad companies, and general contractors that develop income producing properties, have set up their subsidiary asset management companies. Additionally, a variety of **financial institutions**, such as banks, trust banks, regional banks, securities companies, insurance companies, etc., have also entered the industry. Foreign private equity firms have also set up their subsidiary asset management companies in Japan.

5-6 不動産ファンド運用事業

Q：**不動産ファンド運用事業**とはどのようなビジネスなのですか？

A：不動産ファンド運用事業とは、単独もしくは複数の投資家の資金を預かって、収益不動産に投資するビジネスのことです。この投資運用の役割を担うのが、**資産運用会社（アセットマネジメント会社）**です。資産運用会社は、**アセットマネジャー（AM）、ファンドマネジメント会社、ファンドマネジャー（FM）**と呼ばれることもあります。ですから、このビジネスは不動産アセットマネジメント事業（不動産運用ビジネス）とも呼ばれます。**運用資産残高**は、**投資実績**を投資家に示すもので資産運用会社のビジネスにおいて重要です。

　資産運用会社は、金融商品取引法に基づく**投資助言業**か**投資運用業**のライセンスを得る必要があります。

Q：資産運用会社は誰と契約を結びますか？

A：不動産ファンドで用いられる**特別目的会社**と**アセットマネジメント契約**を締結します。つまり、TK-GK スキームの場合は合同会社、TMK スキームの場合は特定目的会社、REIT スキームの場合は投資法人です。

Q：資産運用会社はどのような手数料を得ますか？

A：不動産を取得した際の**取得報酬**、運用期間中の**運用報酬**、売却した際の**処分報酬**が主な報酬です。運用実績や売却実績に応じた**実績報酬**を得ることもあります。

Q：不動産ファンド運用事業の主要なプレイヤーは誰なのですか？

A：収益不動産を開発する総合不動産会社の多くが資産運用会社を設立しています。また、不動産開発事業を営む商社、鉄道会社、ゼネコンなども参入しています。このほか、様々な**金融機関**（銀行、信託銀行、地方銀行、証券会社、生保、損保）も資産運用ビジネスの一環として参入しています。海外でプライベートエクイティファンドを運用する資産運用会社も日本で子会社を設立しています。

Types of Funds

*The **comingled fund** is for multiple investors. Examples are J-REITs and Private REITs. On the other hand, a **separate account** is usually for only one investor with a large amount of capital. This can also be called a private real estate fund.*

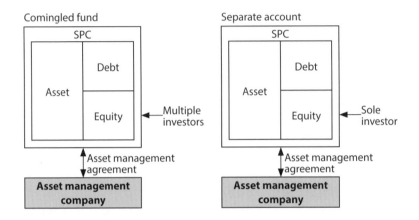

Types of Asset Management Fees

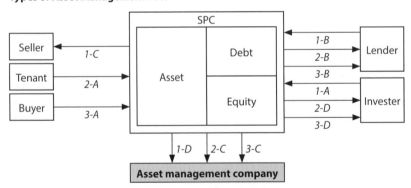

*1-A to 1-D: Acquisition Process (1-D is **acquisition fee**)*
*2-A to 2-D: Management Process (2-C is **management fee**)*
*3-A to 3-D: Disposition Process (3-C is **disposition fee**)*
*If the dividend for investors (2-D and 3-D) exceeds the investor's expectations, a **performance fee** is paid to the asset management company based on the agreement between the investor and the asset management company.*

ファンドのタイプ

コミングルファンドは多数の投資家を対象にしています。例としては、J-REIT や私募REIT が挙げられます。一方、**セパレートアカウント**は通常、豊富な資金を持っている単独投資家のためのものです。私募ファンドの一類型として見られます。

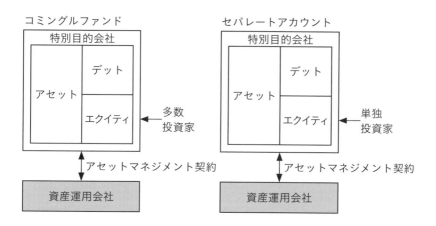

アセットマネジメントフィーのタイプ

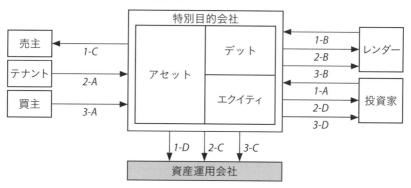

*I-A to ID:取得プロセス（I-Dは**取得報酬**）*
*2-A to 2D:運用プロセス（2-Cは**運用報酬**）*
*3-A to 3D:処分プロセス（3-Cは**処分報酬**）*

もし投資家への配当（2-Dと3-D）が投資家の期待を超えた場合には、投資家と資産運用会社の合意により、**実績報酬**が資産運用会社に支払われることがあります。

5-7 Real Estate Finance Business

Q : What is the primary real estate role of banks in Japan?

A : The main role of banks in Japan relating to real estate is their financing role as **lender**. There are two types of debt financing offered to real estate investors.

The first type is **recourse lending**, whereby traditional corporate loans are made to real estate developers and general real estate companies. The bank usually issues a **mortgage** on the subject property to deal with any potential **default**. In the event the real estate investment is not successful and the sale of the property cannot meet the amount the bank lent, the **borrower** is still responsible for the amount they borrowed, and the bank can seek payment through other properties the borrower owns or through the profits of the borrower's other businesses.

The second type is called **non-recourse lending**, whereby loans are made to real estate investment vehicles like a TMK or GK. The bank issues a mortgage on the subject property or establishes a right of **pledge** over the TBI, which is backed by the subject property. In this case, if the investment fails, the bank cannot seek further payment of the loan beyond the property they agreed to finance. If the investment does fail, the bank can and will take control of the property.

Q : Who are the major **mezzanine lenders**?

A : In Japan, **leasing companies** actively provide **mezzanine loans** to investors. Those loans are also non-recourse loans.

Q : What is the primary real estate role of securities companies in Japan?

A : Regarding J-REITs, the major role of a securities company (Japanese **investment bank**) is to underwrite the **IPO (initial public offering)** and the **PO (public offering)**. **Underwriting** J-REITs means that a securities company first purchases all units issued by an investment corporation in order to resell them to investors.

Securities companies also support private funds including Private REITs, to find equity investors in the capital markets. This role is often called "arranger" in Japan.

5-7 不動産ファイナンス事業

Q：日本の銀行の不動産ビジネスにおける主要な役割は何ですか？

A：日本の銀行の不動産ビジネスにおける主要な役割は、貸し手としての融資の提供です。不動産投資家向けには、2つのタイプの融資（ローン）があります。

1つ目のタイプは、**リコースローン**で、総合不動産会社やデベロッパーに対して提供される伝統的なコーポレートローンです。銀行は、通常、**債務不履行**に対処するために、対象不動産に**抵当権**を設定します。しかし、不動産投資が上手くいかず、不動産を売却しても銀行が融資した額を回収できない場合には、**借り手**は、引き続き融資を受けた額の返済義務を負い、銀行は借り手が保有する他の資産や他のビジネスの利益からの返済を求めることができます。

2つ目のタイプは、特定目的会社や合同会社など不動産投資ビークルへの**ノンリコースローン**です。銀行は、対象不動産に抵当権を設定するか、対象不動産を裏付けとする信託受益権に**質権**を設定します。この場合、もし、不動産投資が失敗に終わっても、銀行は融資の対象となった不動産以外には、その返済原資を求めることができません。投資が失敗に終わった場合に、銀行ができるのは、対象不動産を支配することだけです。

Q：主要な**メザニンレンダー**は誰ですか？

A：日本では、**リース会社**が積極的に**メザニンローン**を投資家に提供しています。このローンもまた、ノンリコースローンになります。

Q：証券会社の不動産ビジネスにおける主な役割は何ですか？

A：J-REITに関しては、証券会社（日本における**投資銀行**）の主な役割は、**新規公募**や公募を引き受けることです。J-REITの**引き受け**とは、投資法人が発行した投資口の全てを、投資家に転売する目的で買い取ることです。

証券会社は、私募REITを含む私募ファンドに対し、資本市場で、エクイティ投資家を探索するサポートを実施しています。このような役割を、日本では、しばしば、アレンジャーと呼んでいます。

Illustrated Real Estate Terminologies

Difference between recourse lending and non-recourse lending

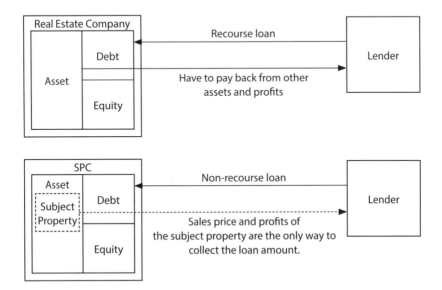

Image of Underwriting Business for J-REITs

After underwriting all units, a securities company will sell the units at an issue price to a variety of investors including domestic institutional investors, domestic retail investors, and foreign institutional investors. Usually, the difference between the underwriting price and the selling price (issue price) is a gross margin (underwriting fee) for the securities company.

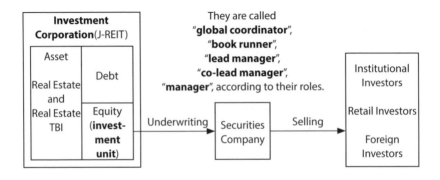

リコースローンとノンリコースローンの違い

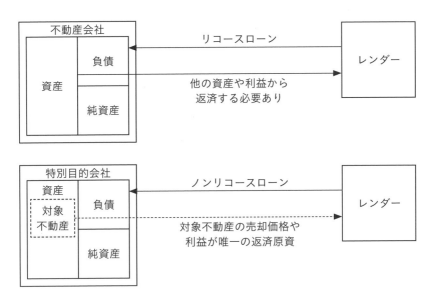

J-REIT の引受業務イメージ

全ての投資口を引き受けた証券会社は、それらを発行価格で様々な投資家に売却します。これらの投資家には、国内機関投資家、国内個人投資家、海外機関投資家が含まれます。通常、引受価額と発行価格の差額が、証券会社の売上、つまり、引受手数料となります。

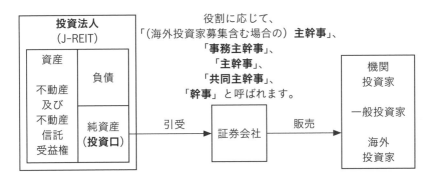

5-8 Real Estate Trust Business

Q : What is the real estate trust business?

A : **Real estate trust** refers to real estate management services when the trust bank acts as the **trustee** on behalf of the **beneficiaries**, which are usually real estate investment vehicles such as investment corporations (J-REIT), TMKs, or GKs. These vehicles hold the **trust beneficiary interests** (**TBI**) and, as such, have the right to receive the profits from the entrusted real estate.

Q : What is a Trust bank?

A : **Trust Banks** are very unique in Japan. They can provide all general banking services and can also provide asset management services for their corporate and individual clients by utilizing trustee functions. Also, unlike **commercial banks**, they can provide real estate related services including real estate brokerage.

Q : What real estate related services do trust banks provide?

A : Other than trust business, trust banks mainly deal with three real estate services: brokerage, real estate finance, and asset management.

Brokerage refers to real estate brokerage services for different kinds of customers including J-REITs, private real estate funds, corporations, and individuals. Brokerage has accounted for a large share of revenues from the real estate business of trust banks.

Real estate finance refers to the business of lending money, which mainly focuses on **non-recourse lending** for real estate investments in Japan.

Asset management includes real estate fund management for **institutional investors** such as **pension funds** and real estate asset management to manage real estate investment vehicles (SPCs).

In addition to the above businesses, trust banks provide REITs with **asset custody services** and general administrative services including accounting work, tax payments, etc. Furthermore, trust banks can be equity investors.

5-8 不動産信託事業

Q：不動産信託業務とは何ですか？

A：**不動産信託**というのは、投資法人、特定目的会社、合同会社といった不動産投資ビークルである**受益者**のために、**受託者**として不動産管理サービスを提供するものです。この場合、これらの投資ビークルは**信託受益権**を持ち、信託されている不動産からの利益を得る権利を有します。

Q：信託銀行とは何ですか？

A：**信託銀行**は、日本特有の銀行です。信託銀行は、法人や個人顧客に対して、通常の銀行業務だけでなく、信託機能を活用した資産運用業務を提供しています。また、信託銀行は、**普通銀行**（**商業銀行**）と異なり、不動産仲介などの不動産関連業務を提供することができます。

Q：信託銀行はどんな不動産関連業務を提供しているのですか？

A：不動産信託業務の他に、信託銀行は、大きく、3つの不動産ビジネスを行っています。仲介、不動産ファイナンス、そして、不動産運用です。

仲介というのは、REIT、私募ファンド、法人、個人などの顧客に対する、不動産仲介サービスです。仲介業務は、信託銀行の不動産ビジネスの中で最大の売上シェアを占めています。

不動産ファイナンスというのは、主に、不動産投資ビークルに対する**ノンリコースローン**の提供です。

運用というのは、**年金基金**などの**機関投資家**のために不動産ファンド運用を行ったり、不動産投資ビークル（特別目的会社）の不動産アセットマネジメントを行ったりすることです。

以上のようなビジネスに加えて、信託銀行は、REITに対して**資産保管業務**や会計事務や納税などの一般事務受託業務を提供しています。さらに、信託銀行はエクイティ投資家になることもあります。

Market Size of Real Estate Trust Business

According to the **Trust Companies Association of Japan**, *the AUM of* **real estate trusts** *is about 56.3 trillion yen as of 2022/9/30. The AUM in 2011/3/30 when the previous version of this book was published was about 24.9 trillion yen.*

Real Estate Business Capabilities of Trust Banks

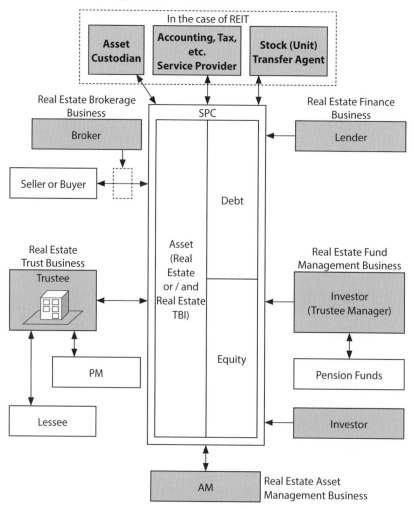

不動産信託業務の市場規模

一般社団法人**信託協会**によれば、2022年9月末時点での不動産信託の総資産は約
56.3兆円です。本書の初版が発行された2011年3月末時点での**不動産信託**の総資
産は、約24.9兆円でした。

信託銀行の不動産ビジネスにおける機能

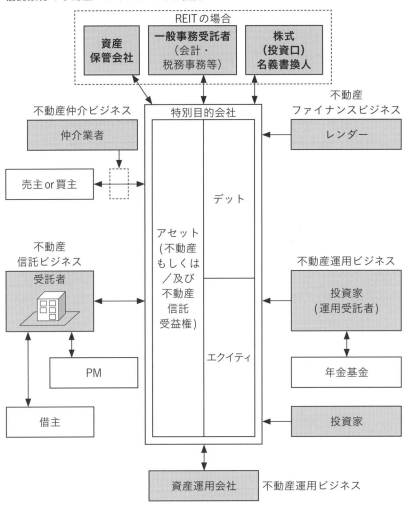

5-9　Real Estate Specialists

Q : Are there any other businesses that are not mentioned in this chapter but are related to real estate in Japan?

A : A variety of real estate specialists are involved in real estate businesses, especially within the real estate fund management sector.

Q : Who deals with real estate registration?

A : **Judicial scriveners** play an important part of the real estate business as they record ownership of a property.

The **registered land and building investigator** and the **land surveyor** play important roles in determining the **boundary lines**. The land and building investigator also records the **registration of the property description**, which includes the size of the land area.

Q : Who is involved in due diligence for real estate transactions?

A : **Engineering reporting firms** and **market reporting firms** emerged in the late 1990's at the beginning of the real estate fund business. These **due diligence** related services, as well as the appraisal service provided by **real estate appraisers**, are critical parts of the real estate investment process.

Q : Who is involved in investment structuring for real estate transactions?

A : **Law firms, tax firms**, and **accounting firms** also play a big role in the real estate fund business and assist with the fund structure and contracts related to purchasing and owning real estate in Japan.

Q : Are there any specialists relating to real estate ESG?

A : More asset managers are considering acquiring **environmental certifications** to attract investors. For this reason, many companies, including trust banks, engineering reporting firms, **architectural design firms**, etc. provide related consulting services.

5-9 不動産専門家

Q：本章でこれまで述べた以外の不動産関連事業にはどのようなビジネスがありますか？

A：様々な不動産の専門家が不動産ビジネス、特に不動産ファンド運用ビジネスに関わっています。

Q：不動産登記には誰が関わりますか？

A：**司法書士**も、不動産の所有権に係る登記を行うことから、不動産ビジネスにおいて重要な役割を果たしています。

土地家屋調査士と**測量士**は、**境界**を確定する上で、重要な役割を果たします。また、土地家屋調査士は、土地面積などの**不動産表示登記**も取扱います。

Q：不動産のデューデリジェンスには誰が関わりますか？

A：**ER作成業者**と**マーケットレポート作成業者**は、不動産ファンドビジネスがスタートした1990年代後半から登場してきました。彼らの**デューデリジェンス関連サービス**と**不動産鑑定士**による鑑定は、不動産投資プロセスにおいて欠かせないものです。

Q：不動産投資のストラクチャリングには誰が関わりますか？

A：**法律事務所**、**税務事務所**、**会計事務所**もまた、不動産ファンドビジネスにおいて大きな役割を果たしており、日本における不動産取得や所有に関連したファンドストラクチャーや契約をサポートしています。

Q：不動産ESGに関連する専門家はいますか？

A：より多くの資産運用会社が投資家にアピールするために**環境認証**を得ることを考えています。ですから、信託銀行、ER作成会社、**設計会社**など多くの会社が関連するコンサルティングサービスを提供しています。

Real estate transactions between parties, including general corporations and individuals

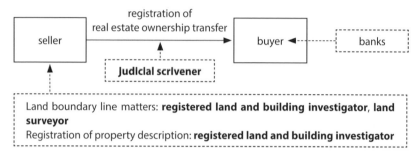

Real estate transactions where an SPC is the buyer

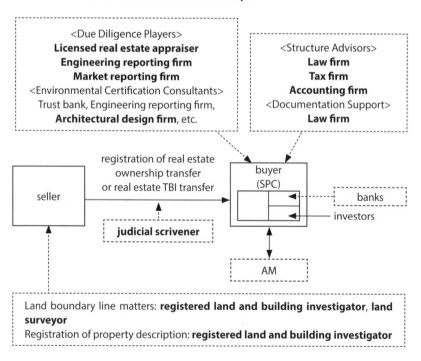

会社や個人間の不動産取引

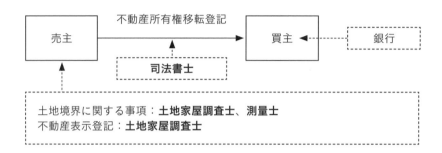

SPCが買主となる不動産取引

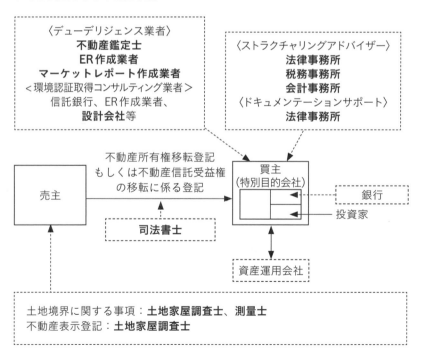

5-10 Other Real Estate Related Parties

Q : What kinds of construction companies are there in Japan?

A : There are mainly two types of **construction companies.** The first is the **general contractor**, who coordinates the entire construction process. The second is the **sub-contractor**, who works under the general contractor and mainly focuses on building systems such as HVAC systems, electrical systems and plumbing systems.

Q : In the real estate fund business, who communicates with construction companies?

A : Property management companies are responsible for a variety of tasks and communication with contractors under the direction of the asset management company. Property management companies are usually asked to repair/fix the damages of the building, the malfunctions of the plumbing, etc., by tenants and are responsible for managing these requests.

Q : What kinds of companies are tenants and end-users of real estate?

A : Almost all companies use real estate for their business, whether as owners or tenants. They need **headquarters buildings** for employees to communicate with each other and their clients. Companies that sell their products through the internet must use a **warehouse** to stock their products.

Q : What kinds of real estate funds are offered to investors?

A : Real estate funds can be divided into several products according to their risk and return characteristics. **Core funds,** like private REITs, provide stable income returns to investors. **Core-plus funds** provide a stable income return and also capital appreciation over the investment period. **Value-add funds** try to increase rental income through renovation work and then pursue a capital gain when they sell. **Opportunity funds** aim to maximize capital gains by buying distressed investment opportunities.

5-10 その他不動産関係者

Q：建設会社にはどのような種類がありますか？

A：大きくは、2つのタイプの**建設会社**があります。1つは、建設工事全体を請け負う**ゼネコン**です。もう1つは、その下請けで主に空調設備、電気設備、給排水設備などの設備工事を請け負う**サブコン**です。

Q：不動産ファンドにおいては、誰が建設会社とコミュニケーションをとりますか？

A：アセットマネジメント会社の指示の下で、プロパティマネジメント会社が、対象建物の各種工事に関して、建設会社と連携をとります。プロパティマネジメント会社は、通常、テナントから建物の修繕や水道設備の故障などの修繕を依頼され、それらに対応します。

Q：不動産のエンドユーザーやテナントにはどのような会社がありますか？

A：ほとんどすべての会社が所有者もしくはテナントとして、自らのビジネスで不動産を利用しています。会社は、従業員がお互いや顧客とコミュニケーションをするために**本社ビル**を必要とします。インターネットで商品を売っている会社もそれらの商品を保管する**倉庫**が必要です。

Q：どのような不動産ファンド商品が投資家に提供されていますか？

A：不動産ファンドは、そのリスクリターン特性に応じて、いくつかの商品に分けられます。私募REITのような**コアファンド**は、安定的なインカムリターンを投資家に提供します。**コアプラスファンド**は、安定的なリターンと長期的な対象不動産の価値向上も図ります。バリューアッドファンドはバリューアップ工事などによる賃料収入の上昇とそれによる売却益を狙います。**オポチュニティファンド**は、不良債権の取得など売却益を狙うファンドです。

Real Estate Fund and Related Parties

A variety of companies dealing with the following businesses are involved in real estate as a seller, tenant, and buyer.

- **Accommodation business**
- **Construction business**
- **Education business**
- **Finance business**
- **Information and communication business**
- **Insurance business**
- **Manufacturing business**
- **Medical business**
- **Real estate business**
- **Restaurant business**
- **Retail business**
- **Service business**
- **Transportation business**
- **Utility business**
- **Welfare business**
- **Wholesale business**

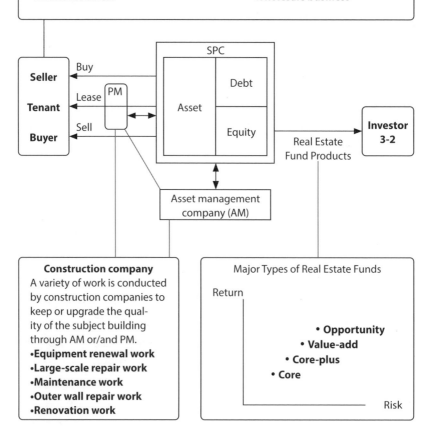

SPC

	Debt
Asset	
	Equity

Seller — Buy
Tenant — Lease — PM
Buyer — Sell

Real Estate Fund Products → **Investor 3-2**

Asset management company (AM)

Construction company
A variety of work is conducted by construction companies to keep or upgrade the quality of the subject building through AM or/and PM.
- **Equipment renewal work**
- **Large-scale repair work**
- **Maintenance work**
- **Outer wall repair work**
- **Renovation work**

Major Types of Real Estate Funds

Return

- **Opportunity**
- **Value-add**
- **Core-plus**
- **Core**

Risk

不動産ファンドと関係者

以下のようなビジネスを営む様々な会社が売主、テナント、買主として不動産に関わっています。

- ・宿泊業
- ・建設業
- ・教育業
- ・金融業
- ・情報通信業
- ・保険業
- ・製造業
- ・医療業

- ・不動産業
- ・飲食業
- ・小売業
- ・サービス業
- ・運輸業
- ・電気・ガス・熱供給・水道業
- ・福祉業
- ・卸売業

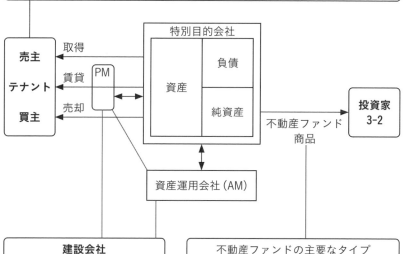

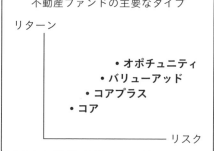

建設会社
対象建物の質を保持したり上昇させたりするためにAMやPMを通じて様々な工事が建設会社により実施されます。

- ・設備更新工事
- ・大規模修繕工事
- ・メンテナンス工事
- ・外壁改修工事
- ・改修工事

不動産ファンドの主要なタイプ

リターン

- ・オポチュニティ
- ・バリューアッド
- ・コアプラス
- ・コア

リスク

How does a real estate fund make money for its investors?

Column

When a **fund management company (FM)** is interested in raising money from investors, it needs to determine the strategy and **target return** of the fund. The FM will try to convince investors that their strategy and returns will be attractive and appropriate for the prevailing market cycle.

In the real estate investment business, there are two kinds of returns that matter the most to investors. The first is called the **cash-on-cash return** and this is the annual percentage return after all fees, expenses and taxes that can be distributed to investors in the form of a **dividend**. Investors in Japan usually look for a 3% to 6% annual cash on cash return. The second kind of return is called the **internal rate of return**, or **IRR**. This is also referred to as the **total return**. The primary difference between the cash-on-cash return and the IRR is time. The IRR calculation considers the amount of time the investment takes from acquisition to disposition of the property and makes the calculation to determine the average annual return over the time period the investment has been made.

The typical **investment period**, or **holding period**, for a fund in Japan is 3 to 7 years. During this time, the FM will do their best to actively manage and increase the performance of the real estate. Usually, the cash-on-cash return will be distributed back to investors **each quarter** or **semi-annually**. At the end of the life of the fund, the FM will hopefully sell the real estate for a **capital gain**, which means the real estate was sold for more money than it was purchased.

After the real estate has been sold, the fees, expenses, taxes, debt finance and the initial equity investment are deducted, and the resulting capital gain is distributed back to the investors. Then the IRR can be calculated by adding in the amount of time that has passed from the start of the investment to the disposition of the property. If the FM has done a very good job, the IRR can reach over 20%. Investors in Japanese real estate funds usually seek an IRR of over 7%.

投資家は不動産ファンドでどのように利益を得ているのか?

　資産運用会社は、投資家から資金を集めようとする場合、ファンドの戦略や**目標利回り**を決定する必要があります。資産運用会社は、彼らの戦略や利回りが魅力的であり、マーケットサイクルの中で適切であるということを投資家に十分に納得させる必要があります。

　不動産投資ビジネスにおいては、投資家は2種類の利回りに関心があります。まず、一つ目は、**キャッシュオンキャッシュリターン**です。これは、全ての手数料、費用、そして税金を控除した後に**配当**という形で投資家に分配できる現金ベースの年当たり投資利回りになります。日本における投資家は、通常、3%から6%程度の年間キャッシュオンキャッシュリターンを求めます。二つ目は、**内部収益率**、つまり、アイ・アール・アール（IRR）です。これは総合利回りとも言えます。キャッシュオンキャッシュリターンとIRRとの主な違いは、時間の概念です。IRRは、不動産に投資してから売却までに要する時間が考慮され、投資期間全体における年平均の投資利回りを意味します。

　日本におけるファンドの通常の**投資期間**、つまり、**保有期間**は、3年から7年です。この間、資産運用会社は、投資家によい配当を提供できるように、不動産を運用していきます。通常、**四半期**ごとに、キャッシュオンキャッシュリターンが投資家に分配されます。資産運用会社は、ファンド期間の終わりに、**売却益**の獲得を目指して不動産を売却します。売却益は、購入価格よりも売却価格が高いことを意味します。

　不動産を売却した後、全ての手数料、費用、そして税金が控除され、当初投資額と一緒にキャピタルゲインが投資家に配当されます。そして、対象不動産の投資から売却までの期間を考慮したIRRが計算されます。もし、資産運用会社が非常によい投資を行った場合にはIRRは20%を超えることもあります。日本での不動産ファンドで投資家が求めるIRRは通常7%超です。

Column | What is the future of real estate investment in Japan?

Japan is one of the largest real estate markets in the world and continues to attract foreign and domestic capital into buildings, developments, and land throughout the country. The **Tokyo Metropolis** remains the most attractive and popular area for investors as Japan continues its trend of inward migration away from the outlying areas and into the major cities of Tokyo, Osaka, Nagoya and Fukuoka.

With the continued influx of people and capital directed toward central Tokyo, **land values** have continued to rise, and new development and office supply continues to be absorbed. The best areas of Tokyo continue to get better and more valuable and the urban ancillary areas have benefited from the new developments and central expansion.

The **J-REIT** market is now turning 20-years old and has continued to mature and expand with consistent interest from foreign and domestic institutional and retail investors. Further consolidations, new listings and acquisitions will propel the Tokyo real estate market forward over the next few decades.

New trends have also emerged during the last 10 years, including property developers pushing into the ultra-high-end luxury residential and hotel markets. Expanding and growing tourism focused on luxury travelers will continue to inspire and influence the next wave of developments in central Tokyo. The possibility of casinos and expanded conference developments will also add to Japan's potential for attracting more high-end visitors.

コラム 今後の日本での不動産投資はどうなるのか?

　日本は世界最大の不動産市場の一つで、日本中の建物、開発、土地に、海外投資家や国内投資家の資金を惹きつけています。**東京都**は、投資家にとって引き続き最も魅力的で最も人気のあるエリアです。なぜなら、日本では、周辺都市から、東京、大阪、名古屋、福岡などの大都市への人口流入の流れが続いているからです。

　人口の流入と資本が東京に向かう中で、**土地価格**は上昇し、供給は消化されています。東京の中心部はよりよく、また、更なる開発や中心部の拡大により、隣接地域もこの恩恵を被るでしょう。

　J-REIT市場は、開設して今や20年となり、海外や国内の機関投資家や個人投資家の継続的な関心を集め、拡大を続けています。更なる合併、新たな上場や不動産取得が、東京の不動産市場を今後数十年の間にさらに活発にすることでしょう。

　また、デベロッパーが超富裕層を対象とした高級住宅やホテルを開発するという新たな流れも過去10年で起こっています。富裕層訪日客を対象としたインバウンドも拡大を続けており、東京の新たな開発に影響を与えていくでしょう。カジノや関連した会議施設の開発可能性もあり、そういった開発があれば、訪日富裕層にとっての日本の魅力はより増すことになるでしょう。

英語索引 (English Index)

English	Synonyms	Japanese	Page
Asset Liquidation Law	Act on the Securitization of Assets	資産の流動化に関する法律、資産流動化法	122, 182
Asset Liquidation Plan	ALP	資産流動化計画	122, 182, 184
asset management agreement	asset management contract	アセットマネジメント契約（書）	178, 180, 212
asset management company	asset manager	資産運用会社、アセットマネジメント会社	110, 112, 118, 120, 126, 138, 190, 212
asset manager	AM, asset management company	アセットマネジャー	210
assuming full occupancy		満室想定	156
AUM	asset under management	運用資産残高	210

English	Synonyms	Japanese	Page
bank		銀行	106, 108, 224
bank account		銀行口座	184
bank transfer	bank remittance	銀行送金	184
bankruptcy remote entity		倒産隔離のための器	120, 124
bankruptcy remoteness		倒産隔離	174, 176
bankruptcy risk		倒産リスク	174
banquet room		宴会場	74
base rate		ベースレート	170
base rate		基準金利	170
bathroom		浴室	92
bathtub		浴槽	92
BCR	building coverage ratio, lot coverage ratio	建ぺい率	34
beneficiary	trust beneficiary	受益者	134, 136, 218
beneficiary certificate		受益証券	108
bid		入札	146
billboard income	billboard revenue	看板収入	156
bond		債券	102
bond agreement		社債契約（書）	180
book runner		事務主幹事	216
book value		簿価	148
borrower	debtor	借り手	214
boundary dispute		境界紛争	148
boundary line	boundary, land boundary line, property line	境界	222
broker	real estate agent company	仲介会社	202
brokerage fee	agent fee, brokerage commission, broker's commission	仲介手数料	202, 204
BTS	Build-to-Suit	BTS型	70
building		建物	14, 16
building age		築年数	148
building completion date		建物竣工年月日	148
building condition		建物状況	162
building construction cost	construction cost	建築工事費	194
building coverage ratio	BCR, lot coverage ratio	建ぺい率	34, 36
building demolition cost		建物解体費用	196

English	Synonyms	Japanese	Page
building design		建物の意匠、建物のデザイン	90
building environmental risk		建物環境リスク	162
building facility		建物の設備	90
building inspection certificate	certificate of occupancy	検査済証	34
building lease contract	building lease agreement	借家契約	48
building maintenance		建物管理	206
building maintenance business	building management business	建物管理事業	206
building maintenance company	building management company	建物管理会社、ビルメンテナンス会社	206, 208
building owner		建物所有者	20
building ownership		建物所有権	18
building permit	building permission, building confirmation	建築確認	34, 90
building registry	building register	建物登記簿、全部事項証明書(建物)	24, 136
Building Standards Law	Building Standards Act	建築基準法	26, 28, 34, 164
building structure		建物の構造、建物構造	90, 148
building tax assessed value		建物課税標準額	158
Build-to-Suit	BTS	ビルド・トゥ・スーツ型	70
bullet repayment	balloon payment, bullet payment	期限一括返済	170
Bunkyo Ward	Bunkyo City	文京区	62, 64
business commencement notification		業務開始届出	184
business district		オフィス街	64
business hotel	economy hotel, budget hotel, limited service hotel	ビジネスホテル	74, 76

C

English	Synonyms	Japanese	Page
CA	NDA, confidentiality agreement	秘密保持契約(書)	50
CAM income	common benefit	共益費収入	154, 156
cancellation notice		解約予告	150
cancellation penalty income		解約違約金収入	156
cancellation request		解約請求	116
CAP rate	capitalization rate	還元利回り、キャップレート	160, 166
CAPEX	capital expenditure	資本的支出	158, 160, 162
capital expenditure	CAPEX	資本的支出	160
capital gain		キャピタルゲイン、売却益	102, 104, 230
capital loss		キャピタルロス、売却損	102
capitalization rate	CAP rate	還元利回り、キャップレート	166
cash		現金	102
cash flow analysis		キャッシュフロー分析	156
cash multiple		キャッシュマルチプル	172
cash on cash return	cash on cash yield	キャッシュオンキャッシュリターン	230
cash reserve		積立金	170
catchment area	market area, trading area, trade area	商圏	66
ceiling		天井	96
ceiling height		天井高	70, 96
Chiba Prefecture	Chiba	千葉県	60, 82, 84

English	Synonyms	Japanese	Page
condominium owners' association	owners' association, home owners' association	管理組合	60, 206, 208
condominium specialized developer		分譲マンション専業デベロッパー	194
confidentiality agreement	non-disclosure agreement	秘密保持契約（書）	50
conflict of interest		利益相反	126
construction business		建設業	228
construction company		建築会社	148, 226
construction management		修繕管理	206
consumption tax	sales tax, Value Added Tax, VAT	消費税	42
contract date	date of contract	契約日	52
contractor		施工会社	90
convention room		会議場	74
co-ownership	joint ownership	共有	18, 20
core fund		コアファンド	226
core-plus fund		コアプラスファンド	226
corporate income tax	corporate tax	法人税	42
Corporate Law	Company Law, Companies Act	会社法	118
corporate tax	corporate income tax	法人税	42, 44, 110, 112, 114, 174, 198
cost approach		原価法	166
covenant		コベナンツ	170
COVID-19		コロナ	58
CP	conditions precedent, loan execution conditions	貸付実行前提条件	170, 182

D			
English	Synonyms	Japanese	Page
D		乾燥機	96
daily necessities		生活必需品	80
data center		データセンター	78
data center operator		DC運営者	78
daytime population		昼間人口	86
DCF Method	Discounted Cash Flow Method	DCF法	166, 168
debt service coverage ratio	DSCR	元利返済金カバー率	170
deemed security		みなし有価証券	138
default		債務不履行	214
delinquent tenant		延滞テナント	150
delivery box		宅配ボックス	92
department store		百貨店	66
deposit*	down payment	手付金	52
deposit*		預金	106
deposit*	security deposit	敷金	156
depreciable asset		償却資産	42, 158
designated confirmation and inspection body		指定確認検査機関	34
detached house	detached housing, single family house, single family detached home, single family housing	戸建住宅	14, 58, 60
development profit		開発利益	194
Direct Capitalization Method		直接還元法	166, 168

＊使い分け方が異なるため、別項目としています。

English	Synonyms	Japanese	Page
direct real estate investment		直接不動産投資	106, 108, 130, 132
disabled people		障がい者	38
discount rate		割引率	166
Discounted Cash Flow Method	DCF method	DCF法	166, 168
discretionary investment management business		投資一任業	140
disposition fee		処分報酬	210, 212
distance from the nearest station		最寄駅からの距離	148
diversification		分散投資	102, 104
dividend	distribution	配当、分配金	102, 120, 128, 230
double taxation		二重課税	118, 126, 174
driver's license		運転免許証	52
drugstore		ドラッグストア	66
dryer		乾燥機	96
DSCR	debt service coverage ratio	元利返済金カバー率	170
due diligence		詳細な調査、デューデリジェンス	50, 134, 152, 222

E

English	Synonyms	Japanese	Page
earthquake insurance		地震保険	164
earthquake reinforcement work		耐震補強工事	162
earthquake resistance	seismic adequacy	耐震性	164
earthquake risk		地震リスク	162, 164
E-commerce		電子商取引	70, 80
economy hotel	business hotel, budget hotel, limited service hotel	ビジネスホテル	76
education business		教育業	228
effective gross income	EGI, effective gross revenue	有効総収入	156, 158
EGI	effective gross income, effective gross revenue	有効総収入	156, 158
elderly people		高齢者	38, 80
electric power company		電力会社	194
electrical systems	electric systems	電気設備	90, 92
elevator	lift	エレベーター	60, 64, 92
elevator hall		エレベーターホール	64
encroachment		越境	148
end tenant		エンドテナント	200
engineering report	ER	エンジニアリングレポート	162
engineering reporting firm	ER writer	ER作成業者	222, 224
entertainment district	downtown area, highly bustling district	繁華街	66
entrance area	entrance hall	エントランス	60, 64
entrusted asset	trust asset	信託財産	134, 136
environmental certification	environmental certificate, green building certification, green certification	環境認証	128, 222
equipment		備品	74
equipment renewal work	plumbing replacement work, HVAC replacement work	設備更新工事	228
ER	engineering report	エンジニアリングレポート	162, 164

English	Synonyms	Japanese	Page
escalator		エスカレーター	64, 92
escrow agent		エスクロー・エージェント	54
escrow system		エスクロー制度	54
ESG investment	ESG investing, sustainable investing	ESG投資	128
estimated sales price		推定売却価格	148
exclusive industrial zone	exclusive industrial district	工業専用地域	32
exclusive negotiation period		独占交渉期間	150
exclusive seller's agent		売主側の単独仲介業者	146
existing rent	current rent, ongoing rent	現行賃料	154
expected rate of return	expected return	期待利回り	160
expiration date		有効期限	150
expressway interchange		高速道路の・インターチェンジ	70
external management		外部運用型	110, 112

F

English	Synonyms	Japanese	Page
facility		設備	62
family office		ファミリーオフィス	106
FAR	floor area ratio	容積率	34
faucet		蛇口	92
fee simple estate	fee simple real estate, real estate, real property	現物不動産	130, 134, 136, 148
FF&E	furniture, fixtures, and equipment	家具・什器・備品	74
fiduciary duty		受託者責任	134
FIEL	Financial Instruments and Exchange Law, FIEA: Financial Instruments and Exchange Act	金融商品取引法	118, 138, 202
finance business	financial business	金融業	228
financial institution		金融機関	210
Financial Instruments and Exchange Law	FIEL, FIEA: Financial Instruments and Exchange Act	金融商品取引法	118, 138
financial product		金融商品	14, 138
fire extinguisher		消火器	92
fire prevention district		防火地域	30
fire prevention equipment		消防設備	90, 92
Fire Protection Law	Fire Service Act, Fire Defense Law	消防法	26
fire sprinkler		スプリンクラー	92
fixed asset tax	property tax	固定資産税	42, 44, 158
fixed asset tax value		固定資産税評価額	158
fixed rate	fixed interest rate	固定金利	170
fixed rent		固定賃料	58, 62, 66, 68, 70, 74, 78
fixed rent with percentage rent	fixed rent with sales-linked rent, variable rent based on sales	売上歩合付固定賃料	66, 68, 74
fixed term building lease right		定期借家権	46, 48
fixed term land lease right	fixed term land leasehold right	定期借地権	46, 48
fixed-term building lease contract	fixed-term building lease agreement	定期借家契約	48
fixed-term land lease contract	fixed-term land lease agreement	定期借地契約	48
fixed-term lease		定借	46, 58, 62, 154

English	Synonyms	Japanese	Page
fixture		什器	74
floating rate	variable rate, variable interest rate	変動金利	170
flood risk		水害リスク	78
floor		床	96
floor area ratio	FAR, floor space index, plot ratio, site ratio	容積率	34, 36
floor plan		間取り図	148
floor weight capacity		床荷重	70
FM	fund management company, fund manager	資産運用会社、ファンドマネジャー	210
foreign investor	overseas investor	海外投資家	186
foreign real estate agent company	foreign real estate brokerage company, global agent	外資系不動産仲介会社	146
foreign visitor		外国人訪日客	80
former earthquake resistance standards		旧耐震基準	164
free-rent period	rent-free period	フリーレント期間	154
FSA	Financial Services Agency	金融庁	122, 126, 134
Fukuoka City	Fukuoka	福岡市	58, 60, 62, 84
Fukuoka Prefecture	Fukuoka	福岡県	60, 84
full service hotel		フルサービス型ホテル	74, 76
fund management company	FM, fund manager	ファンドマネジメント会社	210, 230
fund manager	FM, fund management company	ファンドマネジャー	210
furniture		家具	74

G			
English	**Synonyms**	**Japanese**	**Page**
gas equipment	gas installation	ガス設備	90, 92
gas stove		ガスコンロ	92
gearing ratio	loan to value ratio, LTV	ギアリング・レシオ	140
general contractor		ゼネコン	162, 194, 226
general merchandise store	GMS	総合スーパー	66
general partner		ジェネラルパートナー	120
general partnership	ordinary partnership	任意組合	118, 120
general real estate company	comprehensive real estate company	総合不動産会社	194, 198, 202, 206
GFA	gross floor area	延床面積	22, 148
GHG	greenhouse gas	温室効果ガス	128
Ginza		銀座	66, 68
GK		合同会社	118
global coordinator		主幹事	216
global real estate agent		グローバルエージェント	202
GMS	general merchandise store	総合スーパー	66
Godo Kaisha		合同会社	118
GOP	gross operating profit	営業総利益	74
government-ordinance-designated city	cities designated by ordinance, cities designated by cabinet order, cabinet order designated city, ordinance-designated city	政令指定都市	40, 82
Greater Nagoya Area	Greater Nagoya	中部圏、名古屋圏	72
Greater Osaka Area	Greater Osaka	近畿圏、大阪圏	70, 72
Greater Tokyo Area	Greater Tokyo, Tokyo Metropolitan Area	首都圏、東京圏	58, 60, 70, 72, 82, 84

English	Synonyms	Japanese	Page
green space		緑地面積	38
greenhouse gas	GHG	温室効果ガス	128
grocery store		食料雑貨品店	66
gross floor area	GFA, total floor area, total floor space	延床面積	22, 148
ground rent		地代	20, 160
guest		宿泊者	80
guideline		要綱	38
Guidelines Regarding Appraisal of Securitized Properties		証券化対象不動産の鑑定評価に関する実務指針	166
guaranteed rent type master lease		賃料保証型マスターリース	200

H

English	Synonyms	Japanese	Page
hallway		廊下	60, 64
handrail		手すり	38
headquarters building	head-office building	本社ビル	226
hedge against inflation	inflationary hedge	インフレヘッジ	102
height limit	height restriction	高さ制限	34
high net worth individual	HNWI	富裕層	106
high-rise apartment		タワーマンション（賃貸）	36
high-rise building		高層ビル	36
high-rise condominium		タワーマンション（分譲）	36
high street retail property		大通り沿いの商業店舗ビル	66
Hiroshima City	Hiroshima	広島市	84
Hiroshima Prefecture	Hiroshima	広島県	84
HNWI	high net worth individual	富裕層	106
Hokkaido	Hokkaido Island	北海道	82, 84
Hokkaido Prefecture	Hokkaido	北海道	40, 60, 76, 84
holding period		保有期間	230
Honshu	Honshu Island	本州	82, 84
hotel		ホテル	14
household		世帯	58
HVAC Systems	air conditioning facilities, HVAC (Heat, Ventilation, and Air Conditioning) systems	空調設備	90, 92
Hyogo Prefecture	Hyogo	兵庫県	84

I

English	Synonyms	Japanese	Page
identity verification document	identification document, identity confirmation document	本人確認書類	52
illegal building		違法建築物	34, 148
illegal parking		違法駐車	38
Imperial Palace		皇居	88
income approach	income capitalization approach	収益還元法	166
income gain		インカムゲイン	104
income-producing property	commercial property, investment property	収益不動産、収益物件	14, 16, 112
income tax	personal income tax	所得税	42
indirect real estate investment		間接不動産投資	106, 108, 110
individual unit	living space, exclusively owned area	専有部分	60
indoor fire hydrant		屋内消火栓	92

English	Synonyms	Japanese	Page
indoor wall		内壁	96
industrial zone	industrial district	工業地域	32
industrial zoning district	industrial district	工業地域	30, 32
information and communication business	information and telecommunication industry	情報通信業	228
initial beneficiary		当初受益者	136
initial public offering	IPO	新規公募	214
initial trust set up fee	initial trust fee	当初信託報酬	134
institutional investor	professional investor	機関投資家	98, 106, 108, 114, 126, 218
insurance business		保険業	228
insurance company		保険会社	106, 108
insurance premium	insurance fee, premium	保険料、損害保険料	106, 158, 160
intercom		インターホン	92
interest		利息	102
interest rate		金利	138, 140
internal rate of return	IRR	内部収益率	230
international luxury brand hotel		外資系高級ホテル	76
International Valuation Standards	IVS	国際評価基準	168
investment advisory business		投資助言業	138, 140
investment bank		投資銀行	215
investment corporation		投資法人	110, 126, 128
investment corporation bond		投資法人債	128
investment grade property		投資適格物件	134
investment management business		投資運用業	138, 140
investment period		投資期間	230
investment property	commercial property, income producing property	投資不動産	14
investment return		投資利回り	138, 170, 172
investment security		投資証券	138
investment track record		投資実績	210
Investment Trust and Investment Corporation Law	Act on Investment Trusts and Investment Corporations	投資信託及び投資法人に関する法律、投信法	126
investment unit	investment security, unit	投資口、投資証券	128, 138, 216
investment yield	investment return	投資利回り	98
IPO	initial public offering	新規公募	214
IRR	internal rate of return	内部収益率	230
ISH		一般社団法人	174
IVS	International Valuation Standards	国際評価基準	168

J

English	Synonyms	Japanese	Page
Japanese Generally Accepted Accounting Principles	JGAAP	日本の会計基準	148
Japanese government bond	JGB	日本国債	138

Japanese Real Estate Appraisal Standards	Real Estate Appraisal Standards	不動産鑑定評価基準	14, 166, 168
Japanese Real Estate Investment Trust		日本の不動産投資信託	126
JGAAP	Japanese Generally Accepted Accounting Principles	日本の会計基準	148
JGB	Japanese Government Bond	日本国債	138, 168
joint ownership	co-ownership	共有	18, 20
J-REIT		日本の不動産投資信託	126
judicial scrivener		司法書士	22, 24, 182, 222, 224
Justice Ministry		法務省	22
justifiable reason	just cause, justifiable grounds, good cause	正当事由	46

English	Synonyms	Japanese	Page
loan to value ratio	gearing ratio	負債比率、ローン・トゥ・バリュー	140
LOC	letter of commitment to purchase	買付証明書	50, 52
local financial bureau		地方財務局	122
local government	local municipality	地方公共団体、地方自治体	38, 40
location*		立地	62, 66, 70
location*		位置図	148
location map		位置図	148
logistics property		物流施設	14, 70, 72
LOI	letter of intent	購入意向表明書	50, 52, 54, 150, 152, 186
long term lease		長期賃貸借	78
loop railway line	circle railway line	環状線	86
low interest rate		低金利	170
LTC	loan to cost, loan to cost ratio	総取得コストに対する借入額の比率	140
LTP	loan to purchase price, LTPP	購入価格に対する借入額の比率	140
LTV	gearing ratio, loan to value ratio	負債比率	140, 170
lump sum payment		一括決済	52

M

English	Synonyms	Japanese	Page
machine parking		機械式駐車場	38
mailbox		メールボックス	92
maintenance cost	building maintenance cost, building maintenance fee, building management cost, building management expenses	維持管理費、建物管理費	158, 160
maintenance work		メンテナンス工事	228
mall		モール	66
management contract		運営委託型	74
management fee	asset management fee	運用報酬	210, 212
manager		幹事	216
manufacturing business		製造業	228
market approach	sales comparison approach	取引事例比較法	166
market area population	catchment area population	商圏人口	68
market capitalization	market cap	時価総額	126
market rent		市場賃料、相場賃料	154
market reporting firm		マーケットレポート作成業者	222, 224
market value		市場価値	166, 168
master lease		一括賃貸	200
master lease agreement		マスターリース契約(書)	180
master lessee		マスターレッシー、一括賃借人	180, 200
MB		メーターボックス	96
medical business	medical service industry	医療業	228
medium to small sized building		中小ビル	62
Meguro Ward	Meguro City	目黒区	62, 64
merger and acquisition		合併・買収	126
mezzanine lender		メザニンレンダー	124
mezzanine loan		メザニンローン	124
meter box		メーターボックス	96
Minato Ward	Minato City	港区	62, 64
Ministry of Land, Infrastructure, Transport, and Tourism	MLIT	国土交通省	30
minor repair cost	repair cost, repair expense	修繕費	158, 160

＊使い分け方が異なるため、別項目としています。

English	Synonyms	Japanese	Page
Miyagi Prefecture	Miyagi	宮城県	84
MLIT	Ministry of Land, Infrastructure, Transport, and Tourism	国土交通省	30, 130, 166
modern logistics facility	advanced logistics facility	先進的物流施設	70, 72
monthly rent per tsubo		坪当たり月額賃料	156
mortgage		抵当権	22, 178, 214
Multi-Tenant		マルチテナント型	70
multiple tenants		複数テナント	148
multi-use complex	mixed-use property	複合施設	194
mutual fund	investment trust, unit trust	投資信託	106, 108

N			
English	Synonyms	Japanese	Page
Nagoya City	Nagoya	名古屋市	58, 60, 62, 64, 84
National Land Use Planning Law	National Land Use and Planning Law, National Land Use Planning Act	国土利用計画法	26
natural disaster		自然災害	34
NCF	net cash flow	ネットキャッシュフロー	158, 160
NDA	non-disclosure agreement, CA	秘密保持契約(書)	150, 152
nearest station	nearest train or subway station	最寄駅	58, 66
neighborhood commercial zone		近隣商業地域	32
net cash flow	NCF	ネットキャッシュフロー	158, 160
net lettable area	NLA, net rentable area, leasable area	賃貸可能面積	148
net operating income	NOI	純収益	104, 158, 160
net rentable area	NRA, net lettable area, leasable area	賃貸可能面積	148
new earthquake resistance standards	new seismic standards	新耐震基準	164
newly built property		築浅物件	58
Niseko		ニセコ	76
NLA	net lettable area, NRA, leasable area	賃貸可能面積	148
NOI	net operating income	純収益	104, 158, 160
NOI yield		NOI利回り	160
NOI yield after depreciation		償却後NOI利回り	160
non-disclosure agreement	NDA, confidentiality agreement	秘密保持契約(書)	150
non-life insurance company		損害保険会社	162
non-recourse lending	non-recourse loan	ノンリコースローン	214, 218
NRA	net rentable area, NLA	賃貸可能面積	148
number of floors	number of stories	建物階数	148
number of rooms		戸数	148
nursery school	nursery	保育園	70
nursing care facility	nursing home	介護施設	78
nursing home	pay nursing home, paid nursing home	老人ホーム	14, 78

O			
English	Synonyms	Japanese	Page
OCC	occupancy rate	稼働率	74
occupancy rate		稼働率	148
office building	office property	オフィスビル	14, 62
Okinawa Prefecture	Okinawa	沖縄県	76

English	Synonyms	Japanese	Page
Omotesando		表参道	66, 68
open-end fund	open-ended fund	オープンエンドファンド	114, 116
open-ended real estate fund		オープンエンド型不動産ファンド	114
operational asset		オペレーショナルアセット	78, 80
operator		オペレーター、施設運営者	78
opportunity fund	opportunistic fund	オポチュニティファンド	226
ordinance		条例	38
ordinary building lease contract	ordinary building lease agreement	普通借家契約	48
ordinary building lease right	general building lease right, traditional building lease right	普通借家権	46, 48
ordinary land lease contract	ordinary land lease agreement	普通借地契約	48
ordinary land lease right	general land lease right, ordinary land leasehold right, traditional land lease right	普通借地権	46, 48
ordinary lease	general lease, traditional lease	普通借	46, 58, 62, 154
ordinary share		普通株	124
Osaka City	Osaka	大阪市	58, 60, 62, 64, 76, 84
Osaka Prefecture	Osaka	大阪府	40, 60, 84
other expense		その他費用	158, 160
other income	other revenue	その他収入	154, 156
outer wall repair work	exterior wall repair work	外壁補修工事	228
outlet		コンセント	92
owner		所有者	16, 18
owner-occupied building		自社ビル	62, 64
owners' association fee		管理組合費	160
ownership	title, fee simple estate	所有権	18, 20
ownership structure		所有形態	142
ownership transfer registration		所有権移転登記	52

P

English	Synonyms	Japanese	Page
parking income	parking revenue	駐車場収入	154, 156
parking lot	parking space	駐車場	38
pass-through type master lease		パススルー型マスターリース	200
penalty		違約金	178
pension fund		年金基金	106, 108, 218, 226, 228
pension payment		年金支払い	106
percentage rent	revenue-based rent, sales-linked rent, variable rent	売上歩合賃料	66, 68, 74
performance fee	incentive fee	実績報酬	210, 212
personal income tax	income tax	所得税	42
PGI	potential gross income, potential gross revenue	潜在総収入	156
picture of the building		建物写真	148
pledge		質権	136, 178, 214
plumbing systems	facilities for water supply and drainage	給排水設備	90, 92
PM report		PMレポート	150, 206

PML	probable maximum loss	予想最大損失率	164
PO	public offering	公募	214
potential gross income	PGI, potential gross revenue	潜在総収入	156
power of attorney		委任状	52
prefectural government		道庁、府庁、県庁	40
prefecture		県(府・道)	82
preferential negotiation right	exclusive negotiation right, first refusal right, ROFA: right of first refusal	優先交渉権	150
preferred share	preferred equity, preferred investment security, preference share	優先出資証券	122, 124, 138
preferred TK investor		優先匿名組合員	132
principal repayment method		元金返済方法	170
private equity		未公開株	104
private real estate fund	private fund	私募不動産ファンド、私募ファンド	106, 114, 194, 206
private REIT		私募REIT	114, 116, 126, 128, 198
private treaty	one on one negotiation	相対取引	146
probable maximum loss	PML	予想最大損失率	164
progression of aging society	progress of aging society	高齢化社会の進展	80
property defect		不動産の瑕疵	52
property delivery	closing, property transfer	引渡	50
Property Disclosure Statement of Important Issues	disclosure statements explaining the important points of the property, real estate contract disclosure statement,	重要事項説明書	28, 50, 52, 148
property management		プロパティマネジメント	206
property management agreement		プロパティマネジメント契約(書)	178, 180
property management business		PM事業	206
property management company	PM, property manager	プロパティマネジメント会社	206, 208
property management fee		プロパティマネジメントフィー	158, 160
Property Manager		プロパティマネジャー	208
property name	building name	物件名	148
property tax		不動産保有税	42, 44, 158, 160
property taxes	taxes and dues, taxes and public dues	公租公課	160
property tour	property viewing	物件内覧	50, 152
property yield		不動産利回り	140
proposed purchase price		購入希望価格	152, 160
PSA	purchase and sale agreement, purchase and sales agreement, purchase and sales contract, SPA, sale and purchase agreement	売買契約(書)、不動産売買契約(書)	50, 178, 186
public facility		公共施設	14
public offering	PO	公募	214
public open space		公開空地	36
publicly traded mutual fund		上場投資信託	112
publicly traded real estate company		上場不動産会社	112

English	Synonyms	Japanese	Page
purchase and sales agreement	PSA, purchase and sale agreement, purchase and sales contract, SPA, sale and purchase agreement	売買契約（書）	50
purchase price	acquisition price	取得価格	102, 140

English	Synonyms	Japanese	Page
residential zoning district	residential district	住居地域	30, 32
resort hotel		リゾートホテル	74, 76
restaurant business	F&B business (Food and Beverage business)	飲食業	228
restoration cost	restoration expense	原状回復費	160
restroom		トイレ	64
retail business		小売業	228
retail investor	individual investor	一般投資家、個人投資家	106, 126, 132
retail operator		商業施設運営者	66, 68
retail property		商業施設	14, 66
retail property for daily needs		生活密着型商業施設	66
retailer		小売業者	80, 198
retained earning		内部留保	112
return on investment	ROI	投資利回り	140
RevPAR	revenue per available room	販売可能客室1室当たり売上	74
risk free rate		リスクフリーレート	168
risk premium		リスクプレミアム	168
ROI	return on investment	投資利回り	140
rooftop		屋上	60, 64
room layout	floor plan	間取り	94, 96
running repair	repair cost, repair expense	修繕費	160
rural residential zone	countryside residential district	田園住居地域	32

S

English	Synonyms	Japanese	Page
S		サービスルーム	96
Saitama City	Saitama	さいたま市	84
Saitama Prefecture	Saitama	埼玉県	60, 82, 84
sale and lease back		セール&リースバック	102
sales price	selling price	売却価格	102, 202
same boat investment	alignment of interest	セームボート投資	126
Sapporo City	Sapporo	札幌市	58, 60, 62, 76, 84
SB		シューズボックス	96
seal		印鑑	52
seal registration certificate		印鑑証明書	52
sectional ownership	strata title, unit-ownership	区分所有	18, 20
Sectional Ownership Law	Act on Building Unit Ownership, etc., Act on Sectional Ownership of Buildings, Law Concerning Sectional Ownership of Buildings	建物の区分所有等に関する法律	26, 28
securities company		証券会社	224
security gate		セキュリティゲート	92
security right	security interest	担保権	178
security system		警備設備	92
self-management		内部運用型	110
self-management type		内部運用型	112
self-storage		トランクルーム	78
seller's agent		売主側仲介業者	146
semi-fire prevention district		準防火地域	30
semi-industrial zone	semi-industrial district, quasi-industrial district	準工業地域	32

semi-residential zone	semi-residential district, quasi-residential district	準住居地域	32
Sendai City	Sendai	仙台市	84
separate account		セパレートアカウント	212
service apartment		サービスアパートメント	74
service business		サービス業	228
service room		サービスルーム	96
serviced housing facility for the elderly	serviced senior housing	サービス付き高齢者向け住宅	78
settlement	closing	決済	50
share	stock	株式	108
Shibuya Ward	Shibuya City	渋谷区	62, 64
Shikoku	Shikoku Island	四国	82, 84
Shinagawa Ward	Shinagawa City	品川区	62, 64
Shinjuku Ward	Shinjuku City	新宿区	62, 64
Shinsaibashi		心斎橋	68
shoes box		シューズボックス	96
shopping center		ショッピングセンター	66
signature certificate		サイン証明書	52
silent partnership	anonymous partnership	匿名組合	118, 120, 130, 176
single tenant		単独テナント	148
site inspection		現地調査	162
size		規模	62
smoke detector		煙探知機	92
soil contamination	soil pollution, land pollution, ground pollution	土壌汚染	162
solar panel		太陽光パネル	128
solid ground	firm ground	固い地盤	78
sourcing		ソーシング	148
sovereign wealth fund	SWF	政府系ファンド	106
SPC	SPE, SPV, special purpose company	特別目的会社	108, 122, 190
special agreement		特約事項	170
special purpose company	SPC, SPE: special purpose entity, SPV: special purpose vehicle	特別目的会社	108, 122, 190
Special Taxation Measures Law	Act on Special Measures Concerning Taxation	租税特別措置法	124, 176
specialty shop		専門店	66
specified bond		特定社債	122, 124, 138
specified share	specified investment	特定出資	124, 176
sponsor		スポンサー	126, 128
spread		スプレッド、利ざや	170
stable income		安定的なインカム収入	98
stable power supply		安定的な電力供給	78
stairs		階段	60, 64
stamp tax	stamp duty	印紙税	42
standard floor area		基準階面積	148
station building		駅ビル	66
statutory inspcetion report		法定点検報告書	162
steel structure		鉄骨造、S造	148
steel-reinforced concrete structure		鉄骨鉄筋コンクリート造、SRC造	148
stock		株式	102

English	Synonyms	Japanese	Page
stock exchange	securities exchange	証券取引所	110, 112
stock transfer agent	unit transfer agent	株式(投資口)名義書換人	220
storage room income	storage gross revenue	トランクルーム収入	156
strata-title	sectional ownership, unit-ownership	区分所有	18, 20
structural calculation report	structural calculation sheet	構造計算書	162
student housing	student apartment	学生マンション	58
studio		ワンルーム／1K	94
sub lessee	end tenant	転借人	200
subcontractor		サブコン	226
subject property		対象不動産	152
sublease		転貸	200
suburban retail property	suburban-type retail facility	郊外型商業施設	66, 68
subway		地下鉄	86
sunshine	sunlight	日当たり	34
superficies		地上権	18, 22
SWF	sovereign wealth fund	政府系ファンド	106

T			
English	**Synonyms**	**Japanese**	**Page**
target return		目標利回り	230
tax assessed value		課税標準額	42, 136
tax attorney		税理士	174, 176
tax break	special tax treatment, tax benefits, tax incentive	税の優遇措置	176
tax firm		税理士法人	174, 222, 224
tax incentive	special tax treatment, tax benefits, tax break	税の優遇措置	176
tax liability		税負担	142
tax opinion report	tax opinion	税務意見書	174
tax rate		税率	42
tax return		税務申告	178
tax treaty		租税条約	142, 174
taxable income		課税所得	42, 44, 174, 176
TBI	trust beneficiary interest, trust beneficial interest	信託受益権	118, 130, 134, 138, 148, 190, 218
ten stories above ground and two below	ten floors above ground and two below, ten floors above ground and two basement floors, ten stories above ground and two basement levels	地上10階建地下2階建	148
tenant	lessee, occupier	賃借人、テナント	14, 16
tenant replacement		テナント入替	154
Tenjin		天神	68
term sheet		タームシート	170
terminal station		ターミナル駅	86
terms and conditions		取引条件	54
Three Major Metropolitan Areas	3 Major Metropolitan Areas	3大都市圏	72
title	ownership, fee simple estate	所有権	130
title deed	title	権利証、登記済権利証、登記識別情報	22, 182
TK		匿名組合	118, 176

English	Synonyms	Japanese	Page
wholesale business		卸売業	228
WIC		ウォークインクローゼット	96
witdth of the front road	front road width	前面道路幅員	36
window		窓	96
withholding tax		源泉徴収税	142, 174
work from home		在宅勤務をする	58, 94

日本語索引（Japanese Index）

日本語	英語	類義語	頁
一般事務受託者	accounting, tax, etc. service provider	administrative agent	221
一般社団法人	ISH		175
一般投資家	retail investor	individual investor	107
委任状	power of attorney		53
違法建築物	illegal building		35, 149
違法駐車	illegal parking		39
違約金	penalty		179
医療業	medical business	medical service industry	229
インカムゲイン	income gain		105
印鑑	seal		53
印鑑証明書	seal registration certificate		53
印紙税	stamp tax	stamp duty	43
飲食業	restaurant business	F&B business (Food and Beverage business)	229
インターホン	intercom		93
インフレヘッジ	hedge against inflation	inflationary hedge	103

う

日本語	英語	類義語	頁
ウォークインクローゼット	walk-in-closet, WIC		97
売上歩合賃料	percentage rent	revenue-based rent, sales-linked rent, variable rent	67, 69, 75
売上歩合付固定賃料	fixed rent with percentage rent	fixed rent with sales-linked rent, variable rent based on sales	67, 69, 75
売主側仲介業者	seller's agent		147
売主側の単独仲介業者	exclusive seller's agent		147
売渡承諾書	LOA	acceptance letter, letter of acceptance	51, 151
運営委託型	management contract		75
運転免許証	driver's license		53
運輸業	transportation business		229
運用資産残高	AUM	asset under management	211
運用報酬	management fee	asset management fee	211, 213

え

日本語	英語	類義語	頁
エアコン	air conditioner		93
営業総利益	GOP	gross operating profit	75
駅ビル	station building		67
エスカレーター	escalator		65, 93
エスクロー・エージェント	escrow agent		55
エスクロー制度	escrow system		55
越境	encroachment		149
エレベーター	elevator	lift	61, 65, 93
エレベーターホール	elevator hall		65
宴会場	banquet room		75
エンジニアリングレポート	engineering report, ER		163, 165
延滞テナント	delinquent tenant		151
エンドテナント	end tenant		201
エントランス	entrance area	entrance hall	61, 65

お

日本語	英語	類義語	頁
大阪圏	Greater Osaka Area	Greater Osaka	71, 73

日本語	英語	類義語	頁
大阪市	Osaka City	Osaka	59, 61, 63, 65, 77, 85
大阪府	Osaka Prefecture	Osaka	41, 61, 85
大通り沿いの商業店舗ビル	high street retail property		67
オープンエンド型不動産ファンド	open-ended real estate fund		115
オープンエンドファンド	open-end fund	open-ended fund	115, 117
沖縄県	Okinawa Prefecture	Okinawa	77
屋上	rooftop		61, 65
屋内消火栓	indoor fire hydrant		93
オフィス街	business district		65
オフィスビル	office building	office property	15, 63
オフィスビル賃貸専業会社	rental office building specialized company		199
オペレーショナルアセット	operational asset		79, 81
オペレーター	operator		79
オポチュニティファンド	opportunity fund	opportunistic fund	227
表参道	Omotesando		67, 69
卸売業	wholesale business		229
温室効果ガス	GHG, greenhouse gas		129

か

日本語	英語	類義語	頁
海外投資家	foreign investor	overseas investor	187
会議場	convention room		75
会計事務所	accounting firm		223, 225
外国人訪日客	foreign visitor		81
介護施設	nursing care facility	nursing home	79
外資系高級ホテル	international luxury brand hotel		77
外資系不動産仲介会社	foreign real estate agent company	foreign real estate brokerage company, global agent	147
会社法	Corporate Law	Company Law, Companies Act	119
改修工事	renovation work		63, 229
階段	stairs		61, 65
買付証明書	letter of commitment to purchase, LOC		51, 53
開発許可	land development permission	development permission, permission for development, approval of development	31
開発利益	development profit		195
外部運用型	external management		111, 113
外壁補修工事	outer wall repair work	exterior wall repair work	229
解約違約金収入	cancellation penalty income		157
解約請求	cancellation request		117
解約予告	cancellation notice		151
価格変動の大きさ	volatility	price fluctuation	111, 127
家具	furniture		75
家具、什器、備品	FF&E	furniture, fixtures, and equipment	75
学生マンション	student housing	student apartment	59
核テナント	anchor tenant	key tenant, main tenant	67, 69
貸付実行前提条件	conditions precedent, CP, loan execution conditions		171, 183
貸付手数料	upfront fee		171
貸し手	lender		215

日本語	英語	類義語	頁
ガスコンロ	gas stove		93
ガス設備	gas equipment	gas installation	91, 93
課税所得	taxable income		43, 45, 175, 177
課税標準額	tax assessed value		43, 137
風通し	ventilation		35
固い地盤	solid ground	firm ground	79
合併・買収	merger and acquisition		127
稼働率	OCC, occupancy rate		75, 149
神奈川県	Kanagawa Prefecture	Kanagawa	61, 83, 85
株式	share, stock		103, 109
株式名義書換人	stock transfer agent	unit transfer agent	221
借り手	borrower	debtor	215
川崎市	Kawasaki City	Kawasaki	85
換気扇	ventilation fan		93
環境認証	environmental certification	environmental certificate, green building certification, green certification	129, 223
元金返済方法	principal repayment method		171
還元利回り	CAP rate, capitalization rate		161, 167
観光地（観光名所）	tourist destination	tourist attraction, tourist spot	77, 89
幹事	manager		217
環状線	loop railway line	circle railway line	87
間接不動産投資	indirect real estate investment		107, 109, 111
乾燥機	D, dryer		97
鑑定評価額	appraisal value	appraised value	141, 169
鑑定評価書	Appraisal Report	Real Estate Appraisal Report	169
看板収入	billboard income	billboard revenue	157
管理組合	condominium owners' association	owners' association, home owners' association	61, 207, 209
管理組合費	owners' association fee		161
元利返済金カバー率	debt service coverage ratio, DSCR		171

き

日本語	英語	類義語	頁
ギアリング・レシオ	gearing ratio	loan to value ratio, LTV	141
機械式駐車場	machine parking		39
機関投資家	institutional investor	professional investor	99, 107, 109, 115, 127, 219
議決権	voting right		143, 177
期限一括返済	bullet repayment	balloon payment, bullet payment	171
基準階面積	standard floor area		149
基準金利	base rate		171
既存不適格建築物	legal nonconforming building	grandfathered building	35, 149
期待利回り	expected rate of return	expected return	161
期中信託報酬	annual trust running fee	annual trust fee	135
規模	size		63
希望売却価格	asking price		149
キャッシュオンキャッシュリターン	cash on cash return	cash on cash yield	231
キャッシュフロー分析	cash flow analysis		157
キャッシュマルチプル	cash multiple		173
キャップレート	capitalization rate, CAP rate		167
キャピタルゲイン	capital gain		103

日本語	英語	類義語	頁
購入価格に対する借入額の比率	LTP	loan to purchase price, LTPP	141
購入希望価格	proposed purchase price		153, 161
神戸市	Kobe City	Kobe	85
公募	PO, public offering		215
小売業	retail business		229
小売業者	retailer		81, 199
高齢化社会の進展	progression of aging society	progress of aging society	81
高齢者	elderly people		39, 81
国際評価基準	International Valuation Standards, IVS		169
国土交通省	Ministry of Land, Infrastructure, Transport, and Tourism, MLIT		31, 131, 167
国土利用計画法	National Land Use Planning Law	National Land Use and Planning Law, National Land Use Planning Act	27
個人投資家	retail investor	individual investor	127, 133
戸数	number of rooms		149
戸建住宅	detached house	detached housing, single family house, single family detached home, single family housing	15, 59, 61
固定金利	fixed rate	fixed interest rate	171
固定資産税	fixed asset tax	property tax	43, 45, 159
固定資産税評価額	fixed asset tax value		159
固定賃料	fixed rent		59, 63, 67, 69, 71, 75, 79
言葉の壁	language barrier		187
コベナンツ	covenant		171
コミングルファンド	commingled fund		213
コロナ	COVID-19		59
コンセント	outlet		93

さ

日本語	英語	類義語	頁
サード・パーティ・ロジスティクス	3PL	third party logistics	71
サービスアパートメント	service apartment		75
サービス業	service business		229
サービス付き高齢者向け住宅	serviced housing facility for the elderly	serviced senior housing	79
サービスルーム	S, service room		97
債券	bond		103
在宅勤務をする	work from home		59, 95
埼玉県	Saitama Prefecture	Saitama	61, 83, 85
さいたま市	Saitama City	Saitama	85
債務不履行	default		215
サイン証明書	signature certificate		53
札幌市	Sapporo City	Sapporo	59, 61, 63, 77, 85
サブコン	subcontractor		227
残金支払	remaining payment		53

し

日本語	英語	類義語	頁
市	city		41, 83, 87
ジェネラルパートナー	general partner		121

日本語	英語	類義語	頁
証券化対象不動産の鑑定評価に関する実務指針	Guidelines Regarding Appraisal of Securitized Properties		167
商圏人口	market area population	catchment area population	69
証券取引所	stock exchange	securities exchange	111, 113
詳細な調査	due diligence		51
商社	trading company		195
上場投資信託	listed mutual fund, publicly traded mutual fund		111
上場不動産会社	listed real estate company, publicly traded real estate company		113
消費税	consumption tax	VAT: Value Added Tax, sales tax	43
商法	Commercial Law	Commercial Code	119
消防設備	fire prevention equipment		91, 93
情報通信業	information and communication business	information and telecommunication industry	229
消防法	Fire Protection Law	Fire Service Act, Fire Defense Law	27
照明	lighting		93
条例	ordinance		39
食料雑貨品店	grocery store		67
ショッピングセンター	shopping center		67
所得税	income tax, personal income tax		43
処分報酬	disposition fee		211, 213
所有形態	ownership structure, type of ownership		143, 149
所有権	ownership, title	fee simple estate	19, 21, 131
所有権移転登記	ownership transfer registration		53
所有者	owner		17, 19
新規公募	initial public offering, IPO		215
心斎橋	Shinsaibashi		69
新宿区	Shinjuku Ward	Shinjuku City	63, 65
新耐震基準	new earthquake resistance standards	new seismic standards	165
信託	trust		111
信託会社	trust company		135
信託協会	Trust Companies Association of Japan		221
信託業法	Trust Business Law	Trust Business Act	135
信託銀行	trust bank		119, 135, 147, 203, 219
信託財産	entrusted asset	trust asset	135, 137
信託受益権	TBI, trust beneficiary interest	trust beneficial interest	119, 131, 135, 139, 149, 191, 219
信託配当	trust dividend		137

す

日本語	英語	類義語	頁
水害リスク	flood risk		79
推定売却価格	estimated sales price		149
水道光熱費	utility expense	utility expenses, utilities expenses	159, 161
水道光熱費収入	utility income	utility charge revenue, utility revenue	155, 157
スプリンクラー	fire sprinkler		93
スプレッド	spread		171

日本語	英語	類義語	頁
スポンサー	sponsor		127, 129

日本語	英語	類義語	頁
生活必需品	daily necessities		81
生活密着型商業施設	retail property for daily needs		67
製造業	manufacturing business		229
正当事由	justifiable reason	just cause, justifiable grounds, good cause	47
税の優遇措置	tax break, tax incentive	special tax treatment, tax benefits	177
政府系ファンド	sovereign wealth fund, SWF		107
税負担	tax liability		143
税務意見書	tax opinion report	tax opinion	175
税務申告	tax return		179
税理士	tax attorney		175, 177
税理士法人	tax firm		175, 223, 225
税率	tax rate		43
政令指定都市	government-ordinance-designated city	cities designated by ordinance, cities designated by cabinet order, cabinet order designated city, ordinance-designated city	41, 83
セームボート投資	same boat investment	alignment of interest	127
セール&リースバック	sale and lease back		103
セキュリティゲート	security gate		93
施工会社	contractor		91
施主	client		91
世帯	household		59
設計会社	architectural design firm	architectural design company	91, 223, 225
設備	facility		63
設備更新工事	equipment renewal work	plumbing replacement work, HVAC replacement work	229
ゼネコン	general contractor		163, 195, 227
セパレートアカウント	separate account		213
潜在総収入	PGI, potential gross income	potential gross revenue	157
先進的物流施設	modern logistics facility	advanced logistics facility	71, 73
宣誓供述書	affidavit		53
仙台市	Sendai City	Sendai	85
洗濯機	W, washer		97
全部事項証明書(建物)	building registry	building register	25
全部事項証明書(土地)	land registry	land register	25
洗面台	washbasin		93
専門店	specialty shop		67
前面道路幅員	width of the front road	front road width	37
専有部分	individual unit	living space, exclusively owned area	61

そ

日本語	英語	類義語	頁
倉庫	warehouse		227
総合スーパー	general merchandise store, GMS		67
総合設計制度	comprehensive design system		37
総合不動産会社	general real estate company	comprehensive real estate company	195, 199, 203, 207

日本語	英語	類義語	頁
総取得コストに対する借入額の比率	LTC	loan to cost, loan to cost ratio	141
相場賃料	market rent		155
ソーシング	sourcing		149
測量士	land surveyor	surveyor	223, 225
底地	land with leasehold interest	land, land interest	21
租税条約	tax treaty		143, 175
租税特別措置法	Special Taxation Measures Law	Act on Special Measures Concerning Taxation	125, 177
その他収入	other income	other revenue	155, 157
その他費用	other expense		159, 161
損害賠償	compensation for damage		179
損害保険会社	non-life insurance company		163
損害保険料	insurance premium	insurance fee, premium	159, 161

た

日本語	英語	類義語	頁
ターミナル駅	terminal station		87
タームシート	term sheet		171
第一種住居地域	class one residential zone	category 1 residential district	33
第一種中高層住居専用地域	class one exclusive zone for medium and high-rise residences	category 1 medium-to-high-rise exclusive residential district	33
第一種低層住居専用地域	class one exclusive zone for low-rise residences	category 1 low-rise exclusive residential district	33
大規模修繕工事	large-scale repair work		229
大規模ビル	large sized building	large office building	63
対象不動産	subject property		153
耐震性	earthquake resistance	seismic adequacy	165
耐震補強工事	earthquake reinforcement work		163
代替資産	alternative asset		105
台所	kitchen		93
第二種金融商品取引業者	type II financial instruments business operator	class two financial instruments dealing company	139
第二種住居地域	class two residential zone	category 2 residential district	33
第二種中高層住居専用地域	class two exclusive zone for medium and high-rise residences	category 2 medium-to-high-rise exclusive residential district	33
第二種低層住居専用地域	class two exclusive zone for low-rise residences	category 2 low-rise exclusive residential district	33
太陽光パネル	solar panel		129
高さ制限	height limit	height restriction	35
宅地建物取引業者	licensed real estate agent company	licensed agent, licensed broker, licensed real estate brokerage company	133, 139
宅地建物取引業法	Real Estate Brokerage Law	Real Estate Brokerage Act	27, 29, 51, 203
宅地建物取引士	licensed real estate broker	licensed real estate agent	53
宅配ボックス	delivery box		93
建物	building		15, 17
建物階数	number of floors	number of stories	149
建物解体費用	building demolition cost		197
建物課税標準額	building tax assessed value		159
建物環境リスク	building environmental risk		163
建物管理	building maintenance		207
建物管理会社	building maintenance company		207, 209
建物管理事業	building maintenance business		207

日本語	英語	類義語	頁
建物管理費	maintenance cost	building maintenance cost, building maintenance fee, building management fee, building management expenses	161
建物構造	building structure		149
建物写真	picture of the building		149
建物竣工年月日	building completion date		149
建物状況	building condition		163
建物所有権	building ownership		19
建物所有者	building owner		21
建物登記簿	building registry	building register	25, 137
建物の意匠	building design		91
建物の区分所有等に関する法律	Sectional Ownership Law	Act on Building Unit Ownership, etc., Act on Sectional Ownership of Buildings, Law Concerning Sectional Ownership of Buildings	27, 29
建物の構造	building structure		91
建物の設備	building facility		91
建物のデザイン	building design		91
タワーマンション	high-rise condominium, high-rise apartment		37
単独テナント	single tenant		149
担保権	security right	security interest	179

<table>
<tr><td colspan="4">ち</td></tr>
</table>

日本語	英語	類義語	頁
地下鉄	subway		87
築浅物件	newly built property		59
築年数	building age		149
地上10階建地下2階建	ten stories above ground and two below	ten floors above ground and two below, ten floors above ground and two basement floors, ten stories above ground and two basement levels	149
地上権	superficies		19, 23
地代	ground rent		21, 161
千葉県	Chiba Prefecture	Chiba	61, 83, 85
地方公共団体	local government	local municipality	39, 41
地方財務局	local financial bureau		123
地方自治体	local government	local municipality	41
中央区	Chuo Ward	Chuo City	63, 65
仲介会社	broker	real estate agent company	203
仲介手数料	brokerage fee	agent fee, brokerage commission, broker's commission	203, 205
昼間人口	daytime population		87
駐車場	parking lot	parking space	39
駐車場収入	parking income	parking revenue	155, 157
中小ビル	medium to small sized building		63
中部圏	Greater Nagoya Area	Greater Nagoya	73
長期賃貸借	long term lease		79
超富裕層	ultra HNWI	ultra high net worth individual	107
直接還元法	Direct Capitalization Method		167, 169
直接不動産投資	direct real estate investment		107, 109, 131, 133
千代田区	Chiyoda Ward	Chiyoda City	63, 65

日本語	英語	類義語	頁
電気・ガス・熱供給・水道業	utility business		229
電気設備	electrical systems	electric systems	91, 93
電子商取引	E-commerce		71, 81
転借人	sub lessee	end tenant	201
天井	ceiling		97
天井高	ceiling height		71, 97
天神	Tenjin		69
転貸	sublease		201
伝統資産	traditional asset		105
電力会社	electric power company		195

と

日本語	英語	類義語	頁
トイレ	restroom		65
道	prefecture		83
登記	registration		51, 185
登記識別情報	title deed	title	23
登記済権利証	title deed	title	23
東京23区	Tokyo 23 Wards	Tokyo 23 Cities, 23 Wards, 23 Wards of Tokyo	41, 59, 65, 85, 87
東京圏	Greater Tokyo Area	Greater Tokyo, Tokyo Metropolitan Area	59, 61, 71, 73, 83, 85
東京証券取引所	Tokyo Stock Exchange, TSE		127
東京都	Tokyo Metropolis	Tokyo	41, 59, 61, 83, 85, 231
東京都庁	Tokyo Metropolitan Government, Tokyo Metropolitan Government Office		41, 89
倒産隔離	bankruptcy remoteness		175, 177
倒産隔離のための器	bankruptcy remote entity		121, 125
倒産リスク	bankruptcy risk		175
投資一任業	discretionary investment management business		141
投資運用業	investment management business		139, 141
投資期間	investment period		231
投資銀行	investment bank		214
投資口	investment unit, unit	investment security	109, 129, 139, 217
投資口名義書換人	stock transfer agent	unit transfer agent	221
投資実績	investment track record		211
投資証券	investment security, investment unit, unit		109, 129, 139, 217
投資助言業	investment advisory business		139, 141
投資信託	mutual fund	investment trust, unit trust	107, 109
投資信託及び投資法人に関する法律	Investment Trust and Investment Corporation Law	Act on Investment Trusts and Investment Corporations	127
投資適格物件	investment grade property		135
投資不動産	investment property	commercial property, income producing property	15
投資法人	investment corporation		111, 127, 129
投資法人債	investment corporation bond		129
当初受益者	initial beneficiary		137
当初信託報酬	initial trust set up fee	initial trust fee	135
投資利回り	investment return, investment yield, return on investment, ROI		99, 139, 141, 171, 173

な

日本語	英語	類義語	頁
内部運用型	self-management, self-management type		111, 113
内部収益率	internal rate of return	IRR	231
内部留保	retained earning		113
内壁	indoor wall		97
流し台	kitchen sink		93
名古屋圏	Greater Nagoya Area	Greater Nagoya	73
名古屋市	Nagoya City	Nagoya	59, 61, 63, 65, 85

に

日本語	英語	類義語	頁
二重課税	double taxation		119, 127, 175
ニセコ	Niseko		77
日本国債	Japanese government bond, JGB		139, 169
日本の会計基準	Japanese Generally Accepted Accounting Principles, JGAAP		149
日本の不動産投資信託	Japanese Real Estate Investment Trust		127
入居者	resident		81
入札	bid		147
任意組合	general partnership	ordinary partnership	119, 121

ね

日本語	英語	類義語	頁
ネットキャッシュフロー	NCF, net cash flow		161
年金基金	pension fund		107, 109, 219, 227, 229
年金支払い	pension payment		107

の

日本語	英語	類義語	頁
農地法	Agricultural Land Law	Agricultural Land Act, Cropland Act	27, 29
延床面積	GFA, gross floor area	total floor area, total floor space	23, 149
ノンリコースローン	non-recourse lending	non-recourse loan	215, 219

は

日本語	英語	類義語	頁
売却益	capital gain		103, 105, 231
売却価格	sales price	selling price	103, 203
売却損	capital loss		103
売却物件	real estate for sale	property for sale	51, 147
配当	dividend	distribution	231, 103
売買契約（書）	PSA, purchase and sales agreement	purchase and sale agreement, purchase and sales contract, SPA, sale and purchase agreement	51, 187
柱間隔	column space		71
パススルー型マスターリース	pass-through type master lease		201
バリューアッドファンド	value-add fund	value-added fund	227
バリューアップ工事	value enhancement work	value enhancing construction work, value-upgrading work	63
繁華街	entertainment district	downtown area, highly bustling district	67

販売可能客室1室当たり売上	RevPAR	revenue per available room	75

ひ

日本語	英語	類義語	頁
日当たり	sunshine	sunlight	35
引き受け	underwriting		215
引渡	property delivery	closing, property transfer	51
ビジネスホテル	business hotel, economy hotel	budget hotel, limited service hotel	75, 77
備品	equipment		75
秘密保持契約（書）	CA, confidentiality agreement, NDA, non-disclosure agreement		51, 151, 153
百貨店	department store		67
兵庫県	Hyogo Prefecture	Hyogo	85
表明保証	representations and warranties		187
ビルド・トゥ・スーツ型	Build-to-Suit	BTS	71
昼間人口	daytime population		87
ビルメンテナンス会社	building maintenance company		207
広島県	Hiroshima Prefecture	HIroshima	85
広島市	Hiroshima City	Hiroshima	85

ふ

日本語	英語	類義語	頁
府	prefecture		83
ファミリーオフィス	family office		107
ファンドマネジメント会社	fund management company	FM, fund manager	211, 231
ファンドマネジャー	fund manager	FM, fund management company	211
福岡県	Fukuoka Prefecture	Fukuoka	61, 85
福岡市	Fukuoka City	Fukuoka	59, 61, 63, 85
複合施設	multi-use complex	mixed-use property	195
福祉業	welfare business	social welfare industry	229
複数テナント	multiple tenants		149
含み損益	unrealized profit and loss	unrealized gain and loss	149
負債比率	loan to value ratio, LTV	gearing ratio	141, 171
府庁	prefectural government		41
普通株	ordinary share		125
普通銀行	commercial bank		219
普通借	ordinary lease	general lease, traditional lease	47, 59, 63, 155
普通借地契約	ordinary land lease contract	ordinary land lease agreement	47
普通借地権	ordinary land lease right	general land lease right, ordinary land leasehold right, traditional land lease right	47, 49
普通借家契約	ordinary building lease contract	ordinary building lease agreement	47
普通借家権	ordinary building lease right	general building lease right, traditional building lease right	47, 49
物件内覧	property tour	property viewing	51, 153
物件名	property name	building name	149
物流施設	logistics property		15, 71, 73
不動産	real estate	immovables, real property, property	15, 17, 103, 105
不動産会社	real estate operating company, REOC		113, 133
不動産開発	real estate development		113

不動産開発会社	real estate developer	developer	15
不動産開発事業	real estate development business		191, 193, 195
不動産鑑定士	licensed real estate appraiser, real estate appraiser		163, 167, 223, 225
不動産鑑定評価基準	Japanese Real Estate Appraisal Standards, Real Estate Appraisal Standards		15, 163, 167, 169
不動産鑑定評価書	real estate appraisal report	appraisal report	167
不動産管理事業	real estate management business		191, 193, 195, 207
不動産管理処分信託契約（書）	trust agreement for real estate management and disposal	real estate management and disposition trust agreement, real estate trust agreement for management and disposal	181
不動産業	real estate business		229
不動産取得税	real estate acquisition tax		43, 45, 137
不動産信託	real estate trust		219, 221
不動産信託契約（書）	real estate trust agreement	real estate management and disposition trust agreement, trust agreement for real estate management and disposal	179, 181
不動産信託事業	real estate trust business		191, 193
不動産信託受益権	real estate TBI, real estate trust beneficiary interest	real estate trust beneficiary interest	121, 131, 139
不動産信託受益権売買契約（書）	real estate trust beneficiary interest purchase and sales Agreement	real estate TBI purchase and sales agreement	179, 181
不動産仲介会社	real estate agent company, real estate broker	broker, real estate agent, real estate agent company, real estate broker, real estate brokerage company	15, 51, 139, 147, 149, 203, 205
不動産仲介事業	real estate brokerage business	real estate agent business	191, 193, 195
不動産賃貸事業	real estate leasing business	real estate rental business	191, 193, 195, 199
不動産賃貸市場	leasing market		203
不動産登記	real estate registration		23
不動産登記制度	real estate registration system		23
不動産登記簿	real estate registry		23, 24
不動産登記法	Real Estate Registration Law	Real Estate Registration Act, Real Property Registration Act, Real Property Registration Law	23, 29
不動産投資信託	real estate investment trust, REIT		107, 111, 113
不動産特定共同事業者	qualified real estate specified joint business operator		131
不動産特定共同事業スキーム	Real Estate Specified Joint Business Structure		133
不動産特定共同事業法	Real Estate Specified Joint Business Law	Real Estate Specified Joint Enterprise Law, Act on Specified Joint Real Estate Ventures, Real Estate Syndication Law	119, 131, 133, 135
不動産取引	real estate transaction	property transaction	27
不動産の瑕疵	property defect		53
不動産売買契約（書）	PSA, real estate purchase and sales agreement	purchase and sale agreement, purchase and sales agreement, purchase and sales contract, SPA, sale and purchase agreement	51, 179, 181
不動産表示登記	registration of the property description		223
不動産ファイナンス事業	real estate finance business		191, 193

日本語	英語	類義語	頁
不動産ファンド運用事業	real estate fund management business		191, 193, 211
不動産保有税	property tax		43, 45, 159, 161
不動産利回り	property yield, yield on income producing property		139, 141
富裕層	high net worth individual, HNWI		107
フリーレント期間	free-rent period	rent-free period	155
フルサービス型ホテル	full service hotel		75, 77
プロパティマネジメント	property management		207
プロパティマネジメント会社	property management company	PM, property manager	207, 209
プロパティマネジメント契約(書)	property management agreement		179, 181
プロパティマネジメントフィー	property management fee		159, 161
プロパティマネジャー	Property Manager		209
分割返済	amortization		171
文京区	Bunkyo Ward	Bunkyo City	63, 65
分散投資	diversification		103, 105
分譲マンション	condominium	condo, multifamily housing	15, 59, 61, 97, 207
分譲マンション専業デベロッパー	condominium specialized developer		195
分譲マンションデベロッパー	condominium developer	condo developer	197, 207
分配金	dividend	distribution	121, 129

へ

日本語	英語	類義語	頁
平均客室単価	ADR	average daily rate	75
平均宿泊料	ADR	average daily rate	75
ベースレート	base rate		171
便器	toilet		93
弁護士	lawyer	legal counsel, attorney	175, 177
便所	lavatory		93
変動金利	floating rate	variable rate, variable interest rate	171
変動賃料	variable rent	percentage rent, revenue-based rent, sales-linked rent	67, 69, 75

ほ

日本語	英語	類義語	頁
保育園	nursery school	nursery	71
防火地域	fire prevention district		31
法人税	corporate income tax, corporate tax		43, 45, 111, 113, 115, 175, 199
法定点検報告書	statutory inspcetion report		163
法的拘束力のある書面	legally binding document		153
法務局	Legal Affairs Bureau		23
法務省	Justice Ministry		23
法律意見書	legal opinion report	legal opinion	175
法律事務所	law firm	legal firm	175, 223, 225
法律上の所有者	legal owner		135
簿価	book value		149
保険会社	insurance company		107, 109

保険業	insurance business		229
保険料	insurance premium	insurance fee, premium	107
募集賃料	asking rent		155
北海道	Hokkaido, Hokkaido Prefecture	Hokkaido Island	41, 61, 77, 83, 85
ホテル	hotel		15
保有期間	holding period		231
本社ビル	headquarters building	head-office building	227
本州	Honshu	Honshu Island	83, 85
本人確認書類	identity verification document	identification document, identity confirmation document	53

山手線	Yamanote Line		87

About the Authors

Kazuya Wakimoto

Mr. Wakimoto entered Mitsui Trust Bank (currently Sumitomo Mitsui Trust Bank) in 1992 and has dealt with land trusts, real estate brokerage, real estate trusts, and real estate fund consulting businesses. He has originated and executed various real estate fund transactions, including J-REIT set up and management advisory, private fund origination with pension equity, and J-REIT M&A arrangement. Since April 2012, he has been responsible for cross border real estate transactions such as advisory services for a variety of overseas investors with their investments in Japan, S-REIT set-up consulting, etc. Since April 2022, he has led the inbound and outbound real estate businesses as the General Manager of the Global Real Estate Planning and Promotion Department of Sumitomo Mitsui Trust Bank.

Mr. Wakimoto received a bachelor's degree from Waseda University with a major in law and an MBA from the Drucker School of Management at Claremont Graduate University. He is a licensed real estate appraiser, real estate broker, and ARES master. Mr. Wakimoto has published the following books: "Real Estate Fund Business, Shuwa System, 2006, 2010, 2020," "J-REIT Business, Shuwa System, 2008, 2018," and "Real Estate Fund Business for Beginners, Shuwa System, 2014."

Jon Salyards

Jon entered Chuo Mitsui Trust Bank (currently Sumitomo Mitsui Trust Bank) in 2007 and served as the only foreigner to work in the real estate section covering foreign investment advisory and asset management services. During his 4 years with Chuo Mitsui Trust Bank, Jon helped grow assets under management to 625 million USD and concluded several cross border advisory transactions.

In 2011, Jon joined Savills Japan, a British real estate advisory and asset management firm, and currently leads the Investment Department as Managing Director of Institutional Investment Advisory. Jon has completed over 10 billion USD in transaction volume with over 700 property transactions in Japan. He is a graduate of the University of Arizona with a major in Journalism and a minor in Japanese language.

著者紹介

脇本和也

1992年に三井信託銀行（現三井住友信託銀行）入社。以降、土地信託業務、不動産仲介業務、不動産信託業務、不動産ファンドコンサル業務に従事。不動産ファンドコンサルでは、J-REIT組成・運営サポート、年金資金を活用した私募ファンド組成アレンジ、J-REITのM&Aコンサルなど様々な不動産ファンド関連取引を創出・遂行。2012年4月からは、多様な海外投資家に対する日本不動産投資サポートやS-REIT立ち上げコンサルなど、クロスボーダー不動産取引に係るコンサルティング業務に従事。2022年4月からは、三井住友信託銀行グローバル不動産業務部部長として、インバウンド・アウトバウンド双方に係る不動産ビジネスを統括推進している。
早稲田大学法学部卒業、米国クレアモント大学院大学ドラッカースクールMBA。
不動産鑑定士、宅地建物取引士、ARES不動産証券化マスター。
著書に「不動産ファンドがよ～くわかる本（秀和システム、2006年、2010年、2020年）」「J-REITの基本と仕組みがよ～くわかる本（秀和システム、2008年、2018年）」「不動産ファンドの教科書（秀和システム、2014年）」がある。

ジョン　サリアード

2007年に中央三井信託銀行（現三井住友信託銀行）に入社。不動産部門唯一の外国人として海外投資家への投資アドバイザリーやアセットマネジメントサービスに従事。4年間で6.25億米ドルの運用資産積み上げに貢献し、複数のクロスボーダー取引を遂行。2011年に英国系の不動産アドバイザリー兼アセットマネジメント会社であるサヴィルズ・ジャパンに入社。現在は、プロ向け投資アドバイザリーのマネジングダイレクターとして同社の投資部門を統括している。日本では700物件を超える不動産取引に関与し、総額で100億米ドル超の取引を遂行。アリゾナ大学卒業（主専攻はジャーナリズム、副専攻は日本語）。

図解事典
英語で学ぶ不動産ビジネス [第2版]

発行日　2023年 6月22日　　　　第1版第1刷

著　者　脇本　和也／Jon Salyards

発行者　斉藤　和邦
発行所　株式会社 秀和システム
　　　　〒135-0016
　　　　東京都江東区東陽2-4-2　新宮ビル2F
　　　　Tel 03-6264-3105（販売）Fax 03-6264-3094
印刷所　三松堂印刷株式会社　　　Printed in Japan

ISBN978-4-7980-6830-5 C3033